Praise for *Notes on a Ce...*

"An extraordinary work: erudite, witty, and profound. In summing up his long life in pursuit of knowledge of the region that has fascinated him since childhood, Bernard Lewis has produced a book that will engage, inform, and entertain the scholar and layman alike." —Henry Kissinger

"Whether writing about the early history of the Arabs or the development of the modern Turkish state, Mr. Lewis has always been unusually alert to nuance and ambiguity; he is wary of his sources and tests them against other evidence. . . . He has evinced not only an unswerving commitment to historical truth and a hatred of what he calls 'the falsification of history' but also a passionate, at times obsessive, curiosity about other peoples, other places. . . . No matter how recondite or exotic his subject matter, he writes incisively and with unobtrusive elegance." —*The Wall Street Journal*

"Lewis has led a staggeringly productive life—publishing a jaw-dropping thirty-two books—and seems to have had more fun than any department worth of more somber professors. . . . We are fortunate to have this chatty memoir of reminiscences of scholarly discovery and stimulating encounters with everyone from Isaac Stern to Scoop Jackson to the shah of Iran." —*The Washington Post*

"*Notes on a Century* offers sharp observations on almost a hundred years of change in the Middle East and in Western academia. There are well-honed anecdotes, epigrams, jokes, and puns . . . [and] he chronicles his meetings with the famous." —*The Times Literary Supplement*

"Few could produce a book as witty, erudite, and humorous as this engaging autobiography, which, alongside these lighter characteristics, is also packed with learning and wisdom. It is no exaggeration to say that it is the distillation of a long, attentive, and productive life as a scholar and engaged intellectual. . . . We did not need this book to tell us how impressive an intellect Mr. Lewis has or what a superbly informed historian he is, but it reminds us nonetheless of all this. . . . He can give you an up-close and personal glimpse guaranteed to be as incisive as it is telling." —*The Washington Times*

PENGUIN BOOKS

NOTES ON A CENTURY

Bernard Lewis is the Cleveland E. Dodge Professor of Near Eastern Studies Emeritus at Princeton University and the author of many critically acclaimed and bestselling books, including two number one *New York Times* bestsellers: *What Went Wrong?* and *Crisis of Islam*. *The Middle East: A Brief History of the Last 2,000 Years* was a National Book Critics Circle Award finalist. Internationally recognized as the greatest historian of the Middle East, he has received fifteen honorary doctorates and his books have been translated into more than twenty languages.

Buntzie Ellis Churchill served for twenty-three years as the president of the World Affairs Council of Philadelphia and for a decade hosted the daily radio show *World Views*.

NOTES
ON A
CENTURY

Reflections of a
Middle East Historian

Bernard Lewis

with Buntzie Ellis Churchill

PENGUIN BOOKS

PENGUIN BOOKS
Published by the Penguin Group
Penguin Group (USA) LLC
375 Hudson Street
New York, New York 10014

USA | Canada | UK | Ireland | Australia | New Zealand | India | South Africa | China
penguin.com
A Penguin Random House Company

First published in the United States of America by Viking Penguin,
a member of Penguin Group (USA), Inc., 2012
Published in Penguin Books 2013

Photographs courtesy of Bernard Lewis unless otherwise indicated.

THE LIBRARY OF CONGRESS HAS CATALOGED THE HARDCOVER EDITION AS FOLLOWS:
Lewis, Bernard.
Notes on a century : reflections of a Middle East historian / Bernard Lewis;
with Buntzie Ellis Churchill.
p. cm.
Includes index.
ISBN 978-0-670-02353-0 (hc.)
ISBN 978-0-14-312422-1 (pbk.)
1. Lewis, Bernard.   2. Middle East specialists—Great Britain—Biography.
3. Middle East—Historiography.   4. Middle East—History—21st century.
I. Churchill, Buntzie Ellis.   II. Title.
DS61.7.L48A3 2012
956.0072'02—dc23
[B]   2011049267

Printed in the United States of America
1   3   5   7   9   10   8   6   4   2

Set in Adobe Garamond Pro
Designed by Francesca Belanger

For Buntzie,
without whose inspiration and guidance
this book would not have been written or even started
and without whose presence and participation
this last and best part of my life
could not have been lived.

One grey hair appeared on my head
I plucked it out with my hand.
It answered me: "You have prevailed against me alone—
What will you do when my army comes after me?"

—*Yehuda Halevi*

Lord, of your grace all that I hope is this—
Keep the realm of my pleasure prosperous
Avert from me the calamity of chastity
And keep far from me the doom of repentance.

—*'Ubayd-i Zakani*
Excerpts from *Music of a Distant Drum*

Acknowledgments

I thank my friends and colleagues whose encouragement, over many years and in many places, contributed so much to the life described in these pages.

David Pryce-Jones was kind enough to let me quote extensively from his article "Enough Said," and Adam Garfinkle graciously permitted me to reprint my article from *The American Interest* (spring 2006), with minor changes.

A word of thanks to Mari Steed and Denise Bala for invaluable technical assistance.

Finally, special thanks are due to my editor, Joy de Menil, whose rigorous scrutiny removed defects and added merits to the manuscript.

Contents

NOTES
ON A
CENTURY

The Typewriter

Sometimes the machine stares back at me
Somber, silent
A hint of menace?
Sometimes it works with me,
Anxious, eager
For reassurance.
Sometimes it sits in judgment
Hearing, condemning
Pondering sentence.

Introduction

During my long life I have been principally concerned with the study of the Middle East. This interest began when I was still a schoolboy. It has grown ever since, becoming first a hobby, then an obsession, finally a profession. I have tried from the start to understand the society from within—by learning its languages, reading its writings, visiting its countries, talking—and listening—to its people.

In accomplishing these purposes, I derived considerable advantage from the time, place and circumstances of my birth and therefore of my early education. In England in those days, history was an important part of education, and we were expected to have at least an outline knowledge not just of recent and current events, but of the whole sweep of recorded and remembered history of Western civilization, from classical antiquity to the present day. Not only that, but we were expected to study at least part of it in the original languages, notably French and Latin, to which some of us later added German and Greek. King Alfred, William the Conqueror, Richard the Lionheart and the Crusades were a familiar part of everyday discourse. This did not prepare me for the study of Islamic history; indeed in a sense, by inculcating a Christian, European perception, it biased me against it. But it did give me a better understanding of the nature of the historical process, the purpose and manner of historical research and writing.

In my early studies I was mainly interested in medieval history, in the period when the Islamic Middle East was most different from the West, least affected by the West, and in most respects far in advance of the West. I never lost my interest in medieval Islamic history, but it is no longer my primary concern. The opportunity to enter the hitherto sealed Ottoman archives in 1950 was too good to miss; it provided me with a chance to pursue a topic in which I was already deeply interested—the history of the Ottoman Empire. Most of my published work since then has been on the Ottoman and modern periods, or some combination of the two.

But no specialist on the Middle East, not even an Assyriologist or an Egyptologist, can wholly ignore the contemporary scene. My war service gave me an intimate knowledge of some aspects of modern Middle Eastern life and politics. My travels in Middle Eastern countries, my discussions with Middle Eastern leaders, my meetings with Middle Eastern colleagues, and, perhaps most of all, my encounters with Middle Eastern students, and later with former students, kept me in touch with what was going on. From time to time, I ceded to the temptation to make some public pronouncement on Middle Eastern events, usually in the form of an interview or article in some review or magazine or, occasionally, newspaper. And I have occasionally written at greater length on recent and contemporary topics.

For the study of Middle Eastern history, and at the present time one might even add of world history, some knowledge of Islam's origins and of its scriptures is necessary. Already in my student years I was reading the Koran, the biography of the Prophet, and the extensive literature concerned with them. But at no time did I specialize in these topics. I am not an expert in theology or scripture, and I looked at these, if at all, only with a historian's eye. I am, by vocation and profession, a historian, principally interested in the history of civilization.

Looking back, I see that by this choice I saved myself a lot of trouble. This was not my purpose at the time but I have become well aware of my narrow and fortunate escape from one of the most difficult and dangerous topics of our profession. Even for Muslims, and far more so for non-Muslims, the study of the sacred biography and the sacred text has become highly sensitive, not so much a field of research as a minefield.

This has not prevented my critics from attacking me for my treatment of Muslim scripture and sacred biography. In this as in other matters, the attacks came from both sides. On the one side I am accused of traducing Islam and its sanctities, on the other of defending and even concealing its flaws. As long as the attacks continue to come from both sides, I shall remain confident of my scholarly objectivity.

Once, many years ago when I was traveling in Syria, I had a long conversation one evening with a professional man of religion, discussing such matters as theology and law and other primary Islamic concerns. At one point he interrupted our conversation and exclaimed in astonishment, "I don't understand! You know so much about Islam! Why didn't you become a Muslim?"

Both the question and its possible answers may reveal much about the Islamic world today.

We live in a time when great energies are being devoted to the falsification of history—to flatter, to deceive or to serve some sectional purpose. No good can come of such distortions, even when they are inspired by unselfish motives. History is the collective memory and if we think of the social body in terms of the human body, no history means amnesia, distorted history means neurosis.

Those who are unwilling to confront the past will be unable to understand the present and unfit to face the future. A great responsibility, therefore, falls on historians, whose moral and professional duty it is to seek out the truth concerning the past, and to present and explain it as they see it. I have endeavored to fulfill this responsibility.

1.

Early Days

When I look back over the ten decades of my life, I realize how extraordinarily fortunate I have been. I was a soldier in World War II and I wasn't killed or even wounded. I was a Jew in twentieth-century Europe and I wasn't murdered or even persecuted. The first I can only attribute to the fortunes of war. For the second, I must thank my forebears who chose to live in England. I was born in England and have lived most of my life in England and in the United States, that is to say in countries that enjoy liberty and have no need of liberation. I have always known that I may formulate my opinions as I choose, not regulated by government orders or judicial decisions, and that I may express them in a language unhampered by the rules and regulations of arrogant and fussy philologists. The openness and freedom of Anglo-American society and the glorious anarchy of the English language were privileges which I took for granted, until circumstances drew my attention to the absence of these freedoms elsewhere.

I was born in 1916 in London and that, too, was fortunate, though I didn't realize how fortunate until years later when I arrived in the United States. My parents, Harry and Jenny Lewis, were living at the time in a small town called Maidenhead, up the River Thames not far from London; within commuting distance, but nonetheless a separate town. When my mother was near her delivery time, she decided, as many young mothers did, that she wanted to go to her mother's house. So she went to her mother's home in London and for that reason I was born in London in the same place and, I am told, in the same bed where my mother was born twenty-one years earlier.

Why a narrow escape? Maidenhead. In England people rarely if ever ask you where you were born and if they had asked me and I had said Maidenhead, most English people would know the name of the town. But in America you are asked where were you born all the time, in all sorts of different situations and circumstances, and the reply Maidenhead would have been greeted with open ridicule or with furtive and embarrassed laughter.

My maternal grandmother, Anne Miller, came to England from a town called Grodno, then part of the Russian Empire, in 1895, when she was about eighteen years old. Her family sent her to America to marry her cousin, who had settled there some years previously, and who had written to the family, saying, "I am now established; send me a bride." They chose my grandmother. She was so seasick crossing the North Sea, that having got as far as London, she refused to go any farther. The North Sea was bad enough and she was not going to cross the Atlantic. She argued back and forth with her family. They implored her. At some point her problem was solved. She met and married my grandfather, Joseph Levy, and stayed in England.

It seems that when I arrived I slammed the door behind me, because a couple of years later my mother had a dangerous miscarriage which she narrowly survived. After that no more children were possible; so I grew up as an only child. This has certain obvious advantages and less obvious disadvantages. As I recall, it was sometimes a source of distress. Most of the people I knew had brothers and sisters. I had none. At times I felt lonely. That's the only thing from childhood that I can recall with, shall we say, some pangs.

For at least a year after this miscarriage my mother was seriously ill, most of the time in bed, and I was sent to be looked after by my grandmother. That was one of the reasons why I had a particularly close relationship with my maternal grandmother, who made the most superb yeast cake with cinnamon and raisins.

My grandmother was thirty-nine when I was born and therefore quite young when I was growing up. The difference between my Eastern European grandmother and my English-born mother, at once geographical and generational, could be seen even in such domestic matters as cuisine. One of my vivid recollections of early childhood is of a discussion between my mother and my grandmother. My grandmother was trying to teach my mother how to prepare one of the family's favorite dishes and explained the ingredients and the process in terms of taking a pinch of this, a whiff of that, a touch of the other, and letting the preparation simmer for a while. My grandmother was born in Eastern Europe in the nineteenth century. My mother, who started school in London in 1900, was a child of twentieth-century England and wanted precision, which my grandmother seemed unable to provide. I still remember the agonizing, unanswered questions, "How much is a pinch? How long is a while?"

My mother was undoubtedly more modern and more accurate, but my grandmother's cooking tasted better.

My mother may not have been the best cook but I most certainly benefited from the fact that she was quite fussy about the use of English and was determined that I should speak correctly. I remember asking her, "Can I go out and play with the boys?" to which she replied, "You can, but you may not."

My relations with my paternal grandparents were cool and distant. My father's mother died when he was only five years old, leaving two children, my father and his elder brother, Nat. My grandfather remarried, and in due course begat two more sons and a daughter. When I was a child, relations between the two branches of my grandfather's family were already cool, and at some point a quarrel provided the pretext to break them off entirely. My father remained in close touch with his full brother, Nat, and with his children, Basil and Lily.

My grandfather Lewis had a brother, Samuel, who fell off the roof of the building in which his office was situated, and died. He left a widow, Rose, and six children, four sons and two daughters. The youngest son was almost the same age as I was and was also named Bernard, presumably after the same ancestor. In England my name is pronounced BURR-nerd (no comments, please) and I can tolerate the American Brrr-NAAARD. But, I detest, and am the most unlikely "Bernie."

During the Depression we lived near Aunt Rose and her family and got to know them well. I developed a very close friendship with my cousin Bernard. As luck would have it, we went to the same school and having two Bernard Lewises, roughly the same age, was a source of endless confusion. Fortunately, we were not in the same class.

My earliest political recollection is from the early 1920s, when I was just starting school and there was a general election in England. At that time the two main parties were the Labour Party and the Conservative Party. Between them there was still a vestigial Liberal Party—a remnant of what had once been the only serious alternative to the Conservatives. I remember the boys at school asked me, and each other, for which party our parents were voting. I asked my father and he said, "We vote Liberal." I then went back and told the other boys that we were voting Liberal. This caused some puzzlement, as the overwhelming majority were by then either Conservative or Labour. "Why are you Liberal?" they asked, and I went home and put the question to my father. "Why are we Liberal?" My father, without a moment's hesitation, replied, "Because we have too much money to be Labour and not enough to be Conservative."

My mother was born in 1895, the eldest of four children and the only one who survived—two died in infancy and the third, Auntie Betty, died in her late twenties. When I was a child my mother and her sister Betty would often go on holiday, together with their husbands, and me, somewhere on the English coast. One evening I complained of a very bad bellyache. Children often have bellyaches and normally one wouldn't make too much fuss about that, but since Betty's husband was a doctor, my parents asked him to take a look at me. He did, immediately diagnosed appendicitis, and summoned a surgeon of his acquaintance to deal with it. It turned out the appendicitis was acute and would certainly have killed me if it had not been dealt with expeditiously. The fortunate chance that my uncle was a doctor and holidaying with us saved my life.

My mother's childhood had been a hard one as her parents were very poor and she had to leave school and go to work as soon as she reached the minimum school-leaving age of fourteen. After she died I went through her papers and found she had been very active in her school's activities, especially in sports. She had various certificates indicating her excellence in swimming, one in particular, dated 1908, which I gave, exactly one hundred years later, to my granddaughter, Rachel, who received it with delight.

My mother did not pass along the sports gene to me as I was a miserable failure in every one of the few sports that I dared, or was compelled, to attempt. This is the more remarkable in that my father was also active in sports and was an excellent tennis player. Both my parents were regular readers, but in different ways. My mother read novels, and more especially detective stories, but rarely troubled to read the newspapers. My father read newspapers, sometimes several a day, meticulously, but rarely bothered to read a book.

One morning, shortly after the war when I was again, briefly, living with my parents, I got up earlier than my father and was reading the paper when he came in for breakfast. "What are you reading?" he asked. "An article about UNESCO," I replied. That was just after UNESCO was created, and neither my father nor I nor anyone else had any idea what it was. My father responded, "Oh, who is he? Some corrupt Romanian politician, I suppose." A reasonable response as

UNESCO does sound Romanian and a Romanian as the subject of an article in the English newspapers would almost certainly be a politician and therefore probably corrupt.

Even on his deathbed, when I went to see him and we spoke, literally a few minutes before he died, he was talking very angrily— but in agreement—about an article he had just read in *The Daily Telegraph*.

Each of my parents had hobbies and concerns. My mother spent a great deal of her time knitting and crocheting, producing all kinds of garments, both for us and for the furniture. I particularly recall the antimacassars—Macassar was then a popular, very greasy hair oil, and people sitting back in armchairs often left rather disgusting oily stains. The antimacassar, a doily often with lace edging, became very common. It was placed protectively over the back of the chair and was considered quite decorative.

My father was a collector of paintings of the English Victorian school, the so-called academic painters. I sometimes wondered why. A brief telephone exchange gave me the explanation. I was chatting with my father on the phone and he said, "I've just bought a new painting." I asked, "By whom?" and he mentioned a name and I said, "I've never heard of him." My father replied, "Anyone you've heard of I can't afford." When my parents died I inherited the paintings. I kept two and sold the rest since I was not particularly interested in that genre. They were sold at auction in New York and remarkably, the prices they fetched were almost exactly the prices assessed by Her Majesty's Commissioners of Inland Revenue.

My father was also a soccer fan—at first supporting the Tottenham Hotspurs and then the Arsenal. He used to go every week, religiously, to watch them perform and tried to take me along to interest me in the sport. I was monumentally bored and unable to develop any sort of interest—if anything, it acted as an inoculation.

My father was also very keen on dogs, particularly on what in

England are called Alsatians and in America, German shepherds. He bought an Alsatian bitch, Cora—full name, Lady Cora of Cazenove—with a carefully authenticated pedigree. The next endeavor was to find her a suitable mate. This was duly arranged and after a while Cora produced a fine litter. All her pups were given away or sold, except one, which my father decided to retain. This pup was named after Chicot the Jester, a character in a book my father had just read, one of his rare experiments with books. A whole room in our home was devoted exclusively to the dogs. It was the largest room in the house and totally unfurnished. Its front door was by the street and its back door at the garden.

On one occasion Chicot was almost responsible for my premature death at ten years old. We were taking a walk, I holding the leash, when he suddenly saw a potential lady friend on the other side of the road and dashed across to make her acquaintance. I either could not, or did not, let go of the lead and was dragged across the road, the last part of it on my stomach. Fortunately, there was not much traffic and the drivers saw me and stopped. After this I was no longer entrusted with the task of taking the dogs for a walk. The danger was that if I took them for a walk they would take me for a run.

Needless to say, we never kept cats. The cat lover of the family was my maternal grandmother who always had at least one, and usually two. As an adult I have never kept pets for the simple reason I have spent so much of my time traveling that pet keeping would have been difficult and unkind. Both my children, however, seem to have inherited the love of pets. Melanie likes both cats and dogs and has somehow persuaded them to cohabit peacefully. Michael likes cats—indeed it was a cat who introduced him to the young woman who eventually became his wife, my daughter-in-law, Jessica.

My father began in textiles, particularly woolens and then apparel, and eventually moved into the real estate business. My family was badly hit by the Depression. When I was about thirteen we had to leave the house in North Kensington where I spent my childhood and move to a house in a different neighborhood on a much lower scale. One of the consequences of the Depression was that we ceased to have a resident housemaid. Another was that we had to cut down on our travel abroad. And in general, life became more difficult. It also meant changing my schools since at that time one had to be within walking distance of the school. This continued for several moves and several years until gradually things began to pick up.

The first school I went to was a small private school in Kensington. After that, when we were moving around, I went to various schools, but the important one was the Polytechnic London Day School which I entered at the age of fourteen. Before that, I was at Wilson College, a small private school run by a Devonshire schoolmaster and his French wife, William Brimicombe and Marcelle Manusset. Both had a deep love for and commitment to language, their own and each other's; both felt a kinship with my own attitude to language. They had an enormous educational impact on me, in my use of my English mother tongue and of my first major foreign language, French. As teachers, they were very good on some subjects, utterly hopeless on others. I had an excellent education in English, French, Latin, and history, and they were able to communicate to me the excitement of learning and exploring both modern and ancient languages. Perhaps their most enduring legacy was my knowledge of French, helped by my family's frequent holidays in France. For several years we would go every summer to Le Touquet and sometimes in winter to the Riviera. I recall the mixture of pride, pleasure and satisfaction when, at the age of thirteen, I read my first book in French from cover to cover, *The Count of Monte Cristo,* selected and lent to me by Mrs. Brimicombe.

Unfortunately their course in mathematics was mediocre and there was no course at all in science. Looking back, I think I was very lucky that the school closed down when I was fourteen years old. If I had stayed there I would probably never have been able to meet university entry requirements.

It was not easy to find me another school at that time because schools don't usually accept boys of fourteen. But my parents managed to find me a place at the Polytechnic Day School. I was fortunately able to fit into the class and complete my matriculation. I then went into what in English schools is called the sixth form, where normally one stays for two or three years to prepare for university.

I am greatly indebted to the English master at the Polytechnic, Mr. C. E. Eckersley, who was extremely helpful and effective in recognizing and developing my literary appreciation and capacity. I vividly recall one particular incident. It was the common practice at that time to require students to produce what was known as "the monthly essay." Two or three topics were provided and each student had to choose one. These essays were then examined, ranked, criticized and explained to the class as an exercise in English—how to understand it, how to write it. Each month two essays were picked. Fairly early in my years at the Poly my monthly essay was one of the two chosen, and Mr. Eckersley explained to the class why. He began with the other one and dwelt on its merits and its occasional defects; and then, turning to mine he said, and his words are engraved in my memory, "This first one is an example of a good school exercise. The other one is something more," and proceeded to explain the difference between a good school exercise and literary merit. The monthly essay written under his guidance was a great help in my developing a reasonably good English prose style; his comments brought significant improvement and immense encouragement. Unlike his present-day peers he was not worried about my self-esteem and had no hesitation in criticizing my work when he thought it necessary.

At an early age I made an important discovery: that the pleasure of reading a book could be greatly increased and renewed at will if one actually owned it. To begin with, one could choose the time and place of reading the book, unconstrained by the need to return it to a library or other lawful owner. While reading, appreciation of any particular passage is enhanced by the comfortable awareness that it will always be there—the same words, the same lines, the same pages—whenever one might choose to return to it. And even when not actually reading the book, merely looking at it on the shelf evokes that special pleasure which one derives from the ownership of some beautiful and cherished object.

I began collecting books when I was quite young. In those days there were many secondhand bookshops in London neighborhoods where families like mine resided, with boxes on display in which books were arranged according to price: one penny, twopence, and for the rare moments when my normally exiguous pocket money was increased for some special occasion, sixpence. In this way, I acquired the collected works of most of the major English poets of the past and a quite respectable collection of Victorian novelists. Many of the books, indeed most of them, were in poor condition—broken-backed, dog-eared, scarred, sometimes underlined or obscurely annotated in the margins, sometimes falling apart. But they were always complete. On the very rare occasions when I picked up a book and found a couple of pages missing, the shocked bookseller immediately withdrew it from the box and disposed of it elsewhere. "If even one page is missing," he said, "it is not a book and we only sell books here."

When I was twelve my father got me a set of the *Encyclopaedia Britannica* which I started reading avidly. I remember at one period thinking that I would like to be a paleontologist because I had just read the article on paleontology. Another time I thought I wanted to go into metaphysics and so on.

My father was a great lover of Italian opera and a competent, albeit amateur, performer of it. He did actually undergo some professional training, but never became a professional. My mother did not like the idea and her wishes prevailed. From early childhood, I grew up listening to my father performing (most often in the bathroom in the morning) some of the major arias from *Rigoletto, I Pagliacci, The Barber of Seville* and the rest. He also spent much time singing in the evening and during the weekend while my mother accompanied him on the piano. My father did not know Italian, but as is usual with singers, he was able to memorize and reproduce the sounds with fair accuracy. Like most children, I imitated my father's performance, uttering sounds that were one step further from reality. I knew no Italian, but from school French and Latin I was able to get some idea of what the text was about. At the age of fourteen I decided to learn Italian. This language was not taught at my school, nor was there anyone in our family or circle of acquaintances who knew any Italian, but this did not daunt me. My father found me an Italian grammar in English, and with his sometimes questionable help on phonetics, I happily set to work. I began with his librettos, of which he had a good collection. After a few months, I was given an Italian book, *La Vita Militare* by Edmondo de Amicis. At first reading it was a hard struggle, but after a while, I began to enjoy it. When I had finished reading this book, I decided to try another, and, consumed with insane ambition, I asked my father to procure me a copy of *The Divine Comedy*. This opened a new and wonderful world. Before long, I had a rather better knowledge of Italian than my father did, though, of course, I never approached his capacity for making very convincing Italian noises.

I did not actually set foot in Italy until 1937, when I spent a few days in Rome on my way to Egypt. I never attained much skill in speaking Italian, but my reading knowledge proved invaluable in my subsequent work as a historian of the Middle East. On the one hand, it gave me access to the riches of Italian scholarship in the field; on the other, to the vast Italian historical documentation, so important for the history of the Levant and more especially of the Ottoman Empire where Venice was commercially and therefore also politically active.

. . . .

Along with most Jewish children, in my thirteenth year I was given
elementary instruction in Hebrew, or to be more precise, in the Hebrew alphabet, to enable me to recite a few lines from the book of
Leviticus for my Bar Mitzvah, a ceremony in the synagogue for boys
who, on reaching the age of thirteen, are initiated as full members of
the Jewish community. At that time and in that place, preparing for
Bar Mitzvah implied only learning the alphabet, memorizing the
tunes, and acquiring a sufficient command of the Hebrew script to
read the prayers, provided that they were vocalized. In the normal
course of events, no more than that was expected of pupils; no more
was provided by teachers.

The teacher whom my family found to instruct me in my Bar
Mitzvah portion of the Bible and how to chant it was no ordinary
teacher, but a true scholar. Leon Shalom Creditor was a native of
Dvinsk, in Latvia, who had settled in London many years previously.
A journalist in both Hebrew and Yiddish, for whom teaching was a
sideline, he initiated me into medieval and modern as well as biblical
and rabbinic Hebrew, and enabled me to make the joyous discovery
that Hebrew was not merely a kind of encipherment of prayers and
rituals to be memorized and recited parrot fashion, but a language, at
once classical and modern, written and spoken—which could be
learned in the same way as French or Latin, and which held a more
direct appeal for me than either of them.

At my Bar Mitzvah party I had, as was usual, to deliver a little
speech which was heavily edited for me by my parents and my teacher.
I did however add an improvisation which started with:

> My parents I can ne'er repay
> For how they've helped me on my way.
> What e'er I say will be quite crude
> Compared with my real gratitude.

I wanted to continue my Hebrew studies under Mr. Creditor's direction after the completion of the Bar Mitzvah ceremony. My family thought it odd, but I insisted. My parents agreed, and Mr. Creditor was delighted to continue my instruction. In the course of the years we proceeded from Bible to Talmud, which involved some Aramaic. Years later, when he was elderly and retired, Mr. Creditor published a book and presented a copy to my parents. He inscribed it "To the parents of Bernard Lewis. He was my pupil, and now I am his." It was a touching moment.

My study of Hebrew led inevitably to the Old Testament and of course to the established English translations of the Hebrew Bible. The English Bible known as the "Authorized Version" contains a number of mistranslations, some of which have been corrected, others not. Let me take two examples from the best-known passage in the whole Hebrew Bible, the Ten Commandments. The word translated as "kill" in "Thou shalt not kill" does not mean kill but murder, a much more specific and restricted meaning. This has been corrected in various revised versions. Another mistranslation in the Ten Commandments, "Thou shalt not commit adultery," goes in the opposite direction. In the commandment the Hebrew word rendered as "adultery" has a much wider meaning. Adultery in English is limited and specific—a sexual act between a married person and another who is not his or her spouse. The Hebrew word *na'af* is a broad general term covering all sexual offenses including homosexuality and masturbation. This error, as far as I am aware, has not been corrected in any of the revised versions. Another mistranslation may be attributed to the prejudices of the translator. In the Song of Solomon 1:5, the Authorized Version reads: "I am black, but comely." The Hebrew says, "I am black and comely."

By the time I was sixteen I had a reasonably good command of both written and spoken Hebrew. I did, however, feel the lack of anyone with whom to speak the language. The only person with whom I could converse at all in Hebrew was my Hebrew teacher. I did not know anyone else who possessed that skill. I eventually found a very small number of other people about my own age who were learning to speak Hebrew. I took the step of creating a new group called "Dovre Ivrit," "Speakers of Hebrew," to meet once a week and speak Hebrew. One member was a young lady, Minna, about a year younger than I was. This was my first encounter with the opposite sex and I fell madly in love. Hoping to gain her attention I expressed that love in a series of poems that, insanely ambitiously, I wrote in Hebrew. Our relationship was entirely innocent and of brief duration, but it was my first encounter and experience with "love." We remained good friends until her death, many years later.

During the summer of my sixteenth year I went to Karlsbad with my mother, who wanted to take the waters. One of our fellow guests at the hotel was a lawyer from Tel Aviv, whom we then called a Palestinian but whom today we would call an Israeli. The point was that he was a Hebrew speaker. This was a golden opportunity to speak Hebrew with an adult other than Mr. Creditor. I jumped at it. We were speaking, of course, in English but I expressed a desire to try my Hebrew to which he graciously responded. We had some conversation, not always easy, but on the whole fairly successful. He asked me if I were reading any Hebrew books, and I replied with a list probably longer than he wanted to hear. In passing, I mentioned that I was an avid reader of the poems of H. N. Bialik and had, in fact, brought my copy with me. "Oh," he said, "that's interesting. Did you know that Bialik is in Karlsbad now at a hotel not far from here? I know him. Would you like to meet him?" I was ecstatic at this opportunity to meet the greatest living writer in the Hebrew language. A meeting was arranged and, trembling with excitement, I was brought into the presence of the poet. Bialik had no great interest in our conversation and, looking back over the years from the other side of the fence so to speak, I can sympathize with his boredom. But he was gracious and was willing to sign my copy of his book. It remains one of my treasured possessions.

By the time I entered university, I had read widely and deeply in Hebrew, and had even tried my hand, not very successfully, at writing both prose and verse in the language. All this whetted my appetite for more of the same. I had been launched on one of the paths that led to my subsequent career, a fascination with exotic languages.

In the mid-1920s, when I was a schoolboy in England, a great deal of time and effort was spent by our teachers in showing us how to translate. Astonishingly, considering the present-day perspective, we were required to translate not only from but into the languages we were learning; and not only from and into living languages, but also into the classical languages, Latin and Greek. Sometimes the tests went even further and we were required to write what was known as "free composition" in foreign languages, usually in prose, but sometimes even in verse. On one occasion, after a long and deep study of the Latin hexameter, we were told to compose a few lines of Latin verse, in hexameters, to show that we had mastered or at least understood the technique. We were free to choose our own topics for these verses. I chose a German politician with a rather weird outlook who had just made his first appearance in German elections.

Hitlerias

Verba virumque cano, qui primus gente volebat
False Germana exaltare ipsum super omnes;
Canta, pingendi praeclarae nobilis artis
Musa, Jovis nata, acta domum pictoris Adolphi,
Heros, saltem censebat se maximum eorum,
Iste fuit, campos Germanos pingere rubros
Tentavit nigro fascisto sanguinolento
Cruce gammata, Judaeorum atque cruore.
Motu grandi regali tum brachia tollit

Pulchra super caput eius audacter comitatum
Forte salutatum signo collegii eorum.
Salve, Dis altissime valde, tuere fidelem
Legatum hic sollertem atque vicarium adeptum,
Adduce istum tutum rursus denique Hadem.

Eighty years later I find my Latin is not up to the task of a decent line-by-line translation but roughly the poem talks about the house-painter Adolf who wanted to exalt the Germans above all others and flood German fields with swastikas and Jewish blood. It concludes with a prayer to lead him back to hell. His desire was fulfilled and my prayer was answered, finally.

Translating from English into another language was difficult, and I doubt if the results were ever worthy of a second glance from a native user of that language. But it was a useful exercise, and it helped us understand our own literature in our own language. I particularly liked translating poetry, and even tried to render it into English verse or at least into poetic English. That was the origin of an interest which became, at times, an obsession. I began early on to make verse translations from the French and Latin I was learning at school and from the Hebrew that I was learning at home, to which I later added the Middle Eastern languages that I learned at the university. That obsession continued for a long time.

My very first ambition, long before I ever thought in terms of scholarship as a profession or ever as an occupation, was to be a writer. I can't say exactly when, but I recall that by the time I was Bar Mitzvah I was already writing a great deal; I was churning out prose, verse, essays, poems, even a few stories, at an enormous rate. I wrote in English of course but I also tried my hand at writing in Hebrew. That was not a very successful enterprise. I cherished delusions of a literary career, seeing myself first as a poet and then as an essayist, and until my late teens, I thought that this was going to be my vocation.

I wasn't quite sure about which subjects I was going to write but I knew that I wanted to write well. Eventually I realized that, while I did manage to write reasonably well, I didn't really have anything particularly creative to say. I found outlets for my literary impulses in two respects: one was by translating poetry and the other was by writing about history. Writing about history does allow some scope for fulfilling one's ambitions as a writer.

I continued to write poems now and then, but mainly I translated poetry from various languages into English, even, ambitiously, into English verse and, more realistically, into reasonably poetic English prose. The surest test of one's understanding of a text in another language is translating it into one's own. One may believe one has achieved a full understanding of the meaning of a text, only to find, in the process of translation, that one's understanding has serious gaps and even flaws. The task of translating into English was stimulating, challenging, even exciting, and I continued to do it long after I had ceased to be *in statu pupillari*.

I started with Hebrew poetry, of which I translated quite an immense quantity. I think there must have been hundreds of them—mostly short poems, but also some quite long ones. I translated some of Bialik's longer poems, for example, *"Metei Midbar"* and *"Be-Ir Haharega"* and some others. These were all done in my teens and late teens, and some of them were even published at the time in various magazines. Most of them were not published. And later, when I learned Arabic and Persian and Turkish, I translated many poems from those languages too, and I have continued to do so ever since. I've never done it systematically, and I never even set about publishing them systematically; mainly they were published when occasions presented themselves.

When, for example, somebody was doing a Penguin book of Turkish verse in English translation, I was asked to contribute. The editor of the volume took a more favorable view of my work than I took myself, so I appear in that volume under several pseudonyms. I used my own name for the translations I thought were successful, I used another name for some which I thought were far less successful, and the third name was for others which I thought were quite awful, but which the editor nevertheless insisted on including. The same thing happened with an anthology of Hebrew poetry in English translation edited by Avraham Birman, and I'm in that too under various names, my own and at least two others. In recent years when I have been asked to contribute to Festschrifts and I haven't had anything suitable in hand, I have used some of my translations of poems.

At some stage in my schooling the question arose of what career I should follow. My mother, like many Jewish mothers, wanted me to be a doctor, but that was impossible. At the school which I attended until I was fourteen I learned no science at all, and by the time I went to high school it was too late to catch up with the class. In my matriculation exams I did well in mathematics but did not even try chemistry or physics or any science. My father wanted me to be a lawyer and I was willing to go along with that. In accordance with normal practice I could go to university and study whatever amused me, leaving the study of the law to evenings and weekends and, more realistically, to a later stage.

I have always had a great interest in history and even as a child wanted to know the history of the other side. When I was at school, history meant English history, and for centuries this consisted largely of wars with France. From that I developed a curiosity about French history and asked my father to get me a history of France in English. He did so and with that I was able to consider the history of Anglo-French wars from both sides. The Crusades and the Eastern Question, both essential parts of the school's history syllabus, evoked a similar curiosity about the other side. This was no doubt my first step on the path which led to my career as a historian of the Middle East.

The University of London

I had a good academic record at the Polytechnic and my headmaster was very eager for me to try for an Oxford scholarship. However, my father disapproved very strongly and vetoed it. He didn't like the idea of my going to Oxford as he thought it was just a place where students spent all their time drinking and partying. I enrolled at the University of London in 1933.

The University of London was a loose federation of schools and colleges, each running its own affairs. In my first year I was registered at University College but it was perfectly possible to do courses in other colleges on what was known as the intercollegiate system.

The university had a syllabus called an Honours Degree in History. (Honours Degree in the English system is not a measure of accomplishment but a type of syllabus specializing in one particular discipline.) It was possible to do an Honours Degree in History with special reference to the Middle East, which meant that one had to do some European history, a lot of Middle Eastern history, and also some relevant languages. This gave me an opportunity to combine my interests. At the same time I enrolled in the Honorable Society of the Middle Temple, one of the four "Inns of Court." Of this, more later.

In my first year I did Hebrew, Latin, history and some Greek at University College, and at the same time I went to the School of Oriental Studies to do Arabic. In my second and third years I transferred to the School of Oriental Studies (renamed the School of Oriental and African Studies in 1938) where I concentrated on Middle Eastern history, but on the intercollegiate system I took a course on the history of political ideas with Harold Laski at the London School of Economics. He was an excellent lecturer and it was an illuminating experience. My B.A. degree was in history with languages, and as I chose Middle Eastern history, Arabic was a requirement.

During my undergraduate years I had an encounter of some linguistic significance with a particularly attractive young lady named
Ada, the daughter of a former Soviet Commissar, by then a fugitive
and an exile. I was impressed that before the family's emigration they
had been close to Lenin and that as a child Ada had been dandled on
his knee. They were Jewish and their position regarding Jewish affairs
was, by my standards at least, rather odd. They were profoundly religious and strictly observed all the rules that the Jewish religion im-
poses on its followers. They were also profoundly and fervently anti-
Zionist and rejected the idea of reviving and speaking Hebrew. They
did however place great emphasis on Yiddish which they saw as the
authentic language of the Jewish common people.

My knowledge of Yiddish at that time was limited to a few odd
words and phrases which still floated around in my family. Ada insisted on remedying what she saw as this basic defect and demanded
that I learn Yiddish, not only to understand but also to read it. She
therefore instructed me in the rules of Yiddish orthography, and provided me with a supply of literature in Yiddish. Eventually we parted
but I am grateful to her for enriching my life with some knowledge
of an interesting language and the fascinating culture expressed in it.
It was also invaluable in that I now can understand the punch lines
of Jewish jokes.

There is one other thing that I recall about Yiddish. Many languages have some sort of suffix, added at the end of a word, for a
variety of purposes—smallness, affection, intimacy, etc. In English
we use only two: -let and -kin (e.g., booklet, lambkin) and both spar-
ingly. German makes much more extensive use of *-lein* and *-chen*
(e.g., *fraülein, mädchen*). Italian has a wide range, notably *-ino, -etto,
-ello* and, to magnify rather than reduce, *-one.* A similar effect is
achieved in Arabic not by adding a suffix, but by a change of
vowels—from Hassan to Husayn, from ʿAbd to ʿUbayd, as in the
names ʿAbdallah and ʿUbaydallah. Yiddish has a wide range of such

suffixes, but one in particular, *-inyu,* caught my attention. It is attached to three words and to no others. The three words are father (*tatinyu*), mother (*maminyu*) and God (*Gottinyu*). Clearly, these are not diminutives—the message is not diminution but intimacy. I thought this remarkable. The same theological attitude of intimacy is expressed in a familiar Jewish joke about the hard-up businessman who prays, "Oh God, you help complete strangers! Why can't you help me?"

As a student of the Middle East, my interests were primarily historical rather than, as with most of my predecessors, teachers and contemporaries, philological and literary. I did however serve a brief apprenticeship in these disciplines and am profoundly grateful for having done so. The first and most rudimentary test of the historian's competence is that he should be able to read his sources. This is not always easy, as for example when the language is classical Arabic or the writing is a crabbed Ottoman bureaucratic script. And that is not all. The historian of a region, of a period, of a group of people, or even of a topic, must know something of its cultural context, and for this literature is an indispensable guide.

The teachers of Near and Middle Eastern history were mostly not professional historians, and some, I think I can say now, were not any kind of historian at all. They were philologists; people who followed the old-fashioned philological, textual approach to these subjects. They taught courses on history because they were required to do so. I subsequently learned some of the courses which I took had been specially put on because there was this young nuisance who came and said that he wanted to take them. If the syllabus listed a course they were required to teach it, even if only one student wanted it.

Of those who influenced me, among my Middle Eastern history teachers, certainly Sir Hamilton A. R. Gibb was the most important. He did not have a Ph.D. as in those days it wasn't essential in British university life. The Ph.D. was optional and came in rather late. He had an M.A. In British universities you are not a professor until you are what in American universities is called a "full professor." There is no such thing as an assistant or associate professor. The equivalent titles are lecturer and reader. So until Gibb was appointed to a chair, he was Mr. Gibb to his students. After learning a certain amount of Arabic, his students came to know him as *Amir al-mu'minin al* Mister Gibb *billah* (Commander of the Faithful Mister Gibb in God—a pun never translates well). Gibb was well aware of the fact that he was not really a historian although he studied, taught, and occasionally wrote history. This was a point to which he referred again and again in his conversation and even occasionally in his writings. He had—I wouldn't call it an inferiority complex, that would be an inappropriate expression for Gibb—let's say he had an awareness that he was not a real historian. He was a textual scholar, a philological scholar, a literary scholar, a historian of ideas—but he did not feel that he was approaching his subject as a professional historian.

Another professor in the University of London at that time, Norman H. Baynes, occupied the chair of Byzantine history. Under University of London regulations you could not do Middle Eastern history without doing Byzantine history. The Byzantine and Islamic courses were part of the same program; which I think was an excellent idea, and I'm very grateful for the fact that I did two years of Byzantine history and was required to learn some Greek, neither of which I would otherwise have done. That was very useful for a better understanding of medieval history and civilization. More important than that, it meant that I worked closely for two years with Norman Baynes, who was a professional historian of the highest level. He didn't teach me any Islamic history, Gibb and others taught me that, but Baynes taught me how to study history, particularly how to study the history of a medieval society; an alien society with an alien and difficult language.

At the University of London at that time if you majored in history, you were required by university regulations to choose a special subject: a very limited topic, maybe fifty years of history, which had to be studied in the original documents. I chose the "Eastern Question," as it was called at that time, the problems generated by the decline and eventual fall of the Ottoman Empire and the disposal of its various provinces, mainly in Eastern Europe. For that I was sent to a "special subject" course at the School of Slavonic and East European Studies of the University of London, taught by R. W. Seton-Watson, who was a great teacher. I was told that I should study the original documents, which meant British documents, French documents, German documents, Austrian documents and Russian documents. And in my youth and innocence I asked, What about the Turkish documents? I was told that they were not important, and anyway there weren't any. I found this an unsatisfactory answer. There had to be some Turkish documents. In the books that I read on the Eastern Question, Turkey was a stage and a backdrop and all the actors were Europeans. I felt this needed further investigation. So I learned Turkish, or at least enough to read some documents.

Both Baynes and Seton-Watson were historians in the truest and deepest sense of that word, and gave me my basic training in, and understanding of, historical method. They supplemented each other. From Baynes I learned how to deal with medieval history, based on chronicles and inscriptions; from Seton-Watson I learned how to deal with modern diplomatic history based on documents in embassies and archives. Both were superb teachers, and contributed profoundly to my professional training.

With Seton-Watson I was one of a small class. Since Byzantine history was not a particularly popular subject I was usually alone with Baynes or with one other student. Our personal relationship was therefore much closer and his influence far more profound. I remained in touch with him for the rest of his life.

During my graduate studies, I came across an Arabic text which described a Byzantine palace revolution in rather interesting terms. I translated this into English and showed it to Professor Baynes, asking him whether this was of interest. He said that it was, and insisted that I prepare it for publication. This I did, with considerable help from him, and the article was published in 1939—my third.

I should mention the first two. The very first was an article on the Islamic guilds, published in 1937, to which I will return. My second article was an aspect of the Isma'ili studies in which I was engaged for my Ph.D. thesis. In studying Isma'ili documents, I came across what I thought was an interesting interpretation of the story of the fall of Adam. With some encouragement from my teachers, I published this in the *Bulletin of the School of Oriental and African Studies* in 1938.

Legal Studies

Although I had always been interested in the Middle East, it never occurred to me, while studying for my degree, that one could actually earn a living or make a career out of that interest. My original intention, my family's choice rather than my own, had been to go into the law after graduating from university. In England there are two legal professions, solicitors and barristers. Solicitors mainly do office work—contracts and wills and corporate work and suchlike. Barristers are mainly concerned with litigation. My family thought I would do better as a barrister than as a solicitor. I always liked to talk.

To be called to the bar, two requirements had to be met. The first, in accordance with an old custom dating back centuries, was to "keep terms." To do this one had to be enrolled as a student member of one of the four Inns of Court, or societies of barristers, and to "dine in hall." There were four terms a year and one was required to dine in the great hall of the society at least three times a term (for those who had a university degree), or six times (for those who did not), for twelve terms. The dinners were sumptuous, with five courses, well irrigated with sherry before, brandy after, and two wines with the meal, and all for only 5 shillings. They were obviously well subsidized. The idea was that somehow when judges, barristers, and students dined together like gentlemen (and later also ladies), the mores and ethics of the profession, and perhaps also some knowledge of the law, would reach the students by a kind of social and gustatory osmosis.

Sometime in the nineteenth century a second requirement was added—attending courses and passing examinations, but the first requirement, dining, remained. I completed it diligently and successfully. I made a start on the second requirement. I did English constitutional law and history and also Roman law, which at that time was a requirement. Roman law had to be studied in the original Roman sources. So I read the *Institutes* of Justinian and some other Latin texts. Roman law I liked. I mean, this was right down my alley. It also later proved useful for the better understanding of Islamic political and social thought and practice. Then I had to do criminal law, and that was fun too. It helped me understand detective stories to which I was then rather addicted.

During my brief interlude as a law student, in what is becoming an increasingly remote past, I remember learning two new words, which I had never seen before, and which, for that matter, I have not seen since. The two words are "barratry" and "champerty," both denoting legal wrongdoing—that is, actions for which a lawyer, under English law at that time, could be disbarred. "Barratry" means wasting the time of the courts with frivolous litigation. "Champerty" means undertaking a lawsuit on the understanding that if one lost there would be no fee, but in the event of a successful outcome the lawyer would get an agreed percentage of the money paid to his client by the defeated opponent. This was regarded as highly unprofessional and could result in disbarment. I was therefore more than a little surprised to find that this is a common legal practice in the United

States, and is moreover actively promoted by advertising, another professional offense under the British code.

I have been told that champerty, though not by that name, is now acceptable legal practice in Britain. Some of the legal cases I read reminded me of an episode in my early life when I might have profited from champerty. While I was still living in England my doctor diagnosed a polyp on my larynx and sent me to a specialist to have it removed. The specialist said it was a simple matter. He seated me in his chair, gave me an anesthetic and set to work. When I recovered consciousness sometime later, I found that my mouth was badly battered and several of my front teeth were broken. Needless to say, I was in considerable pain. This grew worse when the surgeon informed me that he had been unable to reach the polyp. It was still there, and still needed to be removed.

The swellings and sores in my mouth in due course disappeared, but the broken teeth were a more difficult matter and required extensive and expensive dentistry. It occurred to me that it might not be unreasonable to ask the surgeon to pay my dentist's bill. I wrote to the surgeon accordingly, and he refused. I consulted a lawyer who sent the dentist a letter. He promptly agreed to pay. It never occurred to me then, nor to my lawyer, to ask for anything beyond the payment of that bill. Living in the United States, I realize that had this happened here, I might have become a millionaire.

An Apprenticeship in Paris

In 1936 I took my B.A. (Honours) final examination in history with more than a hundred others. When the list of graduates was published, I not only had First Class Honours, but I was the first among the small number who had First Class Honours out of all the branches of history. My father was stunned. He had been worried about my studies and was convinced I'd do poorly as he thought I had been spending too much time with my girlfriend. Getting that "first" was a delicious moment. Being the first of firsts earned me a prize of 100 pounds, which in 1936 was a considerable sum. The one condition attached to the prize was that I continue with postgraduate studies. I was delighted to do so.

At the time when I was just beginning to do graduate studies I was interested, as were many young people, in radical opposition movements, and the Isma'ilis were the most important radical opposition movement in medieval Islam. This is the sectarian Muslim group of which the present head, by hereditary succession, is the Aga Khan. This was in the 1930s, and like everybody else at that or any other time, I was influenced by what was going on—the French Popular Front, the Spanish Civil War, the rise of Nazism in Germany. One tends to read the past in terms of the present. While I think it is perfectly legitimate to put to the past questions arising from the present, I think one should be cautious in reading answers from the past into the present.

I told Gibb that I wanted to study the Isma'ilis and he said that he didn't feel qualified to supervise a thesis on that subject. Looking back, I realize I should have been grateful to him because it's not all that usual for professors to say, I don't feel qualified to do this, you'd be better off doing it somewhere else. Gibb did, and suggested I go to Paris and work with Louis Massignon, the great French scholar. Both Gibb and Massignon were Orientalists in the classical sense of that term; that is to say their interests were linguistic, literary, cultural and religious. Both wrote history, but only incidentally, and neither really saw himself as a historian.

I was twenty years old and the idea of going to Paris was very attractive. Paris had much to offer besides Massignon. Gibb wrote to Massignon and he also wrote to an extraordinarily brilliant man, Paul Kraus. Unfortunately Kraus had left Paris and was in Cairo. Gibb had a very high regard for Kraus, and I believe he was at least as eager for me to see and consult Kraus as for me to see Massignon. But Massignon had got Kraus a job in Cairo so I didn't see him then.

I did meet Paul Kraus a year or two later in Cairo where he had taken up what I can only call a rather vague appointment. By that I do not mean to imply anything sinister, only that the appointment was limited in both status and remuneration. I developed a close association with him which I found extremely rewarding. He was a superb scholar with a meticulous, detailed philological accuracy equal to that of the most extreme pedants in our profession, combined with a historian's vision of a civilization and its many different aspects. The association was profoundly illuminating and I remain indebted to him. Later, during the war, I was appalled to learn that he had committed suicide. The circumstances and the reasons remain obscure. What a waste!

I spent the academic year 1936–37 in France, working with Massignon and taking courses at various academic institutions.

Louis Massignon was a very distinguished figure, a famous scholar in his day, but also a rather controversial figure. His special field was religious and sectarian history in the Islamic world. He was a moody man and reacted to me in different ways on different days. He had two prejudices against me based on two aspects of my identity; sometimes I was not quite sure what my offense was: was it crucifying Jesus (as a Jew) or burning Joan of Arc (as an Englishman)? He was certainly an effective teacher when he lectured, but my one-on-one sessions with him deteriorated as the year went on. After I left France we maintained occasional contact. As a courtesy I sent him copies of my publications and on one occasion he came to London to give a lecture and I did the honors hosting him.

One of the courses I took was given by Marcel Mauss, one of the great names in the field of sociology. I didn't know then that he was a great name and it wasn't until years later when I remarked that I'd take a course with him and saw the reaction of my sociologist colleagues that I understood.

My French improved dramatically of course, and it now became possible for me to begin my study of Persian and Turkish—in French.

One of my favorite teachers in Paris was Adnan Bey, a Turk. He was the husband of the more famous Halide Edib, modern Turkey's first major female writer. He was a very kind man, a superb teacher, and we got on very well indeed. Adnan Bey had played a prominent role in the Turkish Revolution, but then he and his wife fell out of favor with Atatürk and went into exile. Like other Turks at the time they had no surname, and as they were living in exile, they were not obliged to adopt surnames at the time when the surname law was enacted in Turkey. In the West he was known as Adnan Bey. "Bey" is a title equivalent to "Mister" but in Turkish usage it follows, rather than precedes, the name. When they returned to Turkey they were obliged to adopt a surname and Adnan adopted the name Adivar, which means "He has a name."

While in Paris I had the opportunity to meet the great Hebrew poet Zalman Schneur, who was living there. We spoke in a mixture of French and Hebrew. At some point he asked if I were reading and translating any other Hebrew poets. I said, "Yes," and mentioned those whose works I had translated, notably Bialik and Tchernikhovsky. I also mentioned another poet, whose name brought a snort of indignation from Schneur. "You don't like his work?" I asked. He replied with a couple of words I didn't understand and which he wouldn't explain. I did, however, memorize them, and was later able to ascertain their meaning. He had, in fact, described this other poet's verses as "goat turds."

I attended a seminar in the medieval economic history of Europe with Emile Coornaert, and that was very good for me—and also rather unfortunate in that it led to the publication of my first paper, one of which I am not particularly proud. It was on the Islamic guilds.

Coornaert was giving a seminar on the guilds in medieval France, at a time when I had become interested in the Islamic guilds because of the Isma'ili connection—or rather, I should say, because of the alleged Isma'ili connection; the whole thing is very dubious. I went to Coornaert's seminar, and when you go to a seminar you have to pay for your seat by doing a paper. Professor Coornaert indicated that he expected a paper from me, and he suggested that I do a paper on the Islamic guilds.

I did the paper and he got quite excited. He said, "You know, there's absolutely nothing available on the Islamic guilds and from a comparative point of view it's very useful to have it; why don't you publish this paper?" Imagine being twenty years old, a student, and a professor tells you, "Why don't you publish this paper?" When I managed to come down from the stratosphere, I wrote to Gibb and asked him about the possibilities. Gibb asked me to send him the paper and promised to look into it. I sent him my paper, which was in French of course, and he replied that he had given the paper to Eileen Power, who was at that time the great authority on medieval economic history in England. He said that she was willing to publish it in a journal, *The Economic History Review,* which she edited, provided I simplify it a little and cut out the more technical stuff and the more arcane references. I translated my paper and tidied it up a bit and then she cut it down a bit and published it. I was in seventh heaven.

But it is a poor article. I was unduly influenced by Massignon, a man of magnetic personality with much charisma. He had many ideas and he could be very persuasive. As the years went by I discarded those ideas one by one, but I was much affected, indeed dominated, by them at the time.

Like other undergraduate Orientalists, I soon became aware that the reading lists provided by the teachers of the various courses I attended included books and articles in French and German, and sometimes also in other languages, and that I was expected to read and understand these. French and German were no problem; I had studied both at high school and had traveled in both French- and German-speaking countries with my parents. My father's operatic interest had enabled me to add Italian, and that brought a rudimentary reading knowledge of Spanish as a freebie.

But there was one other big and important unknown, and that was Russian. At an early stage I came to realize that Russian Orientalists had made a significant contribution to almost every aspect of scholarship on the Islamic world. Sometimes they were kind enough to write in a Western European language; sometimes excerpts or summaries of their work were available in translation. But the most important body of material remained accessible only in the original Russian. Clearly I would have to deal with this problem sooner or later, and set to work to learn this additional language.

My first serious attempt came when I was a graduate student in Paris and I signed on for a course in Russian, which I attended for a brief time. Unfortunately, that time did not last. A change in the schedule brought the Russian course into collision with a Turkish course, and the latter was more important from my point of view. I did however continue my study of Russian, and reached the point where I was able to read Russian texts with blood, sweat and a dictionary. As was my wont, I even tried my hand at translating the great Russian poet Pushkin into English. More seriously, I began to look at Russian learned journals, conference reports and the like, and attempted to read some books.

In the course of my reading, I made an interesting discovery. Much of the discussion of Islam in the Soviet Union was directed, indeed orchestrated, by an organization called The Union of the Militant Godless. It was, of course, a branch of the Soviet government and its task was to conduct antireligious and more specifically atheist propaganda directed against the different peoples of the Soviet Union.

The Union had departments concerned with the religions that had significant followings in the Soviet Union, first Christianity, then Islam. Judaism and other religions were relatively unimportant.

My concern was of course with the Islamic, or rather anti-Islamic, literature, of which I was able to lay my hands on a fairly considerable quantity. Some of it was openly propagandist—tirades directed against the absurdity of religious beliefs, the falsity of religious writings and traditions, and the toxicity of both. Other publications took the form of scholarship—I repeat "form"—with source references, footnotes, etc. Both kinds gave central importance to attacks on the Prophet Muhammad—his mission, his impact, his authenticity, even his historicity. According to one presentation there never was any such person; he was a fabricated myth. This organization was very active in the late twenties and throughout the thirties and produced a considerable body of literature. Not surprisingly, it evoked no response or even criticism within the Soviet Union. That was to be expected. More remarkably, it appears to have evoked no response or even protest in the Islamic world, though Muslim scholars and politicians must have had some knowledge of what was going on.

This is one example of the exemption accorded to the Soviets by those who were ever ready to denounce Western imperialism and its Orientalist ideologues. The same is true of Edward Said and his disciples, who had nothing to say on the devastating critiques in Soviet writings on Islam, or the ruthless Soviet repression of the Muslim peoples under their rule. This privileged, exempt status of the Soviets was revealed even more dramatically in 1979 when the Soviet government, in a clear and naked act of aggression, invaded and conquered Afghanistan.

First Trip to the Middle East

In 1937, after I returned from Paris, I had a conversation with Professor Gibb, who said, "You've now been studying the Middle East for four years; don't you think it's time you saw the place?" I said, "Yes, but . . ." and explained to him that because of the Depression and the generally impoverished state of everybody, including my family, I could no more afford to go to the Middle East than to the moon. He understood and said he thought something could be done about that. The next thing I heard was that I had been appointed to a Royal Asiatic Society traveling fellowship carrying the princely sum of 150 pounds sterling. It took me on my very first trip to the Middle East and enabled me to spend six months there.

My first port of call was Egypt. Arriving in Alexandria, I felt rather like a Muslim bridegroom first seeing his bride, with whom he is to spend the rest of his life, after the wedding. In my three months in Egypt I took courses in Arabic at the American University in Cairo, acquired some colloquial Arabic and enrolled as an "auditor" in the Egyptian University of Cairo. I did what students usually do— attended lectures and meetings, read books and newspapers, talked— and listened. On one occasion I even joined, or rather observed, a student riot.

At first communication was not easy. I had started to learn a couple of Middle Eastern languages, but I had never heard them spoken except, rarely, by fellow students. When I arrived in Egypt the only Arabic I knew was classical Arabic. Colloquial Arabic differs from classical Arabic as much as Italian differs from Latin. To this day, in every Arab country they have two languages, the written language and the spoken. The written language is the same all over the Arab world with very minor variations, but spoken Arabic differs as much as French, Spanish, Italian and Portuguese do. I learned to handle Egyptian Arabic fairly well. Then, when I went to Lebanon and Syria, everyone laughed. They found it most amusing to hear this foreigner speaking Egyptian dialect.

While at the American University in Cairo I had the good fortune to become acquainted with Professor Arthur Jeffery, one of the leading Arabic scholars in the Western world in his time. Originally Australian, he spent some years in Cairo before moving on to a chair at Columbia University in New York.

At one point during his stay in Cairo an incident occurred which caused him profound shock. He had always been interested in the Koran, and in particular had studied the earliest manuscripts of the Koran. In these he found some minor variations in the text, not unlike those found in the earliest manuscripts of the Old and New Testaments. He therefore set to work and produced a study of these early variant readings.

Arthur Jeffery's book was entitled *Materials for the History of the Text of the Qur'an: The Old Codices*, 1937. To his horror, his study was immediately denounced and publicly burnt by order of the leading Muslim religious authorities at Al-Azhar Mosque and University. Professor Jeffery, always respectful of Islamic values, had previously had excellent relations with the people at Al-Azhar, and was the more startled and horrified by their reaction to his book. He pointed out that what he was doing was no different from what the most pious Christians and Jews do to the texts of the Old and New Testaments. To which they replied, "But that is different. The Koran is not like the Bible. The Koran is the word of God." By this they were not merely casting doubt on the authenticity or accuracy of the Jewish and Christian scriptures. They were pointing to the profound difference between Muslim perceptions and Judeo-Christian perceptions of the very nature of scripture. For Christians and Jews, the Bible consists of a number of books, written at different times and in different places, divinely inspired, but mostly committed to writing by human beings. For Muslims, the Koran is one book, divine, eternal and uncreated. It is not simply divinely inspired; it is literally divine and to question it in any way is blasphemy.

Because of the divine perfection of the Koran, it cannot and indeed may not be translated from the original Arabic into any other language. Although for many centuries the vast majority of Muslims have been non-Arabs with little or no knowledge of Arabic, there are no authorized translations of the Koran into Persian, Turkish, Urdu or other Islamic languages, comparable with the Latin Vulgate or the King James Bible in English. Translation is expressly forbidden. There are of course versions in languages other than Arabic, which one might describe as translations, but they are presented as interpretations and commentaries, never as translations, and none of them has any authoritative status.

By collecting and presenting early variants of the oldest surviving Koranic texts, Professor Jeffery was merely trying to do for Muslim scriptures what rabbis and priests had long been doing for the Bible—to provide a more accurate and intelligible text. In Muslim eyes he was impugning the divinity and eternity of their sacred scripture.

A similar question arose from time to time when Western scholars, including some of the notorious Orientalists, pointed out that some of the biblical stories that reappear in the Koran were inaccurately cited, and assumed that the Prophet or his informants got it wrong. To this Muslims responded with what was, in their terms, well-grounded indignation. God does not get it wrong. His Prophet is not "misinformed." If there are differences between biblical stories in the Bible and biblical stories in the Koran, it is because the Christians and the Jews proved unworthy custodians of the scriptures that had been given to them, and either lost or corrupted them.

To Palestine, Syria and Turkey

After the three months in Egypt, I spent a couple of weeks in what was then the British-mandated territory of Palestine. My parents came to join me in Egypt and we went together on our first visit to the Holy Land, where we spent about two weeks. We were able to go to Safed and Haifa but to our disappointment we were advised not to go to Jerusalem as this was deemed dangerous. My parents and I stayed in Tel Aviv at the Hotel Samuel, where I would return much later. From there I went on a tour of Syria and Lebanon. By that time I was already working on my thesis on the Isma'ilis and thought it might be useful to visit the Isma'ili villages in Syria. These villages were in the central part of the country, both east and west of the city of Hama. In Crusader times, they had been the bases of the dreaded Assassins from which they launched their attacks on chiefly Muslim but occasionally Crusader targets. The power of the Assassins ended in the thirteenth century, but some Isma'ili communities remain to the present day. It was these Isma'ili villages to which I went in the hope of being able to find additional material for use in my doctoral dissertation.

My first book, *The Origins of Isma'ilism*, had been published by the firm of Heffer in Cambridge in 1940. Looking back, I am not very proud of it. A Ph.D. thesis is normally written with an eye on the board of examiners, without much consideration of a wider readership. Even the best theses usually need editing and expansion before they are ready for publication in book form.

But this was a different situation. War had broken out and I was about to leave the academic life for war service with an uncertain, even problematic, outcome. There was no way that I could undertake the necessary revision and editing of my thesis to prepare it for publication. The University of London publication fund, no doubt in recognition of this situation, offered me a grant to facilitate the publication of the thesis, and with this in hand, it was not difficult to find a publisher. This subsidized publication was an edition of five hundred copies. Unsurprisingly, in time of war, its immediate impact was minimal, and it was over ten years before this five-hundred-copy edition ran out of print. One thing however did give me some pleasure. The thesis was well received in the Arab world by Arab scholars and—to my utter astonishment—an Arabic translation was published in Iraq.

After the war I learned that Jean Sauvaget, one of the great masters of my subject, had written some very kind words about *The Origins*. The fact that he was writing in wartime, in German-occupied France, about a book published in England, may have made him more indulgent than he might otherwise have been.

By the time I returned to academic life at the end of 1945, my interests had turned to other, quite different subjects, and I was content to leave the origins of Isma'ilism where they were. My return to Isma'ili studies came in the early 1950s when I was approached by Professor John L. LaMonte, a distinguished American medievalist, who asked me to contribute a chapter on the Assassins to a multivolume syndicated history of the Crusades which he and some colleagues were planning to edit and publish. I readily accepted and produced a chapter entitled "The Isma'ilites and the Assassins" which appeared in Volume I of *A History of the Crusades,* published in Philadelphia in 1955. After my chapter was published I did some short studies on various aspects of the topic, e.g., the Arabic and other sources for the history of the Syrian Assassins, the curious tale of the relations between Saladin and the Assassins, and an edition and translation of a short, unpublished Arabic biography of one of the Assassin leaders.

All these were, of course, concerned with the Assassins in Syria. But their history could not be fully understood in isolation from the headquarters of the Assassin order in Iran. I therefore decided to devote a book to the Assassins, dealing with their place in European folklore and scholarship, their origins in the Middle East, their activities in both Iran and Syria, including their dealings with the Crusaders, and a concluding chapter which I called "Means and Ends," dealing with the terrorist tactics of the Assassins and the revolutionary strategy of their leadership. The book was published in London in 1967, years before a wave of Muslim terrorists gave the book a new relevance, even urgency.

The subsequent bibliographical history of this book is curious. The edition in English was reprinted several times and a French translation appeared in Paris in 1982. Three independent translations into Arabic were made, only one of them authorized. A Persian translation was published twice, both times without authorization, in Tehran, once under the monarchy and again under the republic, with the addition of two other studies on related topics. Translations in Japanese, Spanish, Turkish, Italian and German followed in rapid succession.

The changing nature of interest in the topic is best indicated by the titles used by the translators. The original English text was simply entitled *The Assassins: A Radical Sect in Islam.* In the French edition, the first foreign version, this became *The Assassins, Terrorism and Politics in Medieval Islam;* in Italian, *The Assassins: A Radical Islamic Sect, the First Terrorists in History;* in German, *The Assassins; On the Tradition of Religious Murder in Radical Islam.*

The purpose of all this was clear—to suggest a parallel between the movements and actions described in this book and those that are convulsing the Middle East and threatening much of the world at the present time.

The story of the Assassins, who appeared in Iran and spread to the Syrian and Lebanese mountains and flourished from the eleventh to the thirteenth centuries, can be instructive. They do not represent the mainstream Islamic tradition or consensus; they were a heresy within a heresy—an extremist offshoot of the Shi'a movement, itself a deviation from mainstream Sunni Islam. Their practices and beliefs were rejected by mainstream Sunni and Shi'a alike, and were eventually abandoned even by that small minority which retained their distinctive beliefs. There is a misapprehension, common in the West since medieval times, that the anger and weapons of the Assassins were directed against the Crusaders. This is not true. There were relatively few Crusaders among their victims, and even these were usually marked down as the result of some internal Muslim calculation. The vast majority of their victims were Muslims, because their attack was directed not against the outsider, but against the dominant elites and dominant ideas of Islam.

The chosen victims of the medieval Assassins were the rulers of Islam, monarchs, ministers, generals, and major religious functionaries. The weapon used was almost always the same, the dagger, wielded by the appointed Assassin in person. It is noteworthy that they made virtually no use of such safer weapons as were available to them at the time—the bow, the crossbow, or poison. They chose the most difficult and inaccessible targets and the most dangerous mode of attack. The Assassin himself, having struck down his assigned victim, made no attempt to escape, nor was any made to rescue him. On the contrary, to have survived a mission was seen as a disgrace. In this respect, the Assassins were indeed the forerunners of the suicide bombers of today. Both are in marked contrast to the combination of indiscriminate murder by remote control and blackmail by kidnapping that have become the marks of modern terrorist practice.

Islam, like Christianity or Judaism, is an ethical religion, and murder and blackmail have no place in its beliefs or practices. Nevertheless, then as now, there are groups who practice murder in the name of their religion, and a study of this medieval sect of Assassins may therefore serve a useful purpose—not as a guide to Islamic attitudes on assassination, but as an example of how certain groups gave a radical and violent turn to the basic Islamic association between religion and politics, and tried to use it for the accomplishment of their own purposes. Of all the lessons to be learnt from the Assassins, perhaps the most important is their final and total failure.

The resemblances between the medieval Assassins and their modern counterparts are indeed striking—the Syrian-Iranian connection, the calculated use of terror, the total dedication of the Assassin emissary to the point of self-immolation in the service of his cause and in the expectation of recompense in an eternity of bliss. But there are also significant differences, notably that the medieval Assassins limited their attacks to the targeted victim and always took care not to harm innocent bystanders. Those Assassins made no attempt to escape as it was considered an honor to do the deed and be caught. That tradition, alas, has disappeared.

I was disappointed in what I could find on the Assassins, but in other respects the visit to Syria was interesting and indeed useful, augmenting my knowledge both of Arabic as a spoken language and of the way of life in the Syrian countryside.

My only local contact was the head of a Danish archaeological mission, an acquaintance of my guru, Professor Gibb. I made myself known to him and he was helpful in various ways, one in particular. Syria, at that time, was under French mandate, and the traditional Anglo-French rivalry and mutual suspicion were still alive and well in the Levant. It seems that the local French political officer heard of my visit, but did not believe that a dissertation on the medieval Isma'ilis was the reason for my presence. He suspected that I was a British secret agent engaged in nefarious anti-French activities. The fact that my travel was funded by the Royal Asiatic Society only served to confirm his suspicions. Fortunately, the head of the Danish archaeological mission was able to persuade him of my academic and scholarly bona fides. I managed to complete my stay there unmolested.

During that time I went to visit the famous Crac des Chevaliers, a wonderful Crusader castle on a hill in the north of Syria. I was provided with a guide from the local village. At one point I needed to relieve myself, and asked my guide to direct me to the nearest toilet. He replied in bewilderment that they had no such thing. "Where do you go to relieve yourselves?" I asked. He replied by waving a hand over the fields. I was visibly unhappy with this and then he had an inspiration. He pointed to the castle and said, "The people who built this place were also 'Franks' and probably they built a WC. Let's go and look." (Franks was the general term for Europeans.) Indeed, he was right. The Crusaders had provided themselves with this basic amenity and I was most grateful that they had. (Or perhaps I should say, relieved that they had.)

The very first time I set foot in Turkey, I came from Syria where I had been working on my thesis, and not, like most Western visitors, from the West. My academic training had been as a historian and an Orientalist, specializing in classical Islamic civilization. The fact that my approach was from the past and from the south, instead of the present and the West, gave me a different—and I would claim a better—understanding of the country, its culture, and its problems. Most judgments and evaluations are based on comparison and are inevitably shaped by the elements compared. Mine were markedly different from the usual.

My First Job

By 1938 I had been a postgraduate student for nearly two years and finally settled down to work seriously on my dissertation. At the same time I was studying, intermittently, for my law exams, in order to qualify for a "real profession."

In that year two things happened at about the same time to change the course of my life. First, in my legal studies the next subject was the law of real property and conveyancing, which, as anyone who has studied law knows, is monumentally tedious and boring. Second,

the University of London offered me a position as an assistant lecturer, the lowest form of human life in English universities. Confronted with this choice I did not hesitate for one moment. By then I
realized that I would never be a lawyer. I had enough law to help me
understand a legal civilization, but not enough to turn me into a
lawyer.

In the English universities at that time the procedure for a Ph.D.
examination was very different from the American system. In American universities the really important matter is getting your thesis
approved by your supervisor; the supervisor recommends that it be
submitted to a board of examiners and the rest is ceremonial. In British universities this was not the case. A Ph.D. thesis had to be submitted to a board of three examiners consisting of the supervisor, another
professor from the same university and a professor from a different
university. The board of examiners had three options—accept the
thesis, in which case the candidate was awarded a Ph.D.; reject the
thesis, in which case the candidate went away empty-handed; or, they
could do what was known as "referring the thesis," which meant "Go
away, rewrite this, that and the other thing, resubmit it, and then, if
we like it, we'll give you a Ph.D."

I was appointed assistant lecturer in the history of the Near and
Middle East at the School of Oriental and African Studies in the
University of London (I think Gibb arranged that) at the handsome
salary of 250 pounds a year. My appointment was in the department
of history. The head of the department at that time was a specialist in
Indian history, Professor Dodwell; he welcomed me to the department for its first appointment in Middle Eastern history. When I
went to see him to make myself known, he was looking at my file and
he said, "I see you haven't yet finished your Ph.D." I said that I hoped
to finish it during the coming months. So Professor Dodwell, my
boss, said, "Well, in that case you won't want to be bothered with too
much teaching in your first year. Do you think you could manage to

do one tutorial course?" I replied affirmatively and marveled at my good fortune. How extraordinary!

The first course I taught was therefore a tutorial on the history of the Islamic Near and Middle East. It was taken by four students: one Egyptian, one Palestinian Arab, one Iraqi, and one Iranian—just the four. My father was mystified by this. "You are teaching Middle Eastern history?" "Yes." In a puzzled voice he continued, "To whom?" So I described my first class to him and he said, "I don't understand. Why on earth should the University of London pay you a salary to teach Arab history to Arabs?"

There was a further question: why would Arabs want to come to England to study their own history? This was a question that would come up again sometime later.

2.

The War Years

When in the spring of 1939 the Nazis took over the remaining part of Czechoslovakia, proving that the Munich policy had failed and that war was inevitable, various institutions and individuals began to make preparations for war. The Royal Institute of International Affairs, usually known by the name of the building it occupies, Chatham House, began a series of intensive training programs for its younger members, in which I participated. After war broke out, some of us were sent to the Foreign Office to make ourselves useful as aides and to learn something about the realities of international relations. We were there for about a month, until the opening of the academic year in October. We then went back to our normal pursuits, though no longer in a very normal form.

Much to my surprise I was put down as an expert on Turkey. At that time I had spent altogether about two and a half weeks in Turkey, a few days in Ankara and the rest in Istanbul. That was my only direct knowledge of the country. I had however some knowledge of Turkish, and had of course spent a lot of time studying Turkish history, though not much of it devoted to the recent past.

I have just one vivid recollection of my month-long apprenticeship in the Foreign Office. One day the official to whom I was attached told me that he had an appointment with the Turkish ambassador and asked if I would like to come with him. I was delighted. This was my introduction to this level of international relations. To make it still better, the Turkish ambassador in London at that time was Tevfik Rüştü Aras, until recently the minister of foreign affairs and a close associate of Kemal Atatürk. The conversation, in which of course I was a listener not a participant, took place, rather to my surprise, in French. The Turkish ambassador to England and former minister of foreign affairs could not speak English; the Foreign Office expert who was sent to talk to him could not speak Turkish, and French was their only shared language. At that time, although French was still generally accepted as the international language of diplomacy, it was already on the way out. I cannot imagine such a conversation taking place in French now that English has become the lingua franca.

The subject of their conversation was of course the war which had just begun, and more particularly the role of Turkey, which was in the process of negotiating a treaty of alliance with Great Britain and France. A joint Anglo-Turkish declaration had already been issued on May 12, 1939, which paved the way for the formal Anglo-Franco-Turkish Treaty of Alliance signed in October. But the outbreak of war on September 1 had significantly changed the situation. The ambassador made two points. "We Turks," he said, "have a strong sense of history. We know that a partition of Poland is a threat to Turkey. But . . ." and he went on to explain why Turkey was not about to declare war on the Axis as expected in light of the Alliance with England and France. "It is not our policy," he said, "to undertake commitments for the fulfillment of which we would be dependent on the help of others." Later they invoked the second protocol to the treaty, stating, "The obligations undertaken by Turkey . . . cannot compel that country to take action having as its effect, or involving as its consequence, entry into armed conflict with the U.S.S.R."

This was a plausible excuse at that time, in view of the close relationship between Moscow and Berlin. The same justification for Turkish neutrality was maintained, even when that close relationship was sundered by the German invasion of Russia.

By the summer of 1939 it was already clear that war was imminent. I was asked to serve on an advisory committee for the Foreign Office to prepare reports on the various problems of the Middle East. But obviously this was something very temporary. I wrote to the War Office to offer my services and they wrote back fixing an appointment for me to be interviewed by an officer of the intelligence department. I went to the War Office and was duly interviewed. He asked the usual questions and some unusual questions and then said he thought they could find a job for me and they would be in touch. A little while passed, not very long, and then I was asked to come again for a second interview in which I was told they had decided to accept me and that I would be sent in January to an OCTU (an officer cadet training unit) in the cavalry. I blurted out, "Cavalry, you mean horses?" He nodded yes and I said, "But this is 1939. Who uses cavalry these days?" He gave me a look and said, "Have you ever heard of Lawrence of Arabia?" "Of course," I said. "Well, would he have been able to accomplish what he did if he hadn't been able to ride? We want you to learn to ride properly." I protested that I had never ridden a horse in my life. He said, "So much the better. Then you won't have any bad habits to get rid of."

This was in September 1939, and my call-up was for January 1940, so I thought I'd better do something about this. I hunted around and found a livery stable in Buckinghamshire which was run by a former cavalryman and asked him to teach me to ride cavalry style. So I spent my weekends during the winter of 1939–40 careering around Buckinghamshire on horseback, holding the reins in my left hand and brandishing an imaginary gun or saber in my right hand. I was determined to be prepared for cavalry officer training.

Unfortunately my boss, Professor Ralph Turner, the director of the School of Oriental and African Studies, wasn't having any of it. He was very determined that SOAS should make its own contribution to the war effort as a collective body. He stopped all our call-ups

and volunteering and everything else to make sure that he could retain the entire academic faculty of the school. To my great annoyance
and disappointment my call-up to the cavalry was canceled and I
continued to teach at the school which in the meantime had moved
to Cambridge. We spent the academic year 1939–40 at Christ's College in Cambridge, enjoying the hospitality of that institution. Later
in the year, my call-up finally caught up with me, only this time it
wasn't horses but mechanized cavalry. I did my basic training as a
trooper in a tank regiment.

Either because of my aptitude for languages or my ineptitude
with tanks, I was transferred from the tank corps to the intelligence
corps at the end of 1940 or the beginning of 1941. I spent the rest of
the war doing jobs which, bound by the Official Secrets Act, I am still
not at liberty to discuss in any detail.

When I was transferred to the intelligence corps this was so secret
that I wasn't even told where I was going, nor could I have an address
for any mail to be sent to me. I was given a railway ticket which took
me to Euston Station in London. There I had to report to the military
office where I was told to report to Waterloo Station. I went to Waterloo Station where I reported and was given a ticket to go to Winchester. In Winchester I was met at the station and taken to my new
abode. You can imagine that with all this secrecy I was worried about
my mail. I needn't have bothered. My mail arrived from the tank
regiment with the new address written on the envelope.

In Winchester I completed the basic intelligence training and
then was kept waiting until they found a suitable assignment for me.
This was made more difficult by the fact that I had failed an important component of intelligence training, the motorcycle rough-riding
course. I had never ridden a motorcycle before and had to take a special course to fulfill this requirement. I passed the road test but failed
the rough stuff, climbing up and down a hillside amid trees and
bushes. I therefore had to wait for an assignment that did not involve

this requirement. This excluded me from battlefield intelligence but left many other possibilities.

While I was there they didn't want me to waste my time and they saw from my records that I was a lecturer at the university. They said, "Oh, you teach? Then you can teach." I was immediately attached to the training staff.

One of the things which had to be taught was a subject known in official jargon as O&A, which means organization and administration. Recruits in intelligence usually knew precious little about anything military. They needed intensive training in military matters and I was ordered to do this in a three-week course. In the university we get bored if we do the same course every year. Imagine doing the same course every three weeks! My job was to describe the structure of the British Army in general, and its intelligence corps in particular, to these recruits.

In order to be accepted by intelligence, you had to meet two requirements. You had to have at least two generations of British birth and you had to have a mastery of a foreign language. These two are rarely combined in one person, and the people there fell into some recognizable categories. Probably the largest was the children of mixed marriages. The two generations didn't have to be on both sides (we're not talking about Nazi race laws) so many had one English parent and one foreign parent, and grew up using two languages. Another category was schoolmasters—teachers, particularly of French and to a lesser extent of German. And the third, very large category was people from the colonies, particularly the colonies in Europe—Gibraltar, Malta, Cyprus—and to some extent from some of the Asian colonies, especially Hong Kong and Singapore. They were British by birth and descent since they were imperial subjects, and they usually had another language, their local language. What nobody bothered to find out was how well they knew English.

The most common language among our trainees was Greek,

thanks to the numerous Cypriots who were transferred to us. The second commonest was Maltese. In addition, surprisingly, there were some whose registered language was French—British subjects from the Seychelles Islands which had been colonized by the French but which became British during the Napoleonic Wars. The rather aristocratic white settler population in these islands by now had several generations of British descent, but remained very French by language, culture and in some measure loyalty. This gave rise to questions with some of them—were they supporters of de Gaulle or of Vichy?

What all of these different groups had in common was that they had a native language other than English and this sometimes gave rise to problems.

I remember particularly that when the Germans invaded Greece we had a sudden need for intelligence personnel with a knowledge of Greek. Someone at headquarters went through the files and found quite a number of soldiers in the British Army with a knowledge of Greek who were all immediately shipped off to Winchester for training. They were without exception Cypriot Greeks, impeccably British by birth and descent with an excellent knowledge of Greek but often their English was very limited. A large proportion of them were waiters. One or two were headwaiters and at that time I picked up that the Greek for headwaiter is *archi-garsoni*. On one occasion a department head to whom we sent our trained intelligence personnel sent a message saying, "Send me more waiters and fewer schoolmasters."

My class of Greeks was quite raucous and keeping order was challenging. We had NCO's from the Guards to maintain military discipline. We began each day with a roll call and of course having an ordinary English sergeant from the Guards reading the list of names like Pappadopoulos and Athanasacopoulos, one after another, degenerated into high farce.

I tried to liven up my courses with an occasional wisecrack, not thinking, in my youthful folly, that being disrespectful to the army and its intelligence to an audience of aspiring spooks was not wise. I should have got into trouble, and I found out later why I didn't. My boss, Major Jennings Bramley, of blessed memory, had written one short line in my file that said, "His sense of humor should not be taken as seditious."

Eventually I was posted to Bletchley Park, where I spent a couple of months doing decoding. During my stay there I made use of my knowledge of languages and developed some new skills in how to play with languages. Toward the end of 1941 I was transferred to another branch of the service based in London. The phrase we were instructed to use was "attached to a department of the Foreign Office." You have to be known to be doing something and that was the official formula. Actually we were a branch of MI6 and when, as an innocent beginner in intelligence, I asked what the difference was between MI6 and the more famous MI5, I was told, "The job of MI5 is to stop others from doing to us what MI6 is doing to them." Much of my work was summarizing and/or translating texts, mostly from Arabic. Some were in codes or ciphers. What was interesting were the methods by which the texts were obtained. Some of the texts were fascinating, many were not. For much of the time it was just a desk job.

One of my lifelong friendships began through a meeting with a colleague in the service. Like me, Arthur Hatto was a young academic; his field was German studies, and he specialized in medieval German poetry, particularly in the medieval German epics. As a German speaker he was immediately needed and he was recruited into another branch of MI6. One day out of the blue he called and asked if he could come and see me. Of course I agreed. He came to my office and explained that he was tracking a Syrian who had been recruited into the German espionage service and about whom he knew through his German sources. Was there any way in which I could help him? It so happened that I had become aware of the same Syrian from my Arab sources and we were able to compare notes and combine our information to good effect.

My final posting during the war was in London and I spent the greater part of the blitz years living, working and, more remarkably, sleeping in London. In the early stages of the blitz I went to shelters in the underground stations but I soon got tired of this and decided to stay in my bed and take my chances. One can get used to anything!

Forty years later I was on a visit to Israel when Saddam Hussein started sending Scud missiles into the country, a few of which exploded in the Tel Aviv area. I had been invited to a dinner party in Tel Aviv at that time and turned up at my hostess's home at the appointed time, to her utter astonishment. All her other guests had canceled and she assumed I would do the same though I had not called to say so. She started to praise my courage and determination and in all honesty I had to disclaim any particular heroism. I pointed out that the whole Scud episode would have amounted to a rather quiet evening during the London blitz. We had got used to living our lives in much worse conditions than that.

Ascertaining What They Were Doing

When war broke out in 1939 the only Arab state that was completely independent and free from any kind of imperial control, domination or presence was Saudi Arabia. The Saudis at that time had two embassies abroad—one in London, one in Paris. Curiously, neither of the ambassadors was a Saudi. The ambassador in London, Hafiz Wahba, was an Egyptian; the ambassador in Paris, Fuad Hamza, was a Syrian. Presumably the one was chosen for his skill and experience in speaking English and dealing with Englishmen; the other for his corresponding skill and experience with French and Frenchmen.

At the time of the French collapse and surrender, we were very much concerned about the position of the Saudi Embassy in Paris. Since the French government had surrendered and had in effect become a German satellite, we asked the Saudis to close down their embassy in Paris. They refused, and instead moved it to Vichy where it remained in contact with the German satellite French government based in that city.

The Saudi Embassy in Vichy now became a place of major concern and importance to us. More specifically, it became a major place of contact between the Arab world and the Axis. There were other places of contact, notably Ankara in neutral Turkey, where the German ambassador, Franz von Papen, was able to maintain an extensive network of communications in the Arab world. But the Saudi Embassy in Vichy was of particular interest. We found ways of keeping informed about what was going on there, and more particularly about the contacts between the Saudis and the Germans. We were especially interested in the activities of Dr. Fritz Grobba, a leading Arab expert in the service of the Third Reich. He entered into extensive and detailed contacts with the Saudi Embassy in Vichy and through them with the Arab world in general.

We monitored the embassy's correspondence and telephone calls. Ambassador Fuad Hamza reported to the Saudi foreign minister who was based in Jedda, the only place in Saudi Arabia where foreigners were allowed to be resident and where, therefore, the embassies accredited to the Saudi government were based. The foreign minister, in Jedda, communicated with King Ibn Saud, in Riyad, entirely by telephone. They didn't realize how vulnerable telephone conversations were, and were often surprised at the degree of intimate knowledge that we had of what they were doing, even of what they were thinking.

For several years of my life I began my day's work by reading the previous day's transcripts of telephone conversations and written messages between various people. Because of this experience during the war I developed and still retain an almost neurotic fear of telephone conversations and therefore am extremely reluctant to discuss anything of significance on the telephone.

Dealings with other Arab governments during the war were sometimes quite complicated. King Farouk of Egypt demanded that as a friend and ally he was entitled to know of our military plans and insisted that we provide him with full details. We didn't trust him, and concocted a totally false plan and gave it to him. When we captured the Italian headquarters in North Africa, we found a copy of this plan. At that time Italy was, of course, a member of the Axis and a German ally.

When the French surrendered to the Germans in 1940, most of the French overseas empire was beyond their reach and the governors of the colonies were free to choose between Vichy or de Gaulle in London. The overwhelming majority chose Vichy, including the French-mandated territory of Syria-Lebanon. Under Vichy rule, Syria-Lebanon was wide open to Nazi infiltration and became a Nazi base in the heart of the Arab Middle East. The Germans established themselves there and played a very important role.

From Syria the Germans extended their activities into Iraq where they were able to set up a pro-Nazi regime, headed by the famous, or notorious, Rashid Ali. We felt it was imperative that we do something about that. We dealt first with Iraq. A brief military campaign was sufficient to overthrow the regime of Rashid Ali, who fled to Syria and later to Berlin, where he joined his friend the Mufti of Jerusalem as Hitler's guest. Then, with the aid of the Free French who provided us with a cover of legitimacy, we invaded Syria and Lebanon, defeated the "Vichyssois" and established a new Free French regime there. It was in that campaign that Moshe Dayan, who was serving as a volunteer with the British forces, lost one of his eyes. After the departure of the Vichy people, a new regime was established in Syria-Lebanon under French authority but controlled by the de Gaulle center in London.

I was in Syria about that time and one of my most vivid impressions was of the violent hostility, even contempt, of the Syrians for the French. Like other Arabs they disliked all the imperial powers, but they found the continued French presence particularly humiliating. The rival imperialists were seen as the British and later the Americans on one side, and the Germans and later the Soviets on the other. The French, regardless of whether they were loyal to Vichy or de Gaulle, were seen as the servants of either the Germans or the British. What made them particularly angry was when de Gaulle's Free French, being short of troops, brought Senegalese battalions of the French colonial army into Syria. That was the supreme and ultimate insult. The Syrians protested, "Now we are being ruled not just by the servants of the imperialists, but by the slaves of the servants of the imperialists!" A poster was put up in Damascus at that time showing a black Senegalese soldier with a French kepi and a French uniform and a knife between his teeth saying, *"Je viens te civiliser!"* ("I come to civilize you!")

A Message for Downing Street

Intercepting and decoding messages is a very important part of the intelligence world. During the war, reading mail and more particularly reading telegrams became a crucial part of our intelligence operations. This applied not only to enemies but also to neutrals and sometimes even to those who were, officially at least, classified as friends. In 1929 U.S. Secretary of State Henry Stimson said in horror that gentlemen do not read other people's mail. Nevertheless, we did so extensively during the war and these exchanges were an absolutely invaluable source of information.

Teleprinters were much used in those days and once when I was

on night duty, the teleprinter at the back of the office started clatter-
ing. What came through was an intercepted message in German. I
should explain that one of our main sources of Axis information was
the Japanese Embassy in Berlin. There was no overland contact between Germany and Japan; all their communications had to go by
radio and the Japanese ambassador in Berlin, General Oshima, was
an invaluable source of information about what was happening in
Germany. Our superb code breakers had broken the code and were
reading and translating the stuff, but for some reason, this didn't
come through that channel but through one of our German channels. What came through that night was the text, in German, of a
German-Japanese treaty of alliance against Britain and the United
States. Even though this was just before Pearl Harbor I realized this
was an important document and immediately worked to translate it
from German into English and then I forwarded it by teleprinter to
the Prime Minister's office at 10 Downing Street. I don't know what
happened to it after that.

The great tragedy of my life during the war was that on the one
occasion, the only occasion, when the Prime Minister, Mr. Churchill,
visited my unit, by sheer bad luck I was on leave. I thus lost my only
opportunity to meet Winston Churchill. But we were in contact in
various other ways. A lot of stories about Churchill circulated within
the organization. Some have appeared in print; some have not. Here
are two of my favorites.

When the Germans invaded the Soviet Union in 1941, we suddenly became allies with the Soviets, and Churchill sent a military
mission to Moscow commanded by a dour Scottish general. In true
Soviet style the Russians told him nothing, and showed him nothing.
Our general, being a dour Scot, decided that since he had nothing to
report, he would send no reports. Churchill got rather annoyed; he
had a military mission in Moscow and he was hearing nothing from
them. In typical Churchillian style he sent a rather sharp telegram to

Moscow: "Prime Minister London to Head of British Military Mission Moscow. All that we know is that it's raining in Moscow. Would welcome further information." To which came the reply, from Moscow: "Officer commanding British military mission in Moscow, to Prime Minister London. Interested to learn from your message that it's raining in Moscow. We are not allowed to look out of the window."

Another Churchill story. During the war years we had a number of governments in exile in London from the various countries conquered and occupied by the Axis. One of them was a Greek government which rotated rather uneasily between London and Cairo and which consisted of a coalition of different parties which, not surprisingly with a coalition, kept on breaking up and reforming and breaking up and reforming. Then at a certain point a military strong man appeared, General Plastiras (pronounced PlassTEERaahss), and he formed a government. The hope was that he would be a sort of Greek de Gaulle. Churchill went to inform the cabinet of this, and the way he did it was such that within hours it was all round the establishment and even reached my level. Churchill went in and said to the cabinet, "Well, gentlemen, we have a new Greek Prime Minister, General Plaster ass. Let's hope he hasn't got feet of clay too."

I never met Churchill but on one occasion I was received by the legendary "C," Sir Stewart Menzies, the head of the secret service. I was suitably impressed walking into the office of the head of the secret service and still more impressed by meeting him. He was gracious, welcoming, complimentary and he made me feel extraordinarily good. I can no longer remember what we talked about, but even if I could, I wouldn't be allowed to repeat it.

Being Jewish in the Service

It was more than sixty years ago, but I still remember the occasion and the conversation. It was in the middle of the night, and apart from the routine rumble of shells and bombs, things were relatively quiet. I was on night watch. In the branch of His Majesty's service in which I served, we took it in turns to stay awake, two at a time, all night long, to deal with any emergency that might arise. It so happened that during this night we whiled away the time chatting about nothing in particular. My colleague was from another department, so even our shoptalk was limited by the "need-to-know" restriction and therefore not very interesting. Suddenly my colleague George started a new and very different conversation. "Forgive me," he said, "I don't want to intrude, but am I right in thinking that you are Jewish?"

"You are right. I am Jewish, and there is nothing to forgive."

"Forgive me," he said again, "but I have the impression that you are not a devout and observant Jew."

"You are right again."

"Then, I don't understand," he said. "Why do you bother?"

"Now I don't understand." I said. "What do you mean by that?"

"Let me try to explain," said George. "You must agree that being Jewish is often difficult and sometimes dangerous."

"Yes, indeed," I said—one could hardly deny this statement in a branch of the intelligence service in 1942.

"Then, I don't understand," said George yet again. "I can see that you may be ready to face persecution or death for your religious beliefs. But if you don't hold or live by those beliefs, then, why bother?"

This time I began to understand George's question, even his incomprehension. George obviously thought of Judaism as a kind of sect or cult, like so many others. Membership in such a group was meaningful if one were a devout and practicing member, meaningless if one were not. In such a case there would be no good reason to remain a member, particularly if membership involved inconvenience or worse.

I set to work to try to explain to George, and to myself, why being Jewish meant more than belonging to a community defined by religion, though that was obviously a primary part of it. There were other elements besides belief and worship that mattered, and could somehow survive even the loss of these. Jewishness (I prefer this word to Judaism, which sounds rather theological) is a shared memory and experience of life. It is a many-faceted culture—distinctive, yet compatible and combinable with other cultures. It is an identity, not a whole or exclusive identity, but an important part of the multiple identities that all civilized people bear. Finally, it is a heritage, preserved through millennia by courage, achievement and loyalty, and for all these reasons, a source of legitimate pride to be cherished and passed on to those who come after us.

There have always been some who indeed did "not bother," finding the retention dangerous, difficult, or merely burdensome. For many centuries, hostility against Jews was theologically defined. This gave a Jew freedom of choice. By a simple act of conversion he could escape persecution and even, if he wished, join the persecutors. The racially defined hostility of the nineteenth and twentieth centuries removed this option, and forced even the most vestigial of Jews to remain what he was, if only in name. In our own day, events in the Middle East have provided, for those who need it, a new rationale for Jew-baiting; this in turn has restored, for Jews who want it, the lost option of changing sides.

But for most, even for those whose religious faith is at best tenuous and whose Jewish identity is overshadowed by other, larger identities, denying that Jewish identity would be an act of falsehood, if not to others, then to oneself.

In England there is no legal separation of church and state. The monarch is head of the church, the bishops are members of the upper house of Parliament, and in schools, the army, and other institutions, prayer is an important part of the program. Prayer sessions are primarily Anglican, that is, Church of England, but parallel prayers are organized for other groups that are large enough. During World War II a cousin of mine was serving in the Oxford and Bucks Light Infantry. One day he was summoned by his colonel who barked that he hadn't see him at church parade and he wanted to know why. My cousin explained that he was Jewish and it would therefore not be appropriate for him to attend the Anglican church parade. The colonel said that that was not a reason as there were separate church parades for different groups. He should go to the Jewish church parade. My cousin explained that it so happened that he was the only Jew in that battalion and he couldn't very well have a church parade on his own. The colonel harrumphed, and finally said, "Yes. I see your point. Dismissed." My cousin thought that that was the end of the matter but he was quite wrong. A week later he was once again summoned by the colonel who told him that there was a London regiment thirty miles down the road which had lots of Jews and regular Jewish services. The colonel had arranged for a car and driver to take my cousin there to participate in the Jewish church parade. And so, for as long as my cousin was stationed there, he was taken every week to participate in Jewish worship, something he never did either before or after that interval in his life.

To the Middle East

Late in the war I was ordered to go to the Middle East and was directed to a naval base somewhere on the English south coast. There I boarded a seaplane which we flew first to Malta, paused for a little while, and then continued to Egypt. It was certainly not a comfortable or pleasant journey and it was long. The planes were quite small and carried few people. There must have been only half a dozen others at any one time.

After a short time in Egypt I was told to go to Baghdad. It was the height of summer and the temperature was terribly hot. Stepping out of the plane at the airport was like stepping into a blast furnace. I was taken by car to my hotel, and the first thing I had to do was report to the British Embassy. I asked the hotel concierge how to get to the embassy. He said it was quite near, about a quarter of a mile down the road on the same street as the hotel and he would call a taxi for me. I told him I didn't need a taxi for only a quarter of a mile and that I would walk. He gave me a funny look and said, "Please yourself." I stepped out, walked about five yards, came back and said, "You're right, call a taxi." The temperature was 125 degrees in the shade and it was just physically impossible for me to walk. Iraqis managed it but only with great difficulty and to a minimal extent.

During the war there was a serious shortage of food in North Africa. The Americans with true generosity sent in a large supply of various canned foods, of which a large part included ham and bacon. North Africa is overwhelmingly Muslim and pork is forbidden. Our American allies were startled and even a little offended when they found their generous gifts of canned food were being rejected indignantly by the local population. We explained but in those days not much was known about Islam.

When the American forces landed in North Africa, they discovered that no ice cream was available locally. This was a serious problem for an army that was accustomed to having ice cream regularly, particularly in hot weather, and of hot weather there is no shortage in North Africa. With true American ingenuity, they soon found a solution. When planes went on expeditions over enemy territory, reconnaissance or bombing or whatever it was, there was a man sitting at the back with a tub churning for ice cream. One couldn't do that on the ground in North Africa; it was too hot and there was no refrigeration available. But in a plane high in the air it was possible, and that was how American troops were ensured of at least an emergency supply.

One of my colleagues in intelligence, an officer in a Scottish regiment, was a fluent Arabic speaker. He was serving in Iraq and was sent on what we called "detached duty" to the north. On his way back to rejoin his regiment he was captured by people whom we called "bandits" and who called themselves "patriots." They were very polite but they seized him, handcuffed him and said they were going to kill him but would keep him alive until their chief returned that evening. The chief would want to question him. The Scot acknowledged he was their prisoner and that they would do what they chose, but he asked, as a matter of interest, why they wanted to kill him. They replied that it was obvious. "You are English!" He said, indignantly, that if they had to kill him they should do so but they should not do it for the wrong reason—he was not English. "What do you mean?" they queried. "You are an English officer, you are wearing an English uniform, you are serving in the English army." As the story goes, he said, "No, you've got it wrong. I am a British officer, I am wearing a British uniform, I am serving in the British Army, but I am not English." "Well, what are you?" And he replied, with great pride, "I am a Scot." They had never heard of that and asked what that meant. He fumbled a bit and then had an idea and said, "Look, here in Iraq there is one country called Iraq. You have an Iraqi government and an Iraqi army and you are all Iraqis. But in the north there are Kurds and in the south there are Arabs. You are all Iraqis but a Kurd is not an Arab and an Arab is not a Kurd. This is how it is with us. Scots in the north, English in the south; we are all British, but a Scot is not an Englishman." There was a moment of silence and then one of the "patriots" came up to him with a drawn knife and said, "Don't be alarmed," and cut his bonds. "We wouldn't dream of harming a fellow Kurd. We would however like to invite you to stay for dinner so that our leader may have the pleasure of meeting you when he returns. Would you be willing?" Of course he stayed for dinner, and indeed overnight, and they parted on the friendliest terms.

Some years later I was discussing the Kurdish question in Turkey with a Turkish friend, and told him this story. I asked why the Turks and Kurds couldn't live together in Turkey like the Scots and the English in the United Kingdom. He replied immediately, "The Kurds aren't Scotch; they're Irish."

It was a witty remark but not an accurate one. The Turks and the Kurds are both Muslims; the English and the Scotch are both predominately Protestant. The real Irish problem was the domination of that country, with its huge Catholic majority, by the small Protestant Irish minority. Protestants of Irish background had no difficulty in reaching the highest levels in the British establishment—to cite just two examples, the Duke of Wellington and Field Marshal Montgomery. But all over Ireland, as long as the Union survived, Catholics were excluded from positions of power and the whole country was subject to what is known in Irish history as "the Protestant Ascendancy." One might use the Anglo-Irish issue to help explain the Sunni-Shi'a problem in the Middle East, but not the Turkish-Kurdish or the Arab-Kurdish issues.

Spies and Intercepts

At some point my employers had come into possession of some documents in a language they believed to be Turkish. The documents were accordingly passed to me for translation and analysis. I looked at them and reported that the documents were not Turkish. They said, If it's not Turkish, what is it? I said I didn't know, but I thought it was Albanian. You may ask, why did I think it was Albanian? I knew it wasn't Turkish or Persian or Arabic. It wasn't Greek and it wasn't

Slavic. And Albanian was about the only other language left in that general area. Also, it mentioned Tirana, the Albanian capital. My employers reasoned that since Albania was close to Turkey if I knew Turkish, I could learn Albanian quickly. I didn't entirely agree with this logic, but I was willing to make a try and thought it would make an interesting diversion. I said I was willing to try, and in the words of our great leader, give me the tools and I will finish the job. The tools I needed were an Albanian grammar and an Albanian dictionary. They hunted around and they found me both. The grammar was in German, published in 1913, and was a grammar of the south Gheg dialect of Albanian. I had ascertained in the meantime that Albanian came in three main dialects: Gheg, Tosk and Lyap. This was Gheg and not just Gheg but south Gheg, presumably as opposed to north, east or west Gheg. The dictionary was volume one, A–M, of an Albanian/Serbo-Croat dictionary. I had no Serbo-Croat, but I had a colleague who was a Balkan specialist.

The first thing I did was go through my grammar very rapidly to confirm that the texts were indeed in Albanian. Then I went through the texts. Words beginning with letters M through Z I simply abandoned; words beginning with letters A through M I looked up in the Albanian/Serbo-Croat dictionary and telephoned the Balkan expert to ask what does _____ mean? He asked if there was a chevron on the third "z." I said, what is a chevron? He explained, and I confirmed there was. Then he said that according to the context it could mean yesterday afternoon, bellyache or horse. So I went through the document and came to the conclusion that what one of His Majesty's less official representatives had, shall we say, obtained was the business correspondence of an Albanian carpet merchant. What made this discovery relatively easy was that the Albanian word for carpet is the same as the Turkish word, and various carpets were referred to by name, Shiraz, Bokhara and so on. I reported accordingly. My employers were obviously disappointed, and one of them asked if this couldn't be a disguise, a sort of code for something else. At that point I felt I had to protest. Anything less likely than that the German high command was carrying on its operations disguised as carpet talk in south Gheg would be difficult to imagine. By common consent we dropped the matter.

Many years later I had my first encounter with an Albanian when I was introduced to the Albanian ambassador at a reception. I couldn't resist asking him whether he was Gheg, Tosk, or Lyap and without batting an eyelid he replied that he was Gheg. I couldn't help myself and asked, "South Gheg?" To which he responded with a gesture which I was not able to interpret. Some things just don't translate!

During the war our German enemies, though very effective on the battlefield and in the air, proved remarkably incompetent in the field of intelligence. They had a large and important spy network in Britain, all of whom we knew and were able to follow in detail. We were intercepting and deciphering all their communications, so we knew every one of them from the moment they left their base in Germany until they arrived in England, usually via neutral Spain and Ireland. Normally when one identifies enemy agents one does not arrest them but rather lets them continue their work, taking care to supply them with false information to transmit to their masters. This serves the double purpose of misleading the enemy and saving the trouble of finding the new spies. However at some point, for some reason (I never found out why) our masters decided to arrest the German spies in England. Since we were following all their communications, we were able to measure their reactions to this. Understandably, they were furious. How did the stupid incompetent British manage to find and arrest our superb network of highly competent spies?

They batted this back and forth for a while and finally decided that they had found the answer. The Italians were at fault! The reason we had caught these superbly efficient German spies was the incompetence and negligence of their Italian allies. The Italians must mend their ways and—said one message—they must be forced to adopt German methods. But truth be told the Italians were so good at their job that not only had we not found them; we didn't even know they existed. Now, under pressure from Berlin, the Italian espionage network adopted German methods, so we were able to catch them too.

Alliances and Misalliances

It was during the war that another chapter in my life began and ended, my brief first marriage. Jean was the charming daughter of an Anglo-Jewish family in many ways similar to my own. She was a year younger than I and we were introduced by our parents. It didn't occur to me until much later that both sets of parents had probably discussed and agreed on what was, in fact though not in name, an old-style arranged marriage.

We were married for just a couple of months in 1939 when our marriage was interrupted by my call-up and military service. Later, when I was working in intelligence, I introduced her to some of my colleagues, and they found her a place in the Italian department, where, I was told, she did an excellent job for the rest of the war. Over the course of the war our marriage faltered and failed. We parted company by mutual consent before the end of the war and divorced with neither claims nor accusations.

As every survivor will recall, in wartime there are long periods of intense boredom, where nothing much changes, and there is nothing one can do. Like so many others, I usually carried a little book in my pocket to read when circumstances permitted. I preferred poetry, not only for its own sake, but also, perhaps more especially, because it offered more reading time in relation to weight and bulk than prose. Later, I found that the ratio could be still further improved by reading poetry in a foreign language. It also required greater concentration, some advantage in excluding such distractions as exploding bombs and shells. At some stage I found that I could tilt the balance still further in my favor and dispense with the book entirely, by learning a few poems by heart and then trying to translate them into English. Memorizing poetry was child's play—literally, since as children at school in England we were required to memorize vast quantities. Translation was of course more difficult, but there too, tools acquired in dealing with Virgil and Horace were honed on both the ancient and modern poets of the Middle East.

At first I tried to translate them into English verses and to maintain the metrical pattern and rhyme scheme of the original, but later I abandoned that. The loss of poetic value was far greater than any possible gain in form, and what I've usually done is translate them into English which is poetic but not versified, rhythmic but not metrical. Nowadays, free verse is so much part of the language of poetry that I think this is quite acceptable in poetry; and it can be in prose. It doesn't have to be prosaic, and it can be poetic, without being versified. I have occasionally tried my hand at a metrical translation, but rarely.

In any case, verse translation really has a short life. Every generation has to translate Homer and Dante into its own language. We can put up with Shakespeare's sixteenth-century English, rather remote from our present-day English, because Shakespeare is original, he wrote it. But there is no reason why we should put up with an out-of-date translation of something foreign. Victorian translations nowadays for the most part are unreadable; and even if they are readable, they are not acceptable. Even if you look at the first English translations of, say, Tolstoy and Dostoyevsky, where you don't have the special problem of translating poetry, they just don't work.

My efforts to translate Turkish, Arabic and Hebrew poetry continued intermittently after the war. A Hebrew poet who took my translations seriously was David Rokeah, who published several volumes of his poems translated into English. I was flattered that he included some of my translations.

A French colleague who was perhaps a little disconnected from the everyday world around him as he was a specialist on mysticism and philosophy was in Istanbul during the war. Turkey was neutral, but nevertheless had certain security zones which foreigners were not allowed to enter. My colleague, in his perambulations, wandered by mistake into one of these security zones and was promptly arrested, taken to the police station and interrogated by the inspector. Eventually the inspector satisfied himself that Monsieur was not a spy or a saboteur, and was, in fact, a quite innocuous visitor. The two of them relaxed and had a cigarette and a cup of coffee. When the atmosphere had reached a sufficient level of relaxation, he asked the inspector, why, since there are these forbidden zones, don't you have notices up saying forbidden zone, entry forbidden? The inspector looked at him in astonishment and said, "If we did that, we'd never catch anybody."

By late 1944, it was becoming clear that Germany was losing the war, and that it was only a matter of time until the Allies achieved complete victory. Aware of this, the Turks began to modify their neutrality, finally declaring war on the Axis in late February 1945, just in time for the end of the war.

But even before that formal declaration of war against the Axis, informal cooperation with the Turks began on various levels, notably that of intelligence. We had been following developments in Turkey as closely as possible and were well aware that Turkish intelligence, I suppose inevitably in a neutral country, had not kept up with modern technological developments and had therefore become dangerously porous. We assumed, rightly as it later turned out, that what we could do the Germans could also do and as our relationship developed into a genuine alliance, this was a serious source of danger. It was therefore decided that British intelligence had to send someone to Turkish intelligence as liaison, with the task of explaining to them that as their methods were out of date and their service incompetent, they were a danger to our common goals. I was chosen and looked forward to what promised to be a very interesting task. Then our bosses changed their minds and decided that this was a task requiring a career professional, not a wartime temporary, and I was replaced.

At the time, I was deeply disappointed, even hurt, at having been deprived of this adventure. Looking back, I am profoundly grateful to my bosses for not sending me on that mission. In our service, there was a clearly understood and generally accepted distinction between full-time professionals and wartime temporaries. When the war ended the temporaries went back to their various jobs and never again had any connection with intelligence matters. But, I doubt whether the Turks would have been able to understand and accept that. Had I gone to Turkey at that time in that capacity, I would have been labeled for life as a spy. That would of course have totally changed my relationship with my Turkish friends and colleagues. What seemed a misfortune at the time proved a blessing in the long run.

The Turks were willing to allow a British scholar to work in their archives; they would not have been likely to accord the same privilege to a British spy.

Winding Down

At a certain stage in the war in Italy Mussolini was ousted and fled to the Germans in the north, and the Italian government was taken over by Marshal Badoglio. Italy's status shifted from that of an enemy to an ally. We therefore needed communication with Italians at many levels and had an urgent need for people with a knowledge of Italian. In the British forces there were very few such, but our American allies had no problem as there were many Italian Americans, of whom a large proportion originated in southern Italy and Sicily. Orders were sent out and after a while, numbers of American officers were transferred from other branches of the service to Italy to assist in communication with the Italian authorities. At one point one of the English-speaking Italian liaison officers, a Florentine gentleman, exclaimed in bewilderment, "Who are these people? They look like American officers, and they talk like Sicilian peasants!"

I was in London for most of the war but did a tour of the Middle East in the summer of 1945, the main purpose of which was to wind down our services. By then the war in Europe was over, and the German surrender had taken place. The war with Japan was still going on, which meant that the Middle East was no longer terribly important, at least not in the war effort. We were trying to cut down operations in order to concentrate on the Far East. My tour took me around the whole area: Cairo first, then Jerusalem, Baghdad, Damascus, Beirut and back to Jerusalem, and back to Cairo. Sometimes it was rather funny. In Beirut I went up to Alay, in the hills outside Beirut. We had an army base there, the headquarters of the Ninth Army commanded by a General Holmes. My business was not with the general but with the colonel in charge of intelligence. I saw the colonel and we talked about the purpose of my visit, and I explained that we were trying to close down. I said to him, can we stop this and this and that? He said yes, we could stop them as he didn't need them anymore. That was good news. Then he asked if I would like to meet the general. I had no desire to meet the general but I couldn't very well refuse. So we went in to see the general and chatted about this and that. Then the general asked me what I was doing there. I explained. And he said, "Oh no, we simply can't spare any of those services; we need all of them." He turned to the colonel in charge of intelligence and said, "Isn't that so?" And the colonel said, "Oh yes, oh yes, definitely." We left and the colonel said to me, without batting an eyelid, "You have our answer; we need those services."

I went to Jerusalem after that and was able to visit the Wailing Wall for the first time. It is a Jewish custom to write a message to God on a small piece of paper and slip it into one of the cracks or crevices in the wall. This is believed to ensure delivery. I complied with tradition and the visit was very moving.

While I was in Jerusalem I saw Aubrey Eban, who was stationed there as a major in the South Staffordshire Regiment of the British Army. (I call him Aubrey because that's what he was called in England; "Abba" was an adaptation he assumed when he settled in Israel.) We first met when we were schoolboys and then I got to know him better when we were undergraduates. We were interested in the same things. I saw quite a lot of him during the academic year 1939–40. SOAS had been evacuated to Cambridge so we were both in Cambridge that year. We then went into different branches of His Majesty's service. He had been assigned to the center of Arabic studies, which was maintained by the British government in Jerusalem at that time. When I say Arabic studies I don't mean an academic center. This was an army center for training those military and civilian personnel who needed to learn Arabic and something about the Arab world in order to perform their duties.

I didn't see him again until that visit. We had lunch together and talked about what everybody was talking about in those days and that was: what are we going to do when this is over? It was quite clear by then that the war was coming to an end and within a matter of a few months we expected to be free and we'd have to resume a life that had been interrupted five years previously. Aubrey told me that he'd had three offers. His college at Cambridge had offered him a junior fellowship that would have led in time to a senior fellowship and then to an academic career, the sort of thing that I did. The second came from the Labour Party in England which offered him a constituency to fight which could have led him to the House of Commons and a career in British politics. The third one was from the Jewish Agency in

Jerusalem which suggested he might like to arrange to be discharged from the army in Jerusalem and instead of going back to England to stay and help them with the political struggles that were already looming on the horizon. We know what choice he made. That's now part of history. But at that time he was still hesitating among the three and he was particularly intrigued by the idea of going into the House of Commons. Aubrey was already quite a speaker in those days. I remember he asked me, "Do you think that my style of speaking would be suitable for the House of Commons?" I said, "No, I think your style of oratory would be much more suited to the House of Lords."

The End of the War

On the day that the bomb dropped on Hiroshima I was with a group of colleagues driving from Jerusalem to Cairo. It took some hours and when we got to Cairo we had to report to the town major in order to get accommodations. When we came out our driver said, "The war is over, sir." "What do you mean?" "Some other soldiers passed by and they told me the war was over." It wasn't actually over. The bomb had been dropped on Hiroshima. But it was nearly over and would be over within a few days. It was an incredible moment, to feel that the war was finished and we could go home. The seminal experience of my life had come to an end.

Toward the end of the war, and still more afterward, we gradually became aware of the mass slaughter of the Jews in Nazi-ruled Europe, and, increasingly, of the difficulties encountered by the survivors in reaching a safe haven. As I did from time to time, I tried to express my emotions in verse. In the first appendix I have included the poem I wrote on September 29, 1945, not as a literary attempt, but as a contemporary historical document.

Toward the end of the war my immediate chief was awarded a decoration. In accordance with custom, I called on him to congratulate him, and I vividly remember his words. "Let's not play games. We both know perfectly well that I got this for your work. But, that is how the system works. I earned this in the last war when my chief got it, and you will get it in the next war, when your subordinates will earn it." Fortunately, that has not happened.

When the war ended, I was given an accelerated release from the service because of my profession. Between 1939 and1945 young men and women, one year after another, left high school and went into the forces. There was now an accumulation of several years of would-be university students eager to enroll as soon as possible. This created tremendous pressure in the universities, where we had to deal with an unprecedentedly large number of students all at the same time. There was therefore an absolute urgency to release university teachers from duty so that they could resume their positions. I benefited.

I account myself very fortunate to have had a relatively comfortable war and to have come out of it alive and unscathed. I think that even from the point of view of my development as a historian those five years were not entirely wasted time. Anyone who has served in the army will have a much better understanding of military history, which remains an important part of history. I remember Gibbon, in his autobiography, mentions his service as a volunteer in the Hampshire militia and says that this helped him to understand the great wars of the Roman Empire. Some people have found this rather comic. I don't think it's comic at all. Serving in an army is something which you can never imagine until you've actually done it; and serving in an army in wartime, much more so.

What I did after I was transferred to MI6 in 1941 was particularly enlightening, especially for a historian of the Middle East. One thing I learned was a profound mistrust of written documents, which do not tell the whole story. I learned how to look at sources and how to evaluate a document. Documents are only usable if taken globally; individual documents don't really signify much.

Historians who have participated in events of their time are better as historians, firstly because they have a better and more profound understanding of human actions, human motivations, but also because they have a more skeptical and critical approach to the documentation, the traces left by these processes.

Every historian must inevitably be influenced by the events of his time. A historian, by the very fact of being a historian, is interested in history as it happens as well as the history of the more distant past. We are all creatures of our own time and it is natural that we should put to the past the questions that are suggested to us by the problems of our own time. That is not only legitimate; it is necessary. Otherwise, what does each new generation of historians work for? Rewriting the same subjects and going over the same issues? What is not permissible is shaping one's results in order to serve some political or ideological purpose. That is a betrayal of the ethos of the historian.

3.

In the Ottoman Archives

I was most fortunate, though I did not realize it at the time, in that I was the first professional teacher of Middle Eastern history anywhere in England. Until then the study and writing of Middle Eastern history, more specifically of Arab history, had been undertaken either by historians who knew no Arabic or by Arabists who had a limited understanding of history. Such posts as existed in the universities for Arabic and other Middle Eastern studies were concerned with language, literature, and in some cases theology. The study and therefore the teaching of history were incidental. As my teacher Gibb told me more than once, I was the first professional historian to study, teach and write Arab history—the first, that is, in England. There was already one in France, a historian called Claude Cahen, a fellow pioneer with whom I became acquainted in later years.

In accordance with the normal practice in British universities, the University of London offered a variety of honors degree programs, that is, a two- or three-year program specializing in one field of study. Mine was called "History with special reference to the Near and Middle East." Before my appointment, the history of the Middle East was taught by professors of Arabic, Persian and Turkish; only the Byzantine part and the Eastern Question were taught by professional historians. Over the course of the years the study of the Middle East became more and more urgent and necessary, and whole tribes of new historians, trained both in historical method and in language, appeared. They included a number of my former students. It was very fortunate for me, particularly for my professional advancement, that through no merit of my own I was among the pioneers of this development. That professional development received a second major impulse during the war.

The number of people who knew Arabic was at that time very small, probably fewer than a hundred in the entire United Kingdom, and among these there were very few with a historian's perception of the sweep of Arab history. An issue which acquired sudden importance during the war years was that most of them were Arabs and their allegiance was uncertain. A similar problem arose during the Cold War, when the Arab world was contested between the United States and the Soviet Union, with many Arabs in the region and elsewhere preferring the Soviet Union for the same reason that their predecessors had preferred the Third Reich—because it represented the major challenge to the predominant Western powers.

When I got back to the university in September 1945 I was out of touch in my academic pursuits but intensely up-to-date on what had been happening in the region. The war had parachuted me into the contemporary Middle East and to a quite active involvement. Obviously my employers were not interested in medieval history. They were not interested in studying history but rather in making it. It was a very interesting time in the Middle East and having seen it at close quarters was absolutely invaluable.

Because I had been appointed to a teaching post in the University of London before I went into the army that job was waiting for me at the end of the war, so I was returning to where I had left off. However, I had to learn my job all over again. During the war years I had acquired a very intimate, specialized knowledge of certain limited aspects of the modern history of the Middle East, but that didn't help me very much in teaching undergraduates. I had to return to my books and bone up both on the contents of my subject and on the manner of teaching it. All that was not exactly new but something that I hadn't done for many years and I had to relearn it almost from scratch.

I was one of a generation that was still young in years but prematurely aged in experience and perhaps in wisdom. The immediate postwar period was a good time for young scholars just starting or restarting their careers, a time of rapid and expansive development in the universities. There were six years of students waiting to attend courses and there was money from the government to help things along.

I met Ruth Oppenhejm at a party in London in 1946. She came from a distinguished Danish Jewish family and had been sent to England when she finished high school to improve her English. When war broke out she elected to stay in England rather than return to neutral Denmark—a fortunate choice since the following year Denmark was conquered and occupied, and Danish Jews, including her family, were sent to concentration camps. We married a year after we met. It certainly improved her English.

When my first batch of students graduated, one of them, an Egyptian, gave a little party to which he and his wife invited me and my newly acquired Danish wife. Ruth asked him the subject of his thesis. He told her and she said in bewilderment, "But that's a subject in Egyptian history." "Yes," he said, "I am an Egyptian. What is odd about my studying Egyptian history?" She responded, "There's nothing odd about your studying Egyptian history. What is odd is that you should come to London to study Egyptian history. I can imagine a Dane going to England to study science, or to study some English subject, but the last thing that would occur to any Dane is to go to England to study Danish history."

He was rather startled by this and then he gave what I thought was a very good answer. "There are really three reasons why I would come here. One is that although we have more material in Cairo the material is more readily accessible in London and that is important for completing a project within a limited period of time. The second reason is that here we are trained in modern scientific method, which we don't get at home. And the third reason, to be honest, is that an English Ph.D. counts for more in Egypt than an Egyptian Ph.D." I was very proud of my student; I thought this was an honest and intelligent answer.

My wife said to him: "Well, of the three points you mention, the really important one is the modern scientific method." He said, "Yes, I would agree with that." Ruth then said, "Presumably when you go back and you teach in Egypt, you will teach the modern scientific method that you have learned in England." He replied affirmatively and she said, "So your students will no longer need to go to the West to study their own history." "Right," he answered. Then she mused, "Tell me, how long have Egyptian students been coming to England to study Egyptian history?" There was a deadly silence.

The Arabs in History

In early August 1946, out of the blue, I received a letter that filled me with incredulous delight. It came from the great and famous historian Sir Maurice Powicke, the Regius professor of modern history at Oxford University and a very famous medieval historian. The reader may wonder, as I did, why a medieval historian was the professor of modern history. The explanation given at the time was that at Oxford University modern history begins with the fall of Rome.

The letter from Sir Maurice contained an invitation. He was the general editor, he said, of a new series of short historical books to be published by the house of Hutchinson, and he was actually asking me (and here I quote from his letter)—if I "would be willing to write a short volume of 60,000 words on the Arabs in History" (the title, as the reader will see, was his). He enclosed a document stating in general terms what the series was about, and explained more specifically what he wanted from me for this book. Again I quote, "I don't want either a textbook or a work of compact reference, but rather a live essay, which might become a little classic among a wealth of learned and topical literature—clear, well-proportioned, authoritative and easy to read. I think that it is needed, and you would have the opportunity to be welcomed as a scholar and as a man interested in affairs." (This is the language of 1946, and should not be misunderstood.) Sir Maurice went on to say that if I were "inclined to accept this suggestion," he would be "glad to have some statement about the range and treatment of the book as you envisage it." I replied, of course, accepting the invitation with enthusiasm, and I submitted the general plan for which he asked.

Two weeks after his first letter, Sir Maurice sent me a second letter indicating his satisfaction with my willingness to "write the book on the Arabs" and adding some further advice: "I gladly accept your general idea of its arrangement. I would only beg you to remember the point to which I attach much importance—that it should not suffer as a work of art from too much detail. In such a subject—so large, important and comprehensive—it would both be impossible to do more than give a selection, and fatally easy to spoil the essay in literary form by a relaxation of attention to its purpose. This is a great chance for a young scholar, just because only a scholar can take it."

A few days later the mail brought me an even more astonishing document—a real contract from a real publisher with the promise of an advance, in the princely amount of 75 pounds, payable on the delivery and acceptance of the completed manuscript. Seventy-five pounds may not seem very much today; but at that time it was sufficient to buy me a one-month honeymoon in Sweden, and thus enable me to escape from the austerities of postwar Britain and briefly enjoy the luxuries of neutrality. It may give some perspective if I mention that my initial salary on appointment as an assistant lecturer was

250 pounds a year, and that by this time I had reached the exalted figure of 600 pounds a year. So this advance marked a definite change in my economic status.

Looking back now more than half a century later, I am still amazed and bewildered at two things—at Sir Maurice's trustfulness in issuing this invitation, and at my own temerity in accepting it. After all, I was still very young to be writing a "classic," and still a relative beginner in my profession: and this, from Sir Maurice's description of it, seemed more like the kind of book that should be written after a lifetime of scholarship, of teaching, of reflection. It is true that when I received Sir Maurice's invitation, technically I had been a university teacher for eight years, since my first appointment at the School of Oriental and African Studies in the University of London, but of those eight years, only three were actually spent at the university teaching: the first two and the last. The rest of the time I had been on temporary unpaid leave of absence and engaged in war duty—military and other. My war service had left me with an intimate but highly specialized knowledge of certain aspects of the contemporary Middle East, but it had also left my scholarly skills, both of inquiry and of exposition, sadly depleted.

When Sir Maurice's letter arrived I was just beginning to learn my trade again. My published work was minimal; it consisted of a shortened but otherwise unimproved version of my doctoral dissertation, published not because it was ready for publication but because I was about to go off to the wars and the University of London publications committee offered me what at the time might well have been a last chance. Apart from the thesis, I had published a few other odds and ends; some of them I now look back on with more embarrassment than pride.

Why me? Sir Maurice's reason for sending this invitation to me rather than to anyone else was certainly not my reputation, which at that time was justly nonexistent, but the recommendation of my former teacher, Professor H.A.R., later Sir Hamilton Gibb. His reason for choosing me rather than any of his other disciples to recommend to Sir Maurice was known to me. He had told me many times that, as far as he knew, I was the first professional historian in Britain to study and teach Arab history.

I think that Gibb was a little hard on himself and on some other scholars; names like Christian Snouck Hurgronje and Julius Wellhausen immediately come to mind, who were good Arabists and who were I think historians in the true sense of that word. But in what one might call the trade-union sense, of holding the professional qualifications of a historian—having an honors degree in history or equivalent and holding a full-time appointment in a history department—he was probably right that Claude Cahen in Paris and I were the only ones. My assistant lectureship in "the History of the Near and Middle East," created in the autumn of 1938, was, as far as I am aware, the first and for a long time remained the only such appointment in a history department. And it was not until the great expansion of Oriental and African studies in the late forties and early fifties that many new posts were created in universities in Britain, in the United States and elsewhere in the Western world. I remained an active member of the history school in London University until 1974, when I moved to Princeton and for the first time found myself a professor not of history but of Near Eastern studies.

The writing of the book took three months; but publishing was a slow and difficult business in those immediate postwar years, and it did not actually appear until 1950. Both of the book's godfathers, Sir Hamilton and Sir Maurice, declared themselves satisfied, to my immense relief. It was widely and favorably reviewed in the daily and weekly press in England and, later, in scholarly journals both at home and abroad. I was particularly gratified by the fact that the book received on the whole a friendly welcome in the Arab world. One of the outstanding Egyptian historians of the time, Shafiq Ghorbal, actually made it the subject of a broadcast talk, later published as an article, in which he cited it as an example (and this is deliciously ironic given the later turn of events) of the valuable contribution with which Orientalist scholarship could enrich the Arabs' understanding of their own heritage by placing their history within a larger historical context, at that time little known to them. The book was even translated into Arabic by two respected Arab historians, Nabih Faris and Mahmud Zayid, and published by the optimistically entitled Dār al-'Ilm li'l-Malāyīn (Science for the Millions) in Beirut. Even more surprisingly, it was included by the Information Office of the Arab League in Washington and New York in the short list of recommended reading for Americans wanting to know more about the Arabs and their history. It was translated into several other Muslim languages (Turkish, Malay and Indonesian) as well as into Chinese and Japanese and various European languages, both Eastern and Western and, all but the last chapter, into Hebrew. I was given two different reasons for the omission of the last chapter from the Hebrew translation: one was that the publisher ran out of money; the other that they didn't like the last chapter. I don't know which was the real one; perhaps both. One of the more striking responses was a notification from my Yugoslav publisher that I had an account of 40 dinars in a bank in Zagreb which I was at liberty to collect any time convenient to me. I never actually got round to it.

The welcome to the book was by no means unanimous. It was promptly banned in the newly established Republic of Pakistan because of a disrespectful reference to the Prophet which I had quoted from Dante as an example of medieval European prejudice and bigotry. It is the famous passage in which Dante in his travels in hell encounters the Prophet, condemned as a *"seminator di scandalo e di scisma."* (*Inferno* xxviii, 35). More recently the book has been attacked again, especially and indeed principally by exponents of the new school of epistemology, for similarly weighty reasons.

The English original seems to have been widely read and ran through five editions and a much larger number of impressions. I was then, and to be honest, still remain, puzzled at the continuing success and survival of the book, and even (and this may strike the reader as odd) at times somewhat irritated. This was a book written by a young, immature and inexperienced scholar in three months. I have, after all, written other things since then, based on deeper research and wider knowledge, the fruit of experience and I hope greater wisdom, the preparation of which was measured not in months but in years. Yet until the sudden spike of public interest in the Middle East after 9/11, none of them remotely approached the continuing popularity of this sin of my youth. From the remarks cited above, I am sure the reader will agree that the success of the book owed much to the initial guidance of Sir Maurice Powicke, who pointed me in the right direction, gave me a push and then let me find my own way. Its survival, I suppose, is principally due to the shortage of competing books dealing with Arab history with the same brevity and at the same level of generalization.

The Ottoman Archives

In the autumn of 1949, at the age of thirty-three, I became a full professor and was appointed as the first occupant of the newly created chair of the History of the Near and Middle East in the University of London. I was given a year's study leave to familiarize myself more closely with the countries and peoples whose history it was my business to teach and write. More particularly, I was eager to explore the libraries and archives and other documentation which must necessarily form the basis of such teaching and writing.

When my wife and I set out for Istanbul in the autumn of 1949, the situation in the region had been transformed beyond recognition. Previously, most of the Arab world, except for the Arabian Peninsula, was under British or French control and access was not difficult. The newly independent Arab states were now asking all applicants for visas to indicate their religion and routinely refusing visas to those who declared their religion as Jewish. Some of my Jewish colleagues were able to circumvent this rule, by the use of such carefully ambiguous terms as "Orthodox" or "Unitarian." One ingenious lady from New York City even described herself as a "Seventh Avenue Adventist." Some simply lied. But most of us, even the nonreligious, found it morally impossible to make such compromises for no better reason than the pursuit of an academic career. This considerably reduced the number of places to which one could go and in which one could work. For those interested in North Africa, access was still possible and indeed has remained relatively easy even to the present day but most of the Arab east was closed to Jews.

Since then, there has been some easing of this rule in some Arab countries, but at that time, for Jewish scholars interested in the Middle East, only three countries were open—Turkey, Iran and Israel. The great upsurge of Persian and Turkish studies in Western Europe and the United States in the fifties and sixties may be due in part to this circumstance.

It was in these three countries therefore that I arranged to spend the academic year 1949–50. I began, and indeed spent most of my time, in Istanbul which, because of the unique richness of its libraries and archives, offers special attractions to the historian of the Middle East. I counted on being able to use the collections of Arabic and other Islamic manuscripts in Turkish libraries; I also applied, with little expectation of success, for permission to use the Imperial Ottoman Archives. These archives had been described by various Turkish scholars and a number of its documents had been published, mostly in Turkish journals, in the course of the years. No Westerner had however been admitted to them, apart from a very small number of expert archivists brought in as consultants.

These were the central archives of the Ottoman Empire extending over a period of many centuries and including records from even the most distant outposts. It was known that they contained tens of thousands of bound registers and letter books, and millions of documents. It was obvious that these archives would be a precious, indeed an indispensable source for the history of all the lands that had ever formed part of the Ottoman Empire and even, to a lesser degree, those that had had relations with the empire. Access had only been allowed to a limited number of Turkish scholars.

It was my good fortune, rather than any particular merit on my part, which caused me to submit my application precisely at the moment when the custodians of the archives decided to adopt a more tolerant policy and no longer limit access only to their own nationals. I was both astonished and delighted to receive the coveted permit. Feeling rather like a child turned loose in a toy shop or like an intruder in Ali Baba's cave, I hardly knew where to turn first.

A certain amount of work had been done by Westerners studying the empire and some of it was very good, but it was based on Western archives and sources. The only Ottoman evidence available to them consisted of chronicles and other literary works. The opening of the archives brought a major change in the study and understanding of Ottoman, and, more broadly, European history.

The language of the archives is Ottoman Turkish, which was used during the many centuries of the Ottoman Empire. It has a basically Turkish structure with an immense vocabulary of loan words from Arabic and Persian, as much as, and rather similar to, the vocabulary of Latin, Greek and Norman French words in English. Ottoman Turkish was written in the Arabic script with some additional letters to indicate Turkish sounds that do not exist in Arabic. Different forms of the script were used for different types of documents and for different purposes. The decipherment of these documents presents considerable problems for the modern scholar.

Fortunately, there is a large amount of printed material in Ottoman Turkish, including many documents and some, but not many, dictionaries and grammars. These provide a good starting point for a would-be researcher in the archives.

After World War I, Atatürk's revolutionary modernizing program brought a tremendous change in Ottoman Turkish. The Arabic script was replaced by a modified version of the Latin script and an attempt was made to remove the Arabic and Persian vocabulary and replace it with old or newly invented Turkish words. The extensive linguistic reforms carried out in the early years of the Turkish Republic made the Ottoman language antique and arcane, even to modern Turkish readers. To understand the resulting change one might try to imagine a revolution in English in which all French- or Latin-based words are dropped and replaced by resuscitated or newly invented Anglo-Saxon words and at the same time the alphabet is totally replaced by a new one. To give an example, the "remorse of conscience" would become the "againbite of inwit" (in a different alphabet).

There are several different kinds of records in the archives, and they are divided into two categories by their physical form: registers and papers. A lot of the records consist of bound registers, huge volumes into which scribes copied important documents. The other category, papers, consists of individual documents, and there are literally tens of millions of those.

The archivists, it would seem, never developed an efficient system of preserving and classifying incoming documents; if they survive at all, they are lumped together in miscellaneous collections. They were however aware of this problem and dealt with it by a simple and effective device—each outgoing message begins with a summary of the message or report to which it provides an answer. The outgoing messages were meticulously copied and filed in bound registers.

There are several kinds of bound registers. One category contains copies of orders sent out from the sultan's government. Whether at home or abroad, in the city or in the provinces, wherever, every order issued by the imperial secretariat was copied into a register. There are hundreds of these volumes, in strict date order. Then there are the registers of complaints—of misbehavior by this officer or that governor, by this or that minor official. These complaints were conscientiously investigated and rulings issued. There are literally hundreds of registers of reports on complaints, again classified by region and, within region, by date.

Population and taxation records were meticulously kept. There are registers for various foreign consulates, and the dealings with them. There are special categories, like the different minority communities—Christian registers of various denominations and Jewish registers. There are those devoted to fiscal matters covering every town and village, house by house. For each village there is a financial statement—what they grew, what the yield was and what they paid in taxes. And there is a tremendous amount of material which is still imperfectly known.

The Ottoman Empire ruled over a large part of Europe for almost half a millennium. It held the Balkan Peninsula for centuries; it held half of Hungary for a century and a half. Twice the Ottomans reached as far as Vienna. They landed briefly in Italy and held Otranto for a while and of course, they held the whole of southwest Asia west of Iran and North Africa as far as the Moroccan frontier. It was a very large empire. It was also one which was highly literate and sophisticated. The Ottomans had their history, their historians, their chroniclers, their poets, their writers, and they also were very meticulous keepers of records. The archives in Istanbul document the activities of the government over the centuries and contain very detailed information about the affairs of the empire from Budapest to Basra and from Algiers to Baghdad. Further archives in the provincial centers are only now being discovered and exploited.

Before the opening of the archives one could read in a history book that such and such a sultan had built a mosque. What did that mean exactly? It meant that the sultan had summoned an architect and said, "Build me a mosque." So we could correct the statement and say this architect built the mosque. If we are lucky, contemporary historians who chronicled the period may have said something about the time it took to build the mosque, and, rarely, how much it cost. But we are still not much the wiser. We know the name of the sultan who gave the order and we know the name of the architect who designed and supervised the construction of the mosque. For the historian of architecture there is the mosque, the actual building, which is in what he is most interested. But if you go to the archives, you will find the work sheets of the construction of the mosque; day-by-day records which give you the list of the plasterers, the masons, the carpenters and all the other people who worked on the construction. You will know how many there were and from where they came, what jobs they did and how much they were paid and so on. This is priceless historical information. For the social or economic historian it is a treasure trove of immense importance.

Ottoman imperial bureaucracy functioned pretty well for centuries and then, like everything else in the empire, it began to go wrong. Anyone can watch it going wrong in the archives. You can see them begin to get sloppy, to get careless. Instead of preparing new surveys, they merely repeat the old ones, and suchlike. I remember reading in a history of the time that at a certain date a new chief minister had come in and reorganized things so that they were running properly. This lasted for about twenty years and then he died and things went back to where they were before. If you look in the archives, you can see a change; the documentation suddenly becomes efficient and meticulous again. It lasts awhile, and then reverts to where it was before.

Although as a student I had studied both Turkish and Arabic, my previous work had been much more concerned with the Arab countries than with Turkey, and more with medieval than with Ottoman times. It therefore seemed a good idea to take, for my first project of research in the archives, the Arab lands in the sixteenth century, the first century of Ottoman rule. My studies hitherto, including my doctoral thesis, had concentrated on the Isma'ilis and Assassins, and I decided to begin with the Isma'ili districts in central Syria, and to see how my old friends, whom I knew from Fatimid, Ayyubid and Mamluk times (from the eleventh to the early sixteenth centuries) had fared under the Ottomans. The rich archival documentation offered material of a kind wholly lacking in earlier periods, and therefore of special interest.

Unfortunately I soon ran into a difficulty—the impossibility of revisiting these communities on the ground. I had been to some of these Syrian Isma'ili villages in earlier, easier times and was able to recognize some of them in the documents. There were others I could not identify and there was no way I could return now. I was a Jew, and therefore not welcome. In the meantime I had conceived a rather more ambitious project—a study of the whole of the Fertile Crescent for which I had identified several relevant series of records. I soon decided that the right place for me to start, for both practical and scholarly reasons, was the four southernmost districts of the province of Damascus, namely the *sanjaks* of Safed, Nabulus, Jerusalem and Gaza. A scholarly reason for this choice was that these four districts offered the richest independent documentation, Christian and Jewish travel and religious literature, without parallel in any other province of the Ottoman East. The practical reason was that the greater part of these four districts was included in the newly created State of Israel, where I could enter, travel and study without impediment.

Israel and Iran

In the spring of 1950 I went on a trip from Istanbul to Israel, where I was able to check some of my data and meet Israeli colleagues interested in this topic. Among them were the late J. W. Hirschberg, U. Heyd, and Isaac Ben-Zvi, who used some of my material in his book on Palestine and its Jewish settlements under the Ottomans. It was at that time that I gave my first lectures based on the Ottoman records. One of these lectures, with additional material, was published as a booklet in Jerusalem by the Israel Oriental Society in 1952.

While my principal concern had for some time been mainstream Islamic history, I had never forgotten the Hebraic and Judaic interests and concerns which had first led me into the field of Middle Eastern studies. My first published venture in this field was due to the initiative of a truly remarkable man whom it was my good fortune to meet in London just before the war. Dr. Simon Rawidowicz, a refugee from Poland, made his home in England for several years before moving to the United States.

Rawidowicz was a man of driving energy and immense determination. At a time when the whole of Continental Europe was ruled, cowed, or threatened by Nazi Germany, he was acutely conscious of the position of English Jews as the last free Jews in Europe. He felt this imposed special obligations on them, and one of the most important of these was to safeguard Jewish culture, and in particular, to provide a forum for Hebrew letters and studies. He therefore decided to found a journal, in the Hebrew language, devoted to scholarship and literature.

This was a time when England stood alone and under siege. And in wartime England there were shortages of everything, including paper and printing facilities. To start a new publication required a permit. Very few such permits were given, and then only for publications related to the war effort. With other friends, I told Rawidowicz that he was attempting the impossible, and that we saw no way of persuading harassed civil servants that a journal in Hebrew devoted to scholarship was essential to the British war effort. I vividly remember his answer, "You English don't know about permits. It is all new to you and you don't understand it. Where I come from, we had to have a permit to be born, a permit to grow up, a permit to eat, a permit to breathe, a permit to live, and a permit to die. I know how to get permits."

And he did. To everyone's astonishment he was able to find not only the permit but also the printers, the paper, and the money to produce *Metsuda* (in English, "fortress"), a collection in Hebrew published at irregular intervals in London during the war.

Not the easiest part of his editorial task was finding contributors who had something to say, the ability to say it in Hebrew, and the time to do so. I was persuaded to contribute and devoted some moments of my scanty leisure to writing small contributions on aspects of the history of Jews in Arab lands. I wrote these in Hebrew and Rawidowicz corrected them, something which I found the less wounding in that he also corrected everyone else's Hebrew, including that of native Hebrew speakers. In later years I wrote one or two other articles in Hebrew and even ventured to give a few lectures in that language, but later decided to keep to English. It is only in my mother tongue that I can say exactly what I want to say, and in the way I want to say it. In any other language I am restricted and constrained by the limitation of the words and idioms available to me.

In 1950 I went to Iran for the first time. The history of Iran was part of the syllabus that I was teaching at the university and I felt some direct personal experience was necessary. Iran borders Turkey, so it was not a difficult journey from Istanbul. At that time there was no piped water in Tehran. Water was circulated round the city through open gutters and getting clean water was a problem; you could buy drinking water but not bathwater. You got bathwater and heaters in the hotel—if you were lucky.

I was told that I should register at the British Embassy as soon as I got there and make myself known. I went to the embassy and gave my name and that of my hotel and was given the usual guidance and warnings. Then the embassy clerk suggested I had better see the embassy doctor as there were some things to take note of. An appointment was made and I saw the doctor, who warned me about eating this and not drinking that and then he asked what I was going to do about baths. I concurred that this was a problem. To my astonishment he said that if I wanted to I could bathe at the embassy. The embassy had a private water supply from its own springs and all I would have to do is let them know and they'd arrange it. I was profoundly grateful, thanked him, and regularly took advantage of the offer.

I traveled extensively around the country for a few weeks and found it a fascinating and hospitable place. The people were most tolerant of my fragmentary Persian.

Food

I became interested in the history of food when I was a schoolboy, and learnt with delight how our lives had been enriched by the discovery of America which brought us such previously unknown items as potatoes, tomatoes and chocolate. Our gustatory lives were enriched from the East as well as from the West, by exploration and empire, by commerce and cultivation. At some stage in my Persian studies I learnt the words *sheker* and *qand,* denoting a substance used for sweetening food and drinks. These are of course the roots of sugar and candy. Sugar, unknown in the Greco-Roman world, was introduced from Persia, possibly originating farther East. It became an important part of the trade between the Eastern and Western worlds.

Perhaps the most exciting was the history of coffee. In most cases, the process from the natural product to the end product that we eat or drink is fairly short and simple. The journey from the coffee bean to a cup of coffee is long and complex and one can only marvel at the ingenuity of the people of Ethiopia who first brought this gift to humanity. The earliest documentation is from the beginning of the fifteenth century, when we hear about coffee being imported from Ethiopia to Yemen. From the southern end of the Red Sea it spread northward along both sides, reaching Egypt, Syria and Turkey, where it was discovered, with delight, by Western travelers.

My work in the Ottoman archives opened new doors and revealed new opportunities for the study of the history of food. On the one hand, the detailed records of taxes on agriculture, from villages all over the empire, indicated what food crops were being grown, in what regions, and in what quantities. On the other hand, the archives of the imperial palace in Istanbul, in particular those of the kitchens, showed what foods were being cooked and consumed, in what quantities, and sometimes from what region.

Sometimes the history of food produced amusing details. For example, the bird which in English is known as the turkey was a native of the Western Hemisphere, unknown in the Eastern Hemisphere before the discovery of America. The English called this strange bird the "turkey," naming it after the most exotic country that they could think of. The French, more familiar with the Near East, called the bird *dinde,* literally "from India." When, in the course of time, the turkey was introduced to the Middle East, it was sometimes known as *habashi,* the Ethiopian bird, again using the most exotic name that came to mind. It would have been more accurate to call the bird the "American," but neither the name nor the place was familiar at that time.

Turkish Democracy

One of the most moving experiences of my life happened in that year. That was the time when the Turkish government held a free and genuinely fair election—the election of 1950—in which it was defeated. Even more remarkably, the government then quietly and decently withdrew and handed over power to the victorious opposition. This was a totally new experience for the people of Turkey or indeed of any Muslim country. It was also a profound and informative experience for me to be there and witness it.

I did not visit Turkey during the war, but in the course of my war duties I was kept fully informed of what was happening there. Despite a treaty of alliance with Britain signed in 1939, Turkey remained ambiguously neutral during the war. It was not until late February 1945 that they finally declared war on the Axis. The Turkish record was, to say the least, somewhat dubious, and the democratic achievement of 1950 provided a necessary and welcome corrective.

What followed I can only describe as catastrophic. Adnan Menderes, the leader of the party which won the election, soon made it perfectly clear that he had no intention whatever of leaving by the same route by which he had come. He regarded this as a change of regime and had no respect at all for the electoral process. People in Turkey began to realize this. I vividly remember sitting in the faculty lounge at the school of political science in Ankara after several years of the Menderes regime. We were discussing the history of different political institutions and forms. One of the professors suddenly said, to everyone's astonishment, "Well, the father of democracy in Turkey is Adnan Menderes." The others looked around in bewilderment. They said, "Adnan Menderes, the father of Turkish democracy? What do you mean?" Well, said this professor, "he screwed the mother of democracy."

The Emergence of Modern Turkey

When I returned to London in 1950 I was asked by the Royal Institute of International Affairs, known as Chatham House, and the Oxford University Press to write a book on modern Turkey, to be sponsored by the one and published by the other. It was to be part of a series they were planning on the interrelations between the Islamic world and the West. If I agreed they would finance my future trips to Turkey, as many as necessary. I liked the idea, agreed and eagerly set off for my first trip to Turkey for this project.

My sponsors suggested that it would be useful to make myself known to the British ambassador, Sir James Bowker, which I did. He invited me to lunch; not as good as dinner but better than merely coffee. At lunch, and in accordance with tribal custom, we talked of anything and everything except the business at hand until the coffee was served. Then Sir James asked why I was there and could he do anything for me. I explained my mission, to write a book on Turkey, and that this was the first of what would probably be several visits to collect material. Sir James said, "I'll do anything I can to help you. You will probably want to talk with politicians and government officials—let me know which and I'll set up appointments for you." I said, "Are you sure that would be wise? You know how sensitive people are in this part of the world. I don't know how this book will turn out. They may like it or, on the other hand, they may decide it's insulting and anti-Turkish, in which case it would be an embarrassment for you to have introduced me officially." He replied, "That's a risk we'll have to take. You are a British scholar and I am your ambassador, and it is my duty to help you." Which he did. Fortunately, although the book, *The Emergence of Modern Turkey,* was critical in some respects, the Turks liked it, translated it, and it has been in print for over half a century.

The beginnings of this book date back to my academic year in Istanbul. My main purpose in being there was to work in the Turkish State Archives, but living in Turkey at that time, I could not but be aware of the momentous events that were taking place around me, and be deeply impressed, even inspired, by their rapid development. The invitation from Chatham House and Oxford University Press gave me an opportunity to pursue this new interest in modern and recent history.

In the course of the 1950s I made a number of trips to Turkey of varying duration—partly to read books, periodicals, and newspapers in Turkish libraries not readily available elsewhere, and partly to observe at first hand the continuing process of change. I attended a dinner party in Ankara in 1952 shortly after Turkey was accepted as a member of NATO. In Turkey this was a cause for celebration and most people were very happy and proud to have been accepted as a full member. At this dinner party, one of the guests, a Turkish general, made a memorable remark. Someone asked him what he thought of Turkey's joining NATO and the Turkish general replied, "The real problem with having the Americans as your allies is you never know when they will turn around and stab themselves in the back."

My typescript was completed in 1960 and *The Emergence of Modern Turkey* was published in 1961 by the Oxford University Press. Neither the author nor the publisher had expected a large sale for a book of almost five hundred heavily footnoted pages, dealing with a single, no longer major, country. It was with surprise as well as pleasure that we saw it go through four printings in hard cover. This unexpected success stirred the publisher's generosity to the point of allowing me to make fairly extensive, though still minor, revisions in the second, paperback edition, published in 1968.

The preparation of the second edition confronted me with an important question. Writing in the middle and late fifties, I had chosen, as the cutoff point for my book, the Turkish general election of 1950—the first that was conducted in complete freedom and fairness, and resulted in the transfer of power from the ruling to the opposition party. Since my book was one of history, reaching back to the Middle Ages, and not of current affairs, it seemed right to end it at that point. Trying to cope with the rapidly changing scene in present-day Turkey would have required a different approach.

I remained of the same opinion while preparing the revised second edition. The events at the time of the revision, like those at the time of the original composition, must certainly have colored my perception of earlier periods, but I decided to keep to the 1950 cutoff point, and to use the opportunity of revision to take account of the considerable body of new evidence and new studies that had appeared in the meantime. Reprints of the English text have been based on the 1968 edition, with only minor corrections of a few obstinate misprints that had somehow escaped all previous revisions. The same text served as the basis of three translations which were published in the immediately following years—into Turkish, by the Turkish Historical Society in Ankara; into Polish, by the Academy of Sciences in Warsaw; into Hebrew, by the Hebrew University Press in Jerusalem.

The publication of a French edition in 1988 provided an occasion for another look, both at the book and at the subject with which it deals. Reading my own work, more than thirty years after I started writing it, almost twenty years since I last revised it, was in some ways a chastening, in other ways a reassuring, experience. Inevitably, there were things which I would have arranged or presented differently if I were writing the book now, but these are mainly matters of emphasis and presentation rather than of structure. In a few places, I made small changes to take account of new evidence, of new thinking—both my own and other people's—and of the insights afforded by subsequent events. But the major presentation and interpretation remained as they were, and, despite the passage of time and the increase of knowledge and experience, I was content to leave them so.

Curiously, the French publishers reduced my title to a subtitle and gave the book a new title: *Islam et Laïcité: la naissance de la Turquie moderne* ("Islam and Secularism: the birth of modern Turkey"). When I asked a representative of the publishing house the reason for this, he replied drily, *"L'Islam se vend; la Turquie ne se vend pas"* ("Islam sells; Turkey doesn't"). The new French title, despite the change of emphasis, is not inaccurate, since one of the major themes of the book is indeed the emergence of a secular, democratic republic from an Islamic empire. It was thus all the more remarkable that in the year 1994 a complete Persian translation appeared in Tehran. This was of course published without contract or consent. I heard of it and procured a copy, thanks to the good offices of an Iranian friend. One can only speculate why the Persian publisher and translator thought it worthwhile to translate and publish a lengthy, detailed book on a neighboring country, originally published in 1961, which ended its story in 1950. Was it offered as a model to be followed or as a terrible example to be avoided?

Several factors, it seems in retrospect, determined the basic approach, the dominant conception, and the final conclusions of the book. The first, if I may be excused for putting it in that place, was my own intellectual formation. My academic training had been as a historian and an Orientalist, specializing in classical Islamic civilization. I had studied Arabic and Persian before I approached Turkish. In my historical studies I began with medieval Islam, from which I proceeded to the Ottoman Empire, and then, later, to the Turkish Republic. Certainly, in considering the sustained endeavor to create a secular, modern, and democratic nation-state, I was more keenly aware of the immensity of the task that they were undertaking, the difficulties that they confronted, and, in consequence, more able to appreciate the quality and magnitude of their achievements.

A second determining factor, of at least equal importance, was the world situation during my formative years and during the period when the book was written. For the men and women of that generation, their every thought, their whole lives were dominated and indeed shaped by the titanic struggles in which they had participated or witnessed: the defeat and destruction of fascism by an alliance of democrats and communists, followed by a struggle between these ill-assorted allies which would shape the future of the world. In the fifties, these issues loomed large, and the choices before us still retained something of the clarity, even the starkness, which they had through the war years and which they have subsequently lost.

This clarity of choice gave a special significance to the already dramatic development of events in Turkey at the time when *The Emergence of Modern Turkey* was conceived and written. What could be more illuminating, more in accord with the mood of optimism which victory had brought and which the Cold War had not yet dissipated, than the spectacle of a nation liberating itself from ancient bonds—a country of age-old authoritarian habits and traditions turning to democracy; a regime which had for decades enjoyed a virtual monopoly of power setting to work, systematically, to prepare, organize, and preside over its own electoral defeat?

The Birth of My Children

My daughter Melanie was born in 1952 and two years later my son Michael was born. He arrived rather late and unfortunately it was not possible for me to be in London on the actual day that he arrived. I was one of the hosts of a big international conference in Cambridge and I had to be there. I did however leave instructions that I should be informed immediately. That morning I left the college where I was staying; no news had arrived, but by the time I got to the college where the meeting was being held, news had come, and since I was en route and the conference organizers couldn't reach me, they announced the birth over the loudspeakers. When I arrived at the meeting one of my colleagues came up to me and said: "Congratulations, Father Lewis." Another, standing nearby, said in astonishment: "I didn't know that Lewis was in holy orders."

4.

Cultural Diplomacy

Growing up as a child in London in the 1920s I was proudly aware of the fact that I was part of what was probably the greatest empire in history, certainly the largest at that time, exercising direct or indirect sovereignty over one-third of the globe, and bringing, in different parts of the world, civilization in place of barbarism, and in different parts of the empire, freedom and justice in place of tyrannical or at best authoritarian rule.

This mood of self-satisfaction was not universal or unchallenged. I remember one day when I was fifteen, when our history master came into the classroom and began the class by saying, "Our subject today is British imperial administration. The administration of the empire rests on two principles—the boot and the whip; but to help you pass your examinations I will provide you with some corroborative details."

In the years that followed, belief in the empire and in our positive role in it was attacked from many sides, both at home and abroad. By the end of World War II it had become clear that Britain's imperial age had come to an end. The major change was the withdrawal from India in 1947. With the end of the Indian Empire, the most important single reason for Britain's imperial interest in the Middle East was gone, and the winding down of British imperial rule in that region followed rapidly. This was helped and accelerated by the rise of nationalism in these countries. In England too there was a growing reluctance, even unwillingness, to continue the imperial role—a feeling that we had no right, still more, no duty, to rule other countries and to confront their problems.

In evaluating the impact and effects of European imperialism in Asia and Africa one might begin by comparing the records and achievements, positive and negative, of the major European imperial powers—Britain, France, Russia, the Netherlands, Portugal and Italy. But an even more dramatic comparison, and a more instructive one, can be made by comparing the impacts of the same imperial power on different subject peoples. Hong Kong, Singapore and Aden were all British Crown Colonies. All were liberated from the imperial yoke, and now look very different. An even more dramatic example is the liberation of India from British imperial rule. India, Pakistan, Bangladesh all had much the same experience, but with very different results. Similar comparisons may be made in different parts of the Middle East.

In the immediate postwar years militant terrorist movements attacked British troops and installations in three areas—Cyprus, Palestine and Aden. Their shared purpose was to accelerate the departure of their imperial rulers and thus hasten the achievement of independence. Of the three movements, one was Christian, one Jewish and one Muslim. Although all three were called "terrorist" at the time, if one compares their activities with those of present-day terrorist movements, all three were remarkably gentlemanly. With rare exceptions they confined their attacks to military targets, even sometimes taking care to avoid "collateral damage."

In the absence of any viable regime or organization to which power could be transferred, imperial rule continued for some time longer in most of the African colonies, but even there significant steps were taken to develop political, social and cultural institutions, and to prepare these countries for eventual independence. Part of this process was educational.

Although my career in England covered the last years of the

breakup of the British Empire, I was never part of the imperial service and even my wartime role in British intelligence was concerned with preventing Axis penetration rather than preserving British domination. I did, however, later play some role in quite a different respect. In the British Empire, unlike some others, the imperial authorities devoted great attention to education, and more remarkably, to higher education. The aim was that in every one of the British colonies there should be at least one university and in that university some time and effort should be devoted to teaching the people history, principally the history of their own country. This is in marked contrast with French Africa, for example, where the only university was the French university in Algiers, attended principally by the *colons,* and where the history taught was French history. In the schools for the West Africans the history books would begin with "Our ancestors, the Gauls . . ."

In the British colonies some British and imperial history was taught but the main emphasis was on their own history. In some colonies this created a need to discover and write previously unrecorded and unwritten history. In some of the African colonies a considerable effort was made to find or create a historical record, where possible from internal, usually orally transmitted sources, and otherwise from sometimes conflicting foreign narratives. A committee in London concerned with higher education in the colonies brought together a number of scholars, principally from the University of London, who undertook these tasks. I was one of them, and I must say that I found it both enlightening and rewarding. My principle concern was with Sudan, the one Arabic-speaking, predominantly Muslim, country which was still more or less under colonial administration.

Sudan

When the Arabs, after conquering Egypt in the seventh century, invaded or explored the lands to the south, they adopted a general term for the region between Egypt and Ethiopia, Bilād al-Sūdān, literally the Lands of the Blacks. The name survived through the centuries, and became the official designation of a sovereign, independent state, which in 2011 divided into two. To the Western observer, the name Sudan may seem inappropriate, but not inaccurate, since all the inhabitants, from north to south, are indeed black. Black, that is, from a white perspective. But, as I discovered when I went to Sudan as guest of the University of Khartoum, their own perspective is somewhat more complex. To start with, colors are seen differently. The northerners, whom a Westerner might call brown, are known as "reds" while the southerners, who really are intensely black, are known as "blues."

What one might call a classical Arabic view of the question of color was vividly expressed by an Arabic writer, Ibn al-Faqīh, at the beginning of the tenth century C.E. The ideal color, he wrote, was that of the people of Iraq, "a pale brown color, which is the most apt and proper color. They are the ones who are done to a turn in the womb. They do not come out with something between blond, buff, bleached, and leprous coloring, such as the infants dropped from the wombs of the women of the Slavs and others of similar light complexion; nor are they overdone in the womb until they are burned, so that the child comes out something between black, murky, malodorous, stinking and crinkly-haired such as the Ethiopians and other blacks who resemble them. The Iraqis are neither half-baked dough nor burned crust, but between the two." Needless to say, Ibn al-Faqīh was an Iraqi.

I made use of this and other texts in my little book, *Race and Color in Islam,* published in 1971, and in the expanded version, *Race and Slavery in the Middle East,* published in 1990. As they used to say in Moscow, "It is no accident, comrades," that these two are among the least reprinted and least translated of all my books. The subject is too sensitive to appeal to publishers.

The difference in Sudan is not limited to color. The inhabitants of the northern and central parts of the country are, overwhelmingly, Arabic-speaking Muslims, while the peoples of the deep south speak either English or African languages, and profess either Christianity or African religions. For a long time there have been tensions and occasional conflicts between the two groups of Sudanese, at the personal as well as at the public level. I remember a conversation with a University of Khartoum student who was from the south. The official language of instruction at that time was still English, but the overwhelming majority of the students were Arabic-speaking northerners. The student, a black, or should I say blue, Christian from the south, was one of the very few such students in the university. One of the visitors asked him what sort of problems he had in his associations with the Arabic-speaking Muslim majority of the student population. His answer was striking. His relations with them were difficult, but not because they were Arabic-speaking or Muslims. He soon learned enough Arabic to communicate with them and their Islam was not a problem for him. "The real problem," he said, "is that these people are Orientals." Some clarification is needed here. In American usage the term "Oriental" is usually limited to the Far East. In European, including British, usage which at that time was dominant in Sudan, the Orient begins on the eastern shore of the Mediterranean. What he meant of course was that they were part not just of a different religion, but of a different civilization. By this observation he had put his finger on the essential problem in relations between the north and the south of Sudan. Over the decades that followed, relations between north and south became ever more tense, leading eventually to separation.

In Sudan, the principal institution of higher learning was the University of Khartoum which began as a high school, Gordon Memorial College, and gradually blossomed into a university. My connection with the university lasted for a number of years in the 1960s. Several generations of students came from Khartoum to London to take degrees and in some cases Ph.D.'s in history. Most of these went back and taught at what became the University of Khartoum. We at the University of London had a very close relationship with the University of Khartoum and in particular we had trained a number of Sudanese students who were now professors of Middle Eastern and related history.

I assisted in the examinations every year and one year I was asked to go to Khartoum to participate on the spot. These were for the B.A. degree examinations in the university. Three or four of my former students, then teaching at the University of Khartoum, welcomed me at the Faculty Club and we spent a very pleasant time together. One of them asked if I would like to meet the students. I readily agreed. This had obviously been prearranged; we walked along the Nile bank a short distance and came to the Students' Club. Inside was a gathering of students waiting to receive us. My host turned to them and said, "This is Professor Lewis from the University of London," and then he turned to me and pointed to the students and said, "Your grandchildren." That was a really delicious moment.

When we were suitably relaxed and friendly, they asked me what I thought of their work. Students in Sudan were taught to write down every word the teacher said. They learned it by heart and regurgitated it in the examination papers. As the external examiner I got rather tired of this—the same answers, the same points, the same sequence and with the same examples, one after another. I had written a report a year before my visit in which I had said that it was a great pity that the students merely reproduce what they get from their teachers and their textbooks; I suggested it would be nice for them to have their own opinions on these questions. The following year they did exactly the same thing. They regurgitated what the teacher had told them, the same points, the same illustrations; but each answer began with the words "In my opinion."

So when I met with the students and teachers in Khartoum, as we sat and chatted by the Nile riverbank in a very nice garden club, I asked why they didn't give their own opinions instead of merely giving back what they had been given. The teachers chimed in and said, "We keep telling them that. We keep telling them not just to tell us what we told them, but to think of something for themselves." One of the students asked then how he would know whether the answer was correct. I said, "This is a history examination, it's not a math test where an answer is either right or totally wrong. History is very largely a matter of interpretation of a matter of opinion. On the same facts you might arrive at quite different conclusions from your teacher or your examiner." So he repeated, "But how do we know which is right?" I replied that a right answer is any answer which is based on correct facts and is intelligently argued. What you do with the facts is your business, as long as it makes sense. I don't have to agree with you, I just have to respect the way you put it. One of them argued, "Isn't it much safer to keep with what we know is acceptable to the teacher?" I responded, "If you do it that way, you will be safe for a pass, but you will never get a good degree. I mean you will never get a first or an upper second, in other words you'll never get a high grade, an A or a B, just a safe C." We batted this back and forth for a bit, and then finally one of them said, "It's too dangerous." And the rest of them agreed, and they went on answering questions in the same way.

My host later suggested that I might like to visit the Islamic Institute in Omdurman, not very far from Khartoum. I was delighted to do so and was received by the principal, introduced to various professors, and taken to various classes. Then we had a large gathering in the quad with masses of professors and students there to be introduced to me. I should mention that this was during the month of Ramadan when Muslims fast. My host asked, "Would you like something to drink?" I declined but he insisted and said, "Bring a Pepsi." I didn't particularly like Pepsi but nevertheless I had to take the can and drink it in the quadrangle of the Islamic Institute of Omdurman while the sweating, thirsty professors and students looked at me with mixed feelings.

For many years I maintained a relationship with the department of history of the University of Khartoum. That was weakened by my departure for the United States in 1974, and terminated by the total transformation of Sudanese society and culture under the new regime.

Mission to America

The British Foreign Office periodically arranged for British scholars to lecture at American universities—a type of cultural exchange. While I was working on *The Emergence of Modern Turkey* I was asked to do such a tour and was told that I was perfectly free to disagree with UK policies but I should explain that I was doing so as an individual, not as a spokesman for the Foreign Office. I agreed.

I arrived in the United States for my first visit on February 23, 1954, and sailed for home on April 13. In those seven weeks I lectured in New York, Philadelphia, Cambridge, Waltham, Detroit, Ann Arbor, Spokane, Seattle, Tacoma, Portland, San Francisco, Berkeley, Sacramento, Los Angeles, Riverside, Salt Lake City, Albuquerque, Kansas City, St. Louis, and Washington, D.C. Most of my lectures were at universities, colleges, and societies or councils for world affairs. I also addressed a number of luncheon clubs and community groups. In many of the cities I was interviewed on radio and in New York and Hollywood I took part in television programs.

I was struck everywhere by the friendliness with which I was received, not only on the part of individuals but also, what is more remarkable, of audiences. In most places the lectures were followed by a number of questions, most of which were honest requests for information or opinion. There were very few occasions when I could detect any sign of malice or ill will on the part of the questioner. Only in two places did I encounter strong opposition—at the University of Michigan, Ann Arbor, and at the University of California, Berkeley. In both of these I was subjected to vigorous questioning by Middle Eastern (but not by American) students. At Michigan the questioning turned on some observations I had made on the governmental traditions of Islam and did not really involve any current political issues. In Berkeley, on the other hand, I was cross-examined for over an hour on all the misdeeds perpetrated by the British in the Middle East from Richard the Lionheart to the government of Iraq. I was sometimes able to disarm the questioner by an appropriate quote, in Arabic, from the Koran or some other Islamic source. Many of the questions were quite unrelated to anything that I had said in the lecture, and I was told afterward that a committee of Arab students regularly organizes a welcome of this kind for British and French speakers. By way of contrast the reception accorded to me by the academic faculty at Berkeley was one of the friendliest of the whole tour.

There seemed to be quite a lot of general interest in the Middle East, most of it uncomplicated by any knowledge of the area or by any realization of the complexity of the problems involved. I often thought of Adlai Stevenson's remark that for the Americans every question must have an answer and every story a happy ending. I would add a gloss however: the answer must be a simple one, and the story must have a hero and a villain. There seems to be an underlying belief that basically the Middle East is very much like the Middle West, and if only one could "get together" with people there and get rid of the "bad men" and troublemakers everything would be all right and the difficulties would vanish like the obstacles in the path of a Hollywood hero. This attitude sometimes led to the suspicion that British difficulties in the Middle East or elsewhere were due to British stuffiness and standoffishness, and that if only the British had been able to unbutton and "get together" with other people as the Americans do, all would have been well.

The questions followed fairly constant lines. We were at this point at the height of the Cold War and everyone wanted to know about the Russian threat and what we were to do about it, the prospects of communism in the Middle East, the Suez Canal and Iranian oil. Cyprus turned up in New York but nowhere else, Palestine occasionally but much less frequently than I had expected.

I found quite a lot of sympathy for Britain and for British difficulties, but not very much understanding of what these were. The anti-colonial argument still had quite a lot of effect among some Americans who saw King George III's redcoats behind every bush but I had the impression that this group was of dwindling importance. I found in many quarters a dawn of understanding that things were not exactly as they had thought and even signs of anger at those who had misled them. Ideas still seemed to be rather vague however, the one certain and universal conviction being that there is a magical formula for every difficulty, and that the task of statesmanship is to find it and pronounce it correctly. There was considerable interest in developments in Africa and India, about which Americans knew little but wanted to know more. In several different places I found people quite puzzled by the pro-British observations made shortly before by visitors from India.

One episode may be worth mentioning. In St. Louis I lectured to students at a teachers' training college. The professor of history told me that the previous week they had heard a lecture by an Egyptian student who had had a tremendous effect on them. "They were just about ready to drop the hydrogen bomb on London," he said. He had therefore asked the British consulate for a speaker to give another point of view, and that was how I came to be there. He told me that by far the most powerful factor influencing American students on issues of foreign affairs was the presence of fellow students from the countries concerned. He thought that a few more British students at American universities would elicit more empathy for the British point of view than a number of speakers, however distinguished.

In the course of my travels there was a striking difference between the places where I had personal contacts and those where I had none. In the former, such as Harvard, Columbia, Michigan, Brandeis, Berkeley, and Los Angeles, the lecture meeting was well publicized in advance, was preceded and followed by receptions and lunches or dinners with the faculty, and was generally attended by a large and representative audience. In one or two places, Detroit and Seattle, information or consular officers managed to achieve the same effect, but otherwise my visits seem to have had a much more limited impact. The lectures were in effect to ordinary undergraduate classes and probably made about as much impact as these normally do.

The tour ended in Washington, D.C., where I was invited to give a lecture at the Middle East Institute on the policies of the Western powers in the Middle East. A diplomat from the British Embassy was invited to act as chairman. Earlier that week there had been quite a scandal. President Eisenhower had appointed as his ambassador to Ceylon (whose name after 1972 was Sri Lanka) a wealthy businessman who had contributed generously to his campaign. This was normal practice and the Senate Foreign Relations Committee, which has to approve ambassadorial appointments, was disposed to be friendly. The senators didn't ask him difficult questions. They asked the first thing he would do upon his arrival in Sri Lanka. He replied that he guessed he'd present his credentials to the king. As there was no king it was obvious he hadn't a clue what form of government the country had. Having tasted blood the committee went on to press him and his total ignorance became painfully apparent. The State Department official who accompanied him said that of course he would be receiving guidance and instructions from the department.

It was just a few days after this that I gave my talk at the Middle East Institute. During the question period someone asked what, as a visitor to this country, did I think of the way the U.S. government chooses its ambassadors. This really put me on the spot. I was there as a quasi-official guest under the auspices of the British Embassy with someone from the embassy presiding. I had a sudden inspiration and using a well-known diplomatic formula I said, "All I can say is that your ministers may not be plenipotentiary, but your envoys are certainly extraordinary." That went down rather well and when I revisited Washington ten years later, it was quoted back to me.

This tour was a most interesting and valuable experience. It brought me into contact with teachers and students of my subject in U.S. universities, as well as with other specialists, both official and unofficial, on the area. Incidentally, I received five offers of visiting professorships after the trip, one of which, at UCLA, I later accepted.

A Year in Los Angeles

In the autumn of 1955 I flew from England via New York to Los Angeles to begin a year as a visiting professor at UCLA. The dean of the faculty picked me up at the airport. He drove me to his home in the hills outside Los Angeles where I spent the first night. He remarked that I had had a long trip and suggested I not get up early but stay in bed as long as I liked. I thanked him, went to sleep and slept very well. He had left a car for me and said that when I was ready I should drive to the university and then we could talk. I had to drive from the house to the campus, neither a long nor a complicated drive. The problem was that this was the first time I had driven outside the United Kingdom. I was on the wrong side of the car, the car was on the wrong side of the road; and added to that, the car had automatic transmission and power steering, neither of which I had ever encountered or even heard of before. So this drive down the hill from his house to the campus was a terrifying experience.

I soon learned that in order to live in Los Angeles I would have to acquire a car and that meant that I would have to acquire a California driving license. At that time a British driving license would have been recognized in the United States but in California, as a professor, even a visiting professor at UCLA, I was a state civil servant and a state civil servant is required to have a California driving license and for that I had to take a California test. The time and place were fixed and I went for the test. I sat in the car; the examiner got in next to me and told me to drive around the block. I drove around the block and he said, "That'll do." "Is that all?" He said, "That's enough to show me whether you can drive or not." Then he said, "There is one other thing you have to do." "What's that?" "Parallel park." We came to a place where there was a space between two parked cars and he admonished, "You have to get in there in not more than three moves." I failed miserably. I was on the wrong side of the car, the car was on the wrong side of the road and I just couldn't do it in three moves. I was able to take the test again a week later and, fortunately, pass it.

On my early visits to the United States I was shocked by the level of institutionalized anti-Semitism which would have been inconceivable in England. It was quite normal at that time for some hotels not to accept Jewish guests. In England, any hotel that did that would have lost its license.

During that first trip I had the opportunity to chat with a Jewish lawyer in New York who had never been to England and who asked me various questions about the Jews in England. He asked if there were any Jewish members in Parliament. When I answered yes he wanted to know how many. Normally I wouldn't have been able to answer that, but it so happened that I had recently read an article about Jewish members of the House of Commons, and was able to answer that there were thirty-something. He was astonished and said he didn't know there were that many Jews in England. I replied that there were indeed more than thirty-five Jews in England. "No, no—I mean to elect them." I had to explain that they were not elected by Jews. They happened to be Jews but they were elected as members of their party. "Oh," he said, "that couldn't happen here. The only Jewish members of Congress are elected from heavily Jewish districts. We would never get Jews elected in non-Jewish districts." Although that may have been true at that time, it's no longer true now, and it certainly wasn't true in England. Most of the MPs came from districts with few or no Jews.

He asked how the first Jew came to sit in the House of Commons as for several hundred years they were prohibited from even living in England. Jews were expelled from England, by law, in 1290 and not readmitted until 1656, when Oliver Cromwell agreed to a Jewish request to establish a community and a synagogue. Various reasons have been adduced to explain why he did this. One is that he thought that they would be a useful and productive element. Another, more probable, explanation is that he believed that the dispersion of the Jews had to be completed before the Second Coming. There was no law excluding Jews from the House of Commons, but there was a clause in the Oath of Loyalty, taken by a new member on taking his seat, which included the words "on the true faith of a Christian." This obviously excluded non-Christians.

In the middle of the nineteenth century, a member of the Rothschild family stood as a Liberal candidate for the city of London and was elected. He went to take his seat in Parliament and the clerk of the House tried to administer the oath. Rothschild said he was sorry but as a Jew he could not swear on "the true faith of a Christian." The clerk then referred it to House. The House debated it, and decided that since he could not take the oath his election was not valid and there would have to be a by-election. In the British system, if a seat falls vacant for any reason, they do not have to wait for the next general election, nor is there anyone who is empowered to nominate a member. There is a by-election, an election in just that constituency. So a by-election was ordered and Rothschild ran again and was elected again. The same thing happened the second time. The election was declared invalid. And it happened a third time. After his third election, the House of Commons decided that it couldn't really disregard the wishes of the electorate, so it modified words in the Oath of Loyalty and from that time onward it was possible for Jews to be elected members. Rothschild took his seat in 1858. The region where he was elected was the city of London, which was certainly not Jewish.

In America one has much more contact with Jewish matters than in England. It's very difficult to define how, but both Jews and others in America seem to be aware fully of a distinction. It is not an antagonism or a hostility; it is just a distinction. People are conscious of their differences. I noticed this in my first teaching appointment at UCLA. I was in the history department of UCLA through the academic year and within a couple of months I knew the religious affiliation of practically every member of the department. I had never asked or sought this information, which was really of no interest; but I just knew it because it was part of the common knowledge in the department. I had been teaching in an English university for seventeen years before that without knowing the religious or sectarian affiliations of my English colleagues. It wasn't an issue and nobody gave a damn.

There are Jews in the modern world who accommodate themselves to the majority culture and develop either a great resentment and contempt for it or excessive admiration or even a combination of both. In my case, and others like me, we didn't want or need to accommodate ourselves to the majority culture; we were part of the majority culture. I have no sense of ambivalence toward Western European culture. I am by birth, origin, upbringing, part of it, and my claim to it is no less than that of anyone else who was born and grew up in that culture.

I remember one dinner long ago at the University of London when the main dish was pheasant, which I very much enjoy. One of my colleagues looked at me in puzzlement. "But I thought you were an observant Jew and that pheasant was forbidden," he said. I thought for a moment and then I said, "Yes, that's right, it is, but I don't go that far." "But you always refuse to eat any dish with ham, pork or bacon. If you refuse those you should refuse pheasant, too. What's the difference?" he asked. I replied, "When I was growing up the world was divided into people who ate pig meat and people who didn't." Pork and ham became the basic division of identity. As nobody ate pheasant, it was something else.

I was reminded of this years later when I was dining in a restaurant in the United States with a Reform rabbi who, to my surprise, ordered shrimp, which are, of course, on the forbidden list for an observant Jew. I said to him in astonishment, "You are eating shrimp!" He replied, "Yes, we're Reform and not that strict." "But," I said, "you never eat pork or bacon." "It's not the same," he said. "Shrimp and seafood are *trafe* [the opposite of kosher]; pork and bacon are anti-Semitic."

Choosing a School

In 1957, when my daughter Melanie reached the age of five, my wife and I decided it was time to place her in a day school. We naturally wanted to find the best school possible for her. At that time, there were two day schools for girls in London which were, by common consent, the best in the region. One of them, St. Paul's, was a Church of England school; the other, South Hampstead School for Girls, by a fortunate chance, was five minutes' walk from where we lived. We decided to try both. At St. Paul's, the headmistress said she would like to meet the parents of the girl. We went there; she asked us various questions which we answered and then I said to her: "Don't you want to meet my daughter?" She looked at me in surprise and said: "What could I learn from interviewing a five-year-old child?"

The attitude of the neighboring school was very different. Each year they accepted about thirty girls. They interviewed about a hundred. As parents we had to take our daughters there and then leave them with the teachers who, by various procedures, chose half of the girls and then, some days later, summoned them for a further procedure by which they finally chose the thirty that they accepted. This school was what is known in England as a "direct grant school," a private school which receives some government support. Since it received government support, it was subject to government rules of education, one of which was that they were not allowed to ask applicants their religion. At St. Paul's of course they were entitled to do so, and they did. St. Paul's school was primarily for Anglican children, but they accepted a limited number of pupils of other denominations. At South Hampstead, such selection was strictly forbidden. I had been interested in the fact that over the years this particular school had had a fairly consistent level of approximately one-third of the class being Jewish and I wondered how they managed to maintain this level without asking people their religion. On the last day of the interviews, when they were making their final choice, there was a senior school mistress in charge and she asked various questions about my daughter and then, just as we were leaving, she said: "Just one other thing. As you know, we include a class on scripture as part of the syllabus. Would your daughter be doing both Testaments or just the Old?" Mystery solved.

The first day of school is usually a Wednesday, in order to make the transition easier. On the Saturday after my daughter started school, my parents came as usual to pay us a visit. Melanie was full of her new experience and eager to talk about it. What really astonished me was the immediate and total communication that was established between my daughter and my mother. My mother too had started school at the age of five, more than half a century earlier, but when they talked about school, sharing experiences, procedures, games and all the rest, it was as if they had both been in the same place on the same day. My mother started school in 1900, when Queen Victoria was still on the throne. Melanie started more than half a century later, but the degree of similarity and continuity was remarkable. That would not happen now. There have been too many changes and transformations and the England of today is very different from the England in which I grew up, let alone that of my parents. But the continuity was very clear then. Melanie's mother knew English well, but she had arrived in England for the first time in her late teens and had never been a little girl in England. Nor for that matter had my father or I been little girls. We were fascinated listeners but not participants in this conversation. I cannot imagine an exchange of this kind with any of my grandchildren. It is not only a different age; it is a different country and, in a sense, a different world.

Pakistan

In early 1957 I received an invitation to visit Pakistan. The occasion was the opening of the new campus of the University of the Punjab in Lahore. I was also invited to participate in an international conference of Islamic studies, to be held in Lahore at the same time. The invitation was issued jointly by the University of the Punjab and the government of West Pakistan. (This was before East Pakistan split off and became Bangladesh.) I accepted with alacrity and set off on what was to be my only visit to Pakistan, and the first of a series of visits to the Indian subcontinent.

I began my visit in Karachi where I spent a few days and managed to see some old friends, one of whom I had known when he was a law student during the brief interval when I was a law student myself. He had now reached a position of some importance and invited me to his home for dinner. On my arrival, he opened a cupboard and offered me a drink, a choice of various scotch whiskeys and other beverages. I was astonished since there was, in Pakistan at that time, a strict ban on alcohol—a ban, that is, for Muslims. There were bars in hotels and restaurants and other public places but the only people allowed to drink were non-Muslims and "certified dipsomaniacs" who could make a medical case for their absolute need of booze. I was therefore more than a little surprised when my host, a prominent law officer, opened his cupboard and offered me a drink. I asked if he wouldn't have to prosecute himself. To which he replied, "Oh, no, I am a certified dipsomaniac."

I was also invited to dinner by a prominent local Shi'ite family. At one point in our dinner table discussion my host remarked reproachfully that in my book *The Arabs in History* I had praised Mu'awiya's statesmanship and even, in some measure, endorsed his legitimacy. For the Shi'a he is the archvillain, the main perpetrator of their defeat in the succession of the Prophet; he is a figure of pure evil. To praise him was the equivalent of praising Hitler to Jews. My hosts were very gracious, but left me in no doubt about their feelings. My own feeling was of embarrassment (social, not intellectual).

One of my most vivid recollections from the trip is of a dinner at a Pakistani officers' mess. At one point the conversation turned to the recent war—the 1956 war, known as the Suez Crisis, when Israel, in response to the Egyptian blockade of its shipping in the Red Sea, invaded Egypt with the complicity of Britain and France. President Eisenhower intervened and ordered them to leave, which they did. When I asked my Pakistani host, a general, his view of this episode, his reply was really surprising: "Our position is quite clear. We are strongly opposed to military aggression, especially when left unfinished."

I was reminded of that when the memoirs of the widow of Anthony Eden were published, in the course of which she said that a little after the 1956 war she and her husband were talking to an American diplomat who asked, "Why didn't you go on?" This combination of comments, one from a Pakistani and one from an American, raises interesting questions about what was really intended—but that is another topic entirely.

I went on to Lahore after that, where I was officially received and installed in my hotel, and where the very elaborate proceedings of the occasion began. The university ceremonies celebrated the opening of the new campus. As I was the formal representative of my own university I was in cap and gown and delivered the customary academic platitudes.

The other, more interesting, event to which I was invited in Pakistan was the International Congress of Islamic Studies. This was primarily a gathering of Muslims—representatives, many of them professional men of religion, from Muslim countries and Muslim communities all over the world. I was one of the very small group (about half a dozen or so) of non-Muslim specialists in Islamic studies who had been invited to come as guests and participate in the event. It was at times pleasant, at times difficult, but certainly interesting and informative.

Two incidents remain particularly vivid. At the end of the meeting, Gustave von Grunebaum, professor of Near East history at the University of California, and I were walking out of the building when we were stopped by a Pakistani who asked whether he could have the privilege of giving us a lift to our hotel. We accepted. No sooner had we set off than he came to the point. "I have a question which I would like to put to you two gentlemen, as experts on Islam. Would you be willing to consider my question?" We replied that we would be happy to do so. An uncle of his had recently died, leaving him a considerable fortune. The uncle had no children of his own and our host was his sole heir. The question that was troubling him was as follows. His uncle had accumulated his fortune by buying and selling shares on the stock exchange. Our host was a pious Muslim but not a learned one. He knew that trade and profit were permitted but that loans and interest were forbidden, as was gambling. His question was whether making money on the stock exchange counted as the one or the other—in a word, was it permitted or forbidden? As a pious Muslim, he did not feel that he could accept the money if it had been unlawfully acquired.

I said to him that what he was asking for was not a scholarly opinion but a fatwa, a religious ruling. Surely he would want to turn to one of his own jurists, not to infidel Orientalists. He replied with a grimace of disgust, "Our jurists! If they smell money they will authorize anything. I have more confidence in your scholarship than in their piety."

Gustave and I looked at each other in embarrassment and we gave him the kind of vague and inconclusive answer that comes so naturally to academics. We were trying to make life easier for him without making the cost of doing so too onerous.

The other memorable occasion was when the non-Muslim Orientalists who were present at the conference were invited by the great Islamic ideologue Abu'l-'Ala Mawdudi to visit him in his home. Mawdudi was a leading figure in the Muslim world and we felt both honored and privileged and we were eager to hear what he would have to say.

His opening remarks were not surprising: "You Orientalists, you all make the same mistake."

"Oh dear," we thought. "Here it comes . . ." But we were quite wrong. He went on to say, "You all learn Arabic; many of you learn Persian; some of you learn Turkish. That was all right in its day, but its day has passed. Today, the center of the world of Islam is here in Pakistan, and the dominant language of Islam is Urdu. If you want to know what is happening in the Islamic world, you can do so only through Urdu." A surprising and interesting comment, and by no means entirely wrong. I never attempted to learn Urdu as I had decided early on to limit my specialized studies to the Islamic heartlands of the Middle East.

At the time of my visit Bangladesh was still East Pakistan, and my conference hosts suggested, and I readily agreed, that I might go there as part of my visit to Pakistan. There was no direct land link between West and East Pakistan. One could fly, or travel via India. I had never been to India and this seemed to offer an interesting possibility. Relations between India and Pakistan were at best chilly, and since I was there as a guest of Pakistan, I felt that I should not make a stop in India without asking permission. I therefore spoke with my host at the University of the Punjab, and asked whether he had any objection to my stopping in India briefly on my way to East Pakistan. "Not at all," he said. "On the contrary, we would like you to see for yourself how our Muslim brothers are oppressed in India." So I flew from Lahore to New Delhi and spent a few days there before proceeding to East Pakistan. During that brief visit I established some contacts with the Delhi Muslim community, and of course with the dominant Indian Hindu academic and learned organizations. This led to a series of subsequent visits, mostly to Delhi, once to Bombay, and, for a somewhat longer period, as a visiting professor at the Muslim University of Aligarh.

On one of these visits, in the late seventies, I was invited to lecture by the Institute of Islamic Studies in New Delhi. After the lecture my hosts said that they hoped I would understand that they were unable to pay me the kind of lecture fee to which I was no doubt accustomed but they would like to show their appreciation and had a suggestion to make. They proceeded to explain that they had rented a houseboat on Lake Kashmir and had made arrangements to fly me and my Turkish companion to Kashmir where we were to be picked up and taken to the houseboat which was all ready for our cruise round the lake. It was a fascinating experience, and in many ways the most rewarding remuneration I have ever received for a lecture.

Afghanistan

Sometime in the 1960s the British government signed a treaty for an exchange of cultural activities with what was then the Kingdom of Afghanistan. Having signed this document they wondered what on earth to do next. The answer to that was not very obvious and then someone had the idea of sending me to Afghanistan to give a couple of lectures, talk to some people and explore possibilities. This sounded interesting and as I had never been to Afghanistan and was always willing to add another country to my list, off I went over the summer for a visit of a couple of months.

At that time there was no way to fly directly from England to Afghanistan so I went via Tehran. When I boarded the plane in Tehran I was surprised to see a man from the University of Hamburg whom I knew marginally well. It turned out he was bound for Kabul on a mission identical to mine as the West German government had just signed a cultural convention with the Kingdom of Afghanistan.

Each of our programs began with a major public lecture in the university's largest auditorium and it was my good luck that his lecture came first. On the platform were the minister of education, dignitaries of the university, other VIPs and, in the front row, the staffs of the German, Austrian and Swiss embassies and others from the German-speaking community. The auditorium was packed with faculty and students.

My German colleague began his lecture, in German, and was translated, paragraph by paragraph, by an interpreter. He had been told by his sponsors in Berlin, exactly as I had been told in London, "Show them pictures." So he had some slides, as I did, and as soon as the lights went dim for the slide show there was a stampede for the exits. But the authorities had anticipated this. The exits were bolted and barred and guarded by fierce Pathan warriors who flung the students back into their seats—and the lecture continued. I thought, my God, what am I in for?

The next day it was my turn to give my lecture. I began as my colleague had done and then I also asked for the lights to be dimmed to show my slides. I did this with considerable apprehension. Nothing happened. Nobody moved. The audience remained in their seats and I continued my lecture. It had gone well, I thought. Maybe more people in Kabul knew English than German. That's certainly true, but it wasn't the explanation, which I discovered when the lecture was over. In Afghanistan there is no question period after lectures; there are lectures and that's it. When my lecture was over and I was leaving, several students came up to me and said they would like to thank me for my lecture and then asked, very hesitantly, if they could ask me some questions. I responded affirmatively and they asked their questions most apologetically. They said, "We're sorry to bother you with these questions, but you see, tomorrow we're going to be examined on your lecture." That's one way of keeping students in their seats.

Afghanistan has two national languages, Pashto and Dari. Pashto is a language of the Indian family and it is widely spoken in Pakistan. Dari is Persian by another name. Dari is not identical with the Persian spoken in Iran, but it's closer than English and American. There are, however, some differences. Several examples: my hosts provided me with a car and driver and after a visit with some officials I went outside and there was no sign of the car. I wanted to ask, "Where are my driver and car?" In Iranian Persian, the driver would be *chauffeur-i māshīn; chauffeur* is a driver, *māshīn* is a car, so I said *chauffeur-i māshīn*. Nobody understood. Eventually the driver appeared and it was explained to me: "What you want is the *driver-i motor.*" Obvious!

When I flew to Herat after my stay in Kabul, my luggage disappeared. It was just one case, but all I had. I was worried. I was trying to ask about it and my problem was how to say "luggage." I tried the usual word in Persian; it didn't work. I tried Arabic; it didn't work. I tried a sort of international language, "baggage"; even that didn't work. Eventually someone appeared carrying it. "There it is." "Ah," he said, *"Box-i shumā!"* "Box" is the Afghan-Persian word for luggage.

One of the striking things about Afghanistan at that time, and different from other countries in the region, was the frankness and directness of its people. One day I was meeting with officials of the university, discussing the purpose of my visit, when a young professor turned to me and said, "The real question of Anglo-Afghan cultural cooperation is whether British universities are prepared to recognize our degrees as equal." You can guess the answer to that. As I was trying to think of a diplomatic formulation the minister of education, whom I had come to know over the course of the trip, turned to him and said, "Don't be silly. How could they possibly recognize our degrees as equal?"

Not long after that the minister of education gave a reception to which he invited members of the foreign community in Kabul and their wives, not a large group at the time. One woman, the wife of an American diplomat and a staunch feminist, thought that having the minister of education at her mercy was too good an opportunity to miss. She cornered him and asked why he didn't do more for the education of girls. A fair question. I think that most ministers of education in Third World countries, tackled with such a question, would have said something on the order of, we did so much last year, are doing such and such this year and next year we're going to do so much more. Not in Afghanistan. The minister looked at her in astonishment and said, "Madam, I don't have enough schools for boys;

don't bother me with girls." I deplored his sentiments but admired his honesty.

I began to get used to this frankness and even to operate in the style. The Afghans liked to compare their country to Switzerland as it is surrounded by mountains and shares languages with two of its neighbors, Pakistan and Iran, but has a strong identity of its own. I was on a local flight from Kabul to Herat conversing with the young Afghan sitting next to me when he gave me this line about Afghanistan being the Switzerland of Asia. For me, it was one time too many. I knew by then that I could get away with a not very polite answer. I pointed to my wristwatch and said, "When you can make one like that, I'll believe you." Fortunately, he did not take offense at my bad manners and instead, laughed.

I was provided with a Land Rover and driver to travel around the countryside. One morning as we were driving to the western part of Afghanistan we came to a river which we had to cross. There was no bridge, which was not unusual. The general practice in Afghanistan is to go along the river to a spot where the water is fairly shallow and, with fingers crossed, drive across. We were directed to the nearest "best place" and when we arrived I saw, firmly embedded in the muddy water, an American Jeep and a German Volkswagen. Our British Land Rover drove right across. It was a moment of intense patriotic pride.

As I was in the country on an official mission, I spent a fair amount of time at the British Embassy. Ambassador de la Mare, who had the same name as the well-known writer Walter de la Mare, was from a Channel Islands family. His wife, unusual for ambassadors, was not British but an American from Boston. She missed no opportunity of repeating that she was of pure English ancestry on both sides. One day just the three of us were having lunch and she went on about this at some length, for my benefit. All her ancestors were English on both sides, all the way back to when they first crossed the

Atlantic from England to North America. When she had finished, she turned to her husband, the ambassador, and said, "I'm much more English than you are; after all, you come from the Channel Islands." He took a slow, deep breath and said, "Yes, my dear, you are more English than I am, but I am more British than you are."

My trip lasted several months and appears to have been successful. In the years that followed, cultural relations between Britain and Afghanistan were maintained. Afghan students were awarded scholarships to study in English universities and there were exchanges of experts. At some point Muhammad Shafiq, the deputy minister of justice, came to London on an official visit. Afghanistan had just promulgated a new constitution and the University of London invited him to give a lecture on it. He began by saying, "This is not the first time we've had a constitution in Afghanistan. One was promulgated some thirty years ago, but it didn't work. Neither the government nor the people took any notice of it and it became a dead letter. We decided to try again."

He proceeded to describe the new constitution. When he had finished, questions were invited from the audience. One person asked why, since a previous constitution was not taken seriously by either the government or the people, there was reason to believe that the present constitution would be taken seriously. Shafiq, who had the kind of special straightforwardness and directness which at that time was characteristic of the Afghans, looked him straight in the eye and said: "You didn't listen carefully to what I was saying. I didn't say that the new constitution would be a success, or that it would be taken seriously. I said we had decided to try again. I hope it will be a success; I hope it will be taken seriously, but I can't give you any assurance that it will be."

The next time I met him was several years later when my daughter and I had gone to Cairo to attend the Millennium of the founding of the city. At the big opening ceremony I suddenly felt a slap on my back. I turned around and there was Shafiq. We greeted each other warmly and then I asked him: "What are you doing here?" He said rather plaintively, "I'm the Afghan ambassador to Egypt." I congratulated him, and then he was very kind and very helpful and provided a car and driver for Melanie to tour her around the city. When he went back to Afghanistan, he became foreign minister and then Prime Minister. When the Russians came in 1979, he was hanged in his own garden. A sad end of a good and decent man.

A Conference in Moscow

It was with some trepidation that most of the Western participants made their way to Moscow in 1960 for the XXV Congress of Orientalists.* There had been many alarming rumors in circulation of an organized orgy of propaganda and of massed phalanxes of politically selected delegates from Communist countries. It was therefore with more distress than surprise that we found ourselves ushered into a large hall for the opening session where we were addressed at some length and with great vigor by a group of dignitaries on the platform led by Anastas Mikoyan, then Deputy Premier. The keynote discussed the liberation of the peoples of (non-Soviet) Asia and Africa from colonialism, and the corresponding liberation of Oriental scholarship from the yoke of colonialist Orientalists. The speeches formed a well-orchestrated symphony in three movements. In the first, they insulted their Western guests; in the second, they flattered their Eastern guests; and in the third (the synthesis?), they praised themselves with obvious sincerity and relish.

The proceedings of the Congress developed in the usual feckless and inefficient way, bringing a welcome air of familiarity to the otherwise strange and alien setting in which we found ourselves. Sections

*This description is based on a contemporary report which I wrote for SOAS.

dealing with adjoining subjects were placed at great distances from one another with perhaps half a mile of uncharted country between them, thus making it impossible for us to move with any ease from one to another. Timetables were changed with little or no notice, some papers canceled, and some others, unannounced, inserted in the program. There were some interesting changes in the program, notably the division into sections. Islam, which was a separate section since these congresses started, disappeared entirely and those papers which would have come in the Islamic section were, as a result of this act of disestablishment, distributed among sections dealing with Arab, Persian, Turkish, etc., language, literature and history. In compensation an entirely new section appeared devoted to Afghan studies. These had in previous years been included in the Iranian or Indian sections and it was understood that this new section had been inserted in the program after representations from the Afghan Embassy in Moscow. Members of this section had plenty of free time.

The vast number of papers submitted to the Congress varied greatly in theme and still more greatly in quality. A matter of considerable interest to Western visitors was the very large number of papers submitted by Soviet Orientalists. There seemed to be general agreement that those on language subjects were good and often of considerable importance, that those dealing with archaeology contained useful and interesting material, but that those on history, social science and other subjects liable to political pressure were on the whole poor. Many of these were not only strongly propagandist in character but on a very crude and primitive level. It seems likely that any Russian scholar with a real historical sense, still more any non-Russian Soviet scholar, would take up some subject other than history. Some of the papers, as for example one on Soviet-Turkish friendship during the Turkish war of independence, were read in an atmosphere more reminiscent of a religious ceremony than of an academic session.

The main political effort of our hosts was concentrated on the committee dealing with the crucial questions of the venue of the next Congress, and some of us acquired a sudden flash of insight and a sudden gust of sympathy for those whose task it was to negotiate with Soviet officials.

One of the primary benefits that scholars derive from these gatherings is the opportunities they give for the making and renewal of personal contacts with scholars from other countries. This time, opportunities for personal contacts were limited. No list of participants was circulated until the very end of the Congress, no general reception for all participants was held until the eve of our departure, and no common place of meeting was available except for the hall and exhibition rooms of the university. At that time cafés and bars seemed to be unknown in Moscow, where drinking was a secret vice and eating a distasteful chore. Even communication with my colleagues in the SOAS delegation staying at the same hotel was difficult as no alphabetical list of hotel visitors with room numbers appeared to exist. There was, however, at the sections and at the university generally, some possibility of meeting, and it was with our Soviet colleagues that we were naturally most eager to make some form of contact. The Russians on the whole tended to be correct but rather distant and few of us had the chance of entering even into that kind of shoptalk laced with gossip that is normal between colleagues in the same field. For those of us who were able to speak to scholars from the Soviet Oriental territories in their own languages, this did provide an opportunity for frank and friendly conversation, albeit chiefly limited to scholarly matters. There were however some revealing remarks. One scholar from a Soviet Asian republic, when asked whether he really believed that, in accordance with Marxist dogma, there had been a feudal regime in his country in the Middle Ages, replied, "No, but there is now." Another, asked why he had taken up a particularly remote and obscure topic of research, replied, "Because there is no one in the Soviet Union who can tell me how to do it."

The practical arrangements for our accommodations, transport, etc., were lamentable. As one visitor put it, the first few days at the Hotel Ukraina were very much like one's first few days in the army with the difference that there were no clues at all as to the sense and purpose of it all. Intourist, with the alternating indolence and insolence of its staff and the monstrous and intricate lunacy of its organization, was a nightmare straight out of Kafka.

Perhaps the final comment can be given in the words of an English visitor with considerable knowledge of Soviet affairs. When asked whether our Soviet colleagues didn't care at all what kind of impression they were making on us, he replied, "The really terrifying thing is that they think they are making a good impression."

5.

Why Study History?

When I was still actively involved in teaching, I would assemble each new batch of graduate students around the seminar table and invite them, one by one, to introduce themselves, to say on what subject they proposed to conduct their research, and then, a question which never failed to disconcert them, why? Why did they want to study history? Why did they choose to do their research on this particular topic?

Their answers fell into fairly well-defined categories. A common answer, especially from students coming from Third World countries, was that they wanted to serve their country. This is a perfectly legitimate and acceptable answer, provided of course that it not proceed on the assumption that one serves one's country best by presenting a version of history favorable to whatever happens to be the prevailing ideology or ruling leadership in that country. That, as I see it, is not serving one's country. A discussion of this leads to interesting questions about truth, integrity and objectivity, which of course is not the same as detachment or neutrality. I never asked students to be detached or neutral in matters of profound concern to them. It would be unreasonable to expect this of them. But I did ask them to be honest. The point I often made was that if you look back at the history of your country, your party, your class, your church or whichever group with which you identify for the purposes of the history you are reading or writing—if you look back and find that in every single dispute between your group and other groups, yours has been right and the others have been wrong—then you should reexamine the hypotheses on the basis of which you are conducting your researches, because it is not in the nature of human entities to be always right.

I recall a student who came to me from a certain country which had a territorial dispute with a neighboring country, a quite minor territorial dispute about one small piece of territory that had been an issue between them for a very long time. He wanted to do his doctoral dissertation on this little area, and, he said, show that for thousands of years this little area had always been part of his country and not the other's. I asked how he knew. He replied, "It's well known." I said, "You don't get a Ph.D. for stating what is well known. For a Ph.D. you have to establish something that is unknown." To which he responded, "But, it's never been proven scientifically. I want to prove it scientifically." "If you set out to do a piece of scientific research, you go where it leads you," I said. "What will you do if you discover that it belonged to the other people, and not to yours?" This was a possibility he simply refused to consider, and he went elsewhere for his doctorate.

This was a very simple example; there are others where the pitfalls are better concealed. The problem is a universal one. Feuding tribes have opposing sagas, sung by rival bards, and the same tradition underlies much modern national historiography. Its religious equivalent is sectarian historiography.

There is a sense in which an Arab or an Indian, or for that matter anyone else, will know his own culture as no foreigner, however learned, could ever know it. Obviously they don't come west for that. They come for some quite practical things. One of them is an approach to the study of history that is free from both inherited attitudes and imposed constraints, where one follows the evidence wherever it leads, where one may start a piece of research without a prescribed or in any way predetermined result. This freedom has been significantly diminished in the modern West by political correctness, but not entirely ended.

Today, the historical researcher has at his disposal a range of new and sophisticated techniques for critical scholarship. Part of this is technical, even mechanical. We have devices now which make it possible to read previously unreadable manuscripts and decipher previously indecipherable inscriptions. A fragment of writing in this library can be matched with a fragment at that university thousands of miles away. In a palimpsest, for example, that is to say a manuscript which has been written over more than once, we can now read each version separately by the use of infrared scanners. The amount of information that one can collect, process, and use in a limited time has increased exponentially. The collection of data that in the past might have taken an experienced scholar months or even years can sometimes be done now by a novice in half an hour.

But even more important than the growing technology of research is the greater sophistication of method. Historical research means going to your evidence and asking questions. You ask questions of the evidence, and then, preferably without the use of torture, you extract answers. Our methods of examining and questioning the evidence have become much more sophisticated, and we are using evidence of a kind that was previously just thrown aside. For example, in a catalog of manuscripts in a major Western library, published almost seventy-five years ago, some early medieval documents from Egypt were briefly dismissed as "business letters, and therefore valueless." For the compilers of the catalog, only literary or historical manuscripts were of value. If a manuscript stated that this was the history of such and such kings from this date to that date, it was valuable historical evidence. Business and private correspondence was simply brushed aside. Who was interested in the business files of a merchant who lived in Cairo a thousand years ago?

Modern historians have become very interested in such documents. They have found ways of throwing light on matters about which nothing at all was known previously, by examining what one might call the contents of wastepaper baskets, documents which were discarded because they were no longer needed. They included letters, accounts, and jottings of all kinds. The use of this kind of material has enormously enriched historical scholarship. First developed by Western students of Western history, it has been extended by them and their disciples to other societies, wherever such documentation has survived.

An important example of this is the collection known as "Genizah." I have not worked on this material; I know it only second-hand from books and monographs by scholars who have worked on it. The foremost among them by far, standing head and shoulders above everyone else, was the late Professor S. D. Goitein who was for many years my neighbor and friend at Princeton. He was a truly great scholar, and I would regard his *Mediterranean Society* as the single most important work that has been written in modern times about the medieval Islamic world. I can think of nothing comparable in scope and depth and importance.

Imagine trying to write the history of your university at some fu-ture date. What you would need would be the files in the various of-fices. Now imagine that in some conflagration the files were destroyed and all that was left was an accumulation of wastepaper baskets. What Goitein did was to write a history of the Middle East from randomly surviving miscellaneous wastepaper baskets. He began with the dis-cards of the Jews of Cairo, one minority community in one Middle Eastern country. But because members of this community were en-gaged in all sorts of activities—personal, public, private, family, busi-ness, dealings with government, dealings with other countries, dealings with other communities in the same country, and so on—he was able to extract, from these scattered remnants of this minority community, a comprehensive picture of life in the medieval Islamic world over the centuries covered by these documents. It is profoundly illuminating; far better than anyone else has ever done or is likely to do.

Goitein's background was very much in the classical-philological-Orientalist tradition. As he progressed with his work, he realized that what he was doing was no longer classical Orientalism, but social history and economic history. So he made himself into a social historian and an economic historian. He familiarized himself with the methods, the concepts, and the approaches of disciplines which were entirely new to him, and mastered them sufficiently to do a superb job. Being able to change to that extent at that age is really quite unusual. He was a man of great modesty, completely without claims or pretensions: a true scholar. One of his favorite sayings was that among scholars there were princes and peasants, and he always insisted that he was a peasant. I do not agree.

Propaganda and History

The responsibility, the obligation, of a historian is to tell the truth as he sees it, the whole truth and nothing but the truth. He should not allow himself to be a propagandist or to be used by propagandists. This is the great temptation and the great danger of history as a profession because history is, after all, the case that one makes for almost any political cause. The same sequence of events can be interpreted and presented in very different ways. It's a great mistake to assume that historical truths are like mathematical truths where there is one right answer and all others are wrong. If your history is a simple narrative of events, there are right and wrong answers; but they are of no great interest or value to anyone. History is open to interpretation but even with interpretation there is the need for accuracy. Inaccurate history is worse that no history at all. People can be brought up on illusions and myths.

The modern historian needs access to archives, to public and where possible private papers, and of course good libraries. These are still lacking in many parts of the world. Another necessity, also sometimes missing or restricted, is freedom—the ability to express any opinion, put forward any argument, criticize any point of view. In a free society, scholars can take ideas and bat them back and forth over a seminar table. This constant exchange of ideas is part of the excitement of teaching and of studying. A group of people sit around a table, usually a mixed group of faculty and students, and one tries out an idea and sees how the others respond. Students working on a dissertation will draft a chapter and read the draft to a seminar and their fellow students will tear it to pieces, knowing, of course, that the same thing will be done to them in the following weeks. This freedom of research and debate is another reason why we not only may but should study the history of other peoples, some of whom cannot effectively study their own history, because of constraints—practical, political, ideological, religious or other. And there, perhaps, we have a moral duty to help.

I believe profoundly in the value of history. I am well aware of the defects of historical knowledge and it is precisely those defects which give it value. History is not an exact science. It is based on evidence which is incomplete, fragmentary, inconsistent, often contradictory, full of gaps, and in this way precisely reflects the human predicament. It provides some insight into the side of life and knowledge that is not precise, and not even always clear. Many of the troubles in the modern world have arisen from the fact that some people believe that human affairs can be dissected and directed with the sort of planning that engineers use. But humanity is not capable of such precision; human societies are not susceptible to such direction.

In the twentieth century enormous suffering was caused to countless millions of people by misguided attempts to apply that kind of direction to human society, by what is sometimes call social engineering, the planned and purposeful direction of the course of human events. Obviously, some sort of guidance is possible, and may even be useful. However, the idea that one can direct the course of history seems to me a pernicious and destructive delusion. By the study of history we can arrive at some better understanding of the nature of the human predicament in this universe; of what we can do and what we can't do; of where we are and, with luck, where we are going. History may serve us as a guide or as a teacher. We cannot use it as a tool. Those who condemn history as "irrelevant" and want to make it relevant may be even more dangerous than those who dismiss it as useless.

According to a common view that has evolved in the Western world, the primary objective of all study and of all research is to know, to understand. The desire to know the past is almost universal among human beings; almost but not quite. There are societies that have not attached much importance to history. But most societies have. Islamic societies in particular have always attached great importance to history, but only to their own. For them, history means the history of Islam, and is valuable insofar as it reveals the working out of God's purposes for humanity. Non-Islamic history, including their own pre-Islamic history, was in their perception worthless and therefore received no attention until early modern times.

The aim in teaching history is to get people to ask questions, quite basic questions, and to go through a constant process of self-examination. When I make a note, why do I make that note? What is the hypothesis on the basis of which I copy these three lines into a notebook and not the previous ones and not the following ones? One must be self-questioning and alert for unconscious and unstated assumptions. A good teacher must try to induce in the budding historian some idea of the infinite complexities of the historical process and the endless uncertainties. There's a wonderful remark by Anatole France in one of his books when he says of a certain scholar, "He's a truly great historian; he has enriched his subject with a new uncertainty."

A point which I always tried to impress on young historians is the importance of fairness. It is perfectly legitimate to reject and refute someone else's arguments, but you must not distort his arguments in order to make your task easier. This, alas, is very often done, not merely by some disreputable scribblers who dishonor our profession at the present time, but even, on occasion, by serious historians who cede to this temptation. If you wish to refute an argument, you must take as your target a fair statement of the best case possible for the point of view that you are trying to refute.

Another matter, often necessary to raise in reading draft chapters submitted by graduate students, is that they not convey indirectly what they lacked the evidence, or courage, to say directly. If you have the evidence and are convinced that a certain interpretation of that evidence is true—say so, and give both the evidence and the reasoning. There may be more evidence and less reasoning; there may be less evidence and more reasoning—that doesn't matter. But if you are not satisfied that the evidence and reasoning combined suffice to establish your version, don't try to convey it without actually saying so, by the use of carefully selected verbs and adjectives, of emotionally charged language, or of deliberate ambiguities. There are many uncertainties in historical research and often a major achievement of research may be to raise doubt where there was certainty before. Uncertainty may be beneficial in that it invites further research and further thought. But uncertainty disguised as certainty is dangerous.

Teaching Versus Research

Some people, it is argued, are good at teaching but not at research; others are good at research but not at teaching. This often leads to difficult discussions about allocating academic preferment. It is a familiar dilemma. Over the years I have heard many complaints, particularly from those who believe that university preferment is based almost entirely on research, so that good researchers who may be bad or negligent teachers are promoted, while good and devoted teachers with limited or no research are scorned.

I cannot speak of subjects other than history, nor of levels of the educational process below the university, but as far as the teaching of history at university level is concerned, this strikes me as an artificial dichotomy. In teaching history to university students, what precisely are we trying to teach? What is the purpose of the whole business of holding classes and seminars and guiding university students in their study of history?

At this level, history teaching does not simply mean transferring pieces of factual information about the past. If it were only that, it wouldn't be worth the bother. Factual information is of course necessary, but the students should either have this when they arrive at university or know where to find it. What a university teacher should be doing is conveying to his students an understanding of the processes by which historical knowledge is achieved. Unless the teacher has direct personal experience of that process through past research, or better still through current research of his own, he can't do that.

There are of course good teachers who don't do research, and they have an important function, at lower levels or perhaps in other subjects, but it seems to me that the prime value of history as a university discipline lies precisely in the fact that it is more than a mere accumulation of pieces of information to be acquired, stored and passed on. That kind of history is of very little value. It is mere antiquarianism.

We are all aware of the common phenomenon of the university teacher, whether in history or in any other field, who does one major book, and that's all; one major research project, usually a revised and amplified version of his doctoral dissertation, accompanied and followed by a scattering of articles consisting either of leftovers from the book or further developments of points touched on in the book, and no more. I am not saying that this is bad, or that people who do this are unworthy to be teachers. What I do believe is that the teacher who just reads history books, and teaches history from the books he reads, cannot really be a decent university teacher of history.

Years ago I argued that the historian should not set out to prove a thesis and select material to establish it, but rather follow the evidence where it leads. Some of my colleagues challenged this. "Doesn't one," they asked, "necessarily have in mind a thesis that one wishes to prove by citing evidence? This after all is the way one works in the exact and in the social sciences, by formulating a thesis and then marshaling evidence to prove it. Should one not, does one not, work the same way in history?"

To clarify my point, I would make a distinction between thesis and hypothesis. By a thesis, in this context, I mean a proposition or a series of propositions that the historian has in mind before he starts work. These guide him in choosing the evidence that supports his thesis and enables him to present a case. This is where the honest historian must be very careful. On the other hand it is clearly right that in historical research, as in any scholarly or scientific activity, the researcher has to formulate a hypothesis or hypotheses. After all, every time the scholar takes a note he is formulating a hypothesis; that one item in his source is worth noting, whereas the items before and after are not.

Two conditions are normal in honest historical research. The first is that the hypothesis should be conscious and not unconscious. The second is that the scholar should be ready to modify or even abandon his hypothesis at any stage, i.e., follow the evidence. In most of my books, my ideas underwent several modifications in the course of both my reading and my writing. I did not by any means finish with the same ideas on the subject as when I began; I would have been wasting my time if I had. Any scientific or scholarly research, in history as in the social, exact, and life sciences, involves making hypotheses, but this should be a process of constant modification. The scholar tests his hypothesis against the evidence; he doesn't test the evidence against his hypothesis, and then accept or reject it, according to whether it fits or does not fit that hypothesis.

I have found it important to impress on students a very mundane matter, the techniques of scholarship. What should go into a footnote? What shouldn't go into a footnote? How should a footnote be constructed? What constitutes a chapter? There are all kinds of practical things which can make the difference between a good thesis and a mediocre thesis. Little attention is given to these practical questions nowadays. It's somehow assumed that all this comes to students through the light of nature or that they pick it up.

I believe it was Adolf von Harnack who had a very striking passage in which he talks about the great danger, when one gets to the final phase of writing, of somehow trying to stuff everything in, all these great masses of notes and vast quantities of information that you have accumulated. Some people feel it would be a terrible tragedy to waste all the days spent in the archives or reading a book and making notes on it, and from which one gets either nothing or very little. The point he makes with great insistence is: "Do not try to shove in everything." His rather hard advice is: resign yourself to the process of cremation.

I've generally told my students that I thought that was too severe, and I suggested they keep those excess notes for articles in the future, which I think is kinder advice, and what many articles seem to be.

Muslim History and the Danger of Cultural Arrogance

A historian, like human beings in general, is not free from human failings. Loyalties and prejudices may color his perception and presentation of history, but the critical historian is aware of this and tries to correct it. In the past, a Westerner looking at a non-Western civilization tended to assume that everything Western was good, but at the present time it is more fashionable to assume that everything Western is bad, which is really the same prejudice but turned inside out. People nowadays who find it impossible to say anything good about the West are really being extremely ethnocentric and arrogant. When they claim that everything that goes wrong is the fault of the West they are still maintaining the old claim that the West is the fountain of everything and that everything that happens in the world is determined by the West. They say it is bad, in the past they said it was for good, but it is the same kind of arrogance.

One must guard against the danger of cultural arrogance, the arrogance into which I think we fall all too easily by asking what is profoundly the wrong question: asking why something didn't happen. Why didn't Islam do this? Or, why didn't the Middle East develop that? Meaning, why didn't they do what we did? That is an error. One must ask why things happened, not why things didn't happen. If you want to know, why did the West discover America, that's a reasonable question. But to ask, why didn't the Muslims discover America from their seaports in Spain and Morocco, is not a reasonable one.

In trying, self-critically, to preserve my scholarly impartiality, I knew I had to watch out for three sources of prejudice, the Western, the British, and the Jewish. If I'm writing on Semites and anti-Semites, then obviously it is the Jewish angle I have to look out for. If I'm writing of the Middle East and the West, it's the Western angle I have to look out for. By this I don't mean that I'm just going to turn against my own cultural background; that would be just as silly, in fact, far sillier. There is a question of empathy rather than sympathy. And here I will make what may appear to be a blatantly chauvinistic statement and say that this capacity for empathy, vicariously experiencing the feelings of others, is a peculiarly Western feature. It produces the desire to know other civilizations and the ability to understand them. The cause of suspicion is often incomprehension.

When the first Western archaeologists went digging in the Middle East many Muslims were mystified. They had never paid the slightest attention to the remains of their glorious ancestors lying around, because that was not usable history, not significant history. It was pre-Islamic, and therefore unimportant. They could not comprehend that people would go into danger and discomfort and spend vast sums of money in order to dig up the remains of someone long dead, and therefore they suspected there had to be some other motive. They looked for reasons—espionage, treasure hunting—heaven knows what. There were in fact some Orientalists who were in the service of empire, though most of them were very critical of empire. The true explanation, the quest for knowledge, sounded preposterous.

From a Muslim point of view history has a profound, even a religious, significance. The advent of Islam is an event in history, known through historical evidence. The development of mainstream Islamic law is based on Sunna, the precepts and practice of the Prophet and his companions. Sunna is thus a kind of history, a record of past actions and past sayings. For a Muslim history is therefore religiously important, and it is crucially important that the history be accurate. A hadith, a tradition of the Prophet, is a historical statement, that on this or that occasion the Prophet did this or the Prophet said that. The recording, collection and critique of hadiths are therefore a kind of historiography. From the beginning of Muslim history and civilization there was a profound concern, not only to know the past, but to make sure that what was known was true. Already in early Islamic times, Muslim scholars, greatly concerned about the validity of extant traditions, were at great pains to distinguish between true and false hadiths. They had a more sophisticated classification; not just true and false, but certain, probable, weak, false. They also devised a complex methodology for studying and classifying hadith by content, chain of transmission and reliability.

To ask whether history is true obviously implies that history is sometimes false. Why should it be false? Why, and how, would any-one falsify it? This is one of the great problems of the historians of any society. A thousand years ago Muslim specialists in hadith had a problem of false hadith; they also had a problem of weak hadith. What this distinction meant was that sometimes a hadith was totally fabricated, invented by someone; or, sometimes it might have been based on a true narrative which in the course of transmission was somehow changed. I tell you a story, you tell him that story, he tells it to someone else, and after about the fifth retelling the story has become something quite different, without anybody wanting or try-ing to falsify it. We might call this a natural erosion of truth. There is also a deliberate perversion of truth. Why does one falsify history? Some erosion of historical knowledge is self-explanatory, but why does anybody deliberately distort or invent history?

One of the main purposes and uses of history is legitimization, using the past to legitimize the present. Monarchist history legiti-mizes monarchy; republican history delegitimizes monarchy and le-gitimizes the republic. Colonialist history legitimizes the colonial regime: we brought civilization to the barbarians and raised them to a higher level. Anticolonial history serves exactly the opposite pur-pose: we won freedom by throwing off the yoke of foreign oppression. And, of course, as the present changes, the past changes with it. The idea of the past as something fixed and immutable refers only, if at all, to history in the first of the various meanings I mentioned, that is, history as what happened. But the documentation, study, interpre-tation and presentation of what happened change all the time. Insofar as the purpose of history, or rather of the historian, is to legitimize the present, then, as the present changes, the past must change with it, and official historians constantly rewrite the past to meet new re-quirements.

Official rewriting affects international history even more than internal history. Take the case of a war between two countries. Obviously the history written in one country will differ from the history written in the other, even if they use the same evidence and the same methods. This is a rather primitive kind of history, but for most of the recorded history of mankind, it was the only kind that existed. In some such histories, for example of World War I and World War II in the twentieth century, there may be a hard core of commonly agreed fact. In the national historiography of some more recent wars even that limited agreement is missing, and history is overwhelmed by mythology and ideology.

Context is critical. Gandhi, whom we all admire for his long struggle against British imperialism and his ultimate success, succeeded because he was fighting against a civilized democratic enemy. He wouldn't have lasted a week against Hitler or Stalin or even Saddam Hussein. One is reminded, sadly, of Gandhi's advice to the Jews in German-controlled wartime Europe to deal with Hitler "by passive resistance." He seems to have overlooked the fact that Hitler was not British.

6.

Episodes in an Academic Life

In the midsixties a special message was sent from the Imperial Japanese Academy to the British Academy in London. It was part of a general attempt to improve and strengthen relationships between the two island kingdoms in the postwar period. The Japanese Academy suggested an exchange of visitors. They would invite a British scholar, to be nominated by the British Academy, and host him for a month-long stay in Japan to visit academic institutions and generally acquaint himself with the world of scholarship and culture. In return the British Academy would invite a Japanese scholar to England for a similar visit and a similar purpose. The British Academy accepted and proposed to send one of their Far Eastern experts. To their surprise, the Japanese showed reluctance to accept this suggestion. They were well acquainted with our Far East specialists, and preferred something different. The choice of the Academy directorate fell upon me, since I was at that time the chairman of the section of the Academy concerned with Oriental studies. I accepted with delight. The prospect of a visit to Japan as a guest of the Academy had obvious attractions. The Japanese agreed to this, and as a first step sent a round-trip air ticket for me on Japan Airlines, London-Tokyo-London.

What horrified my colleagues at the Academy was that the ticket was first-class. They had not thought in those terms. Obviously they would have to reciprocate and provide a first-class round-trip ticket for the Japanese visitor, a rather heavy expense for the not very richly financed Academy. But there was nothing that could be done about it, and in due course I was installed as a first-class passenger on a flight to Tokyo in conditions of luxury and indulgence.

At the airport I was met by a representative of the Imperial Japanese Academy who escorted me to my hotel and made sure that I was safely and comfortably installed. All my bills would be paid by the Academy, but to cover out-of-pocket expenses he had been instructed to give me a check and suggested that we go immediately to the neighboring bank to cash it.

Here our problems began. At the bank the teller explained that he could not simply cash a check at sight—it had to be paid into an account and the cash withdrawn from that account. I had no account but I was willing to open one for the duration of my stay. I was told that this was not possible, as temporary visitors to Japan could not open accounts without special permission and that, if given at all, would take a long time. My escort dealt with this with characteristic Japanese efficiency. He asked me to endorse the check to him and immediately opened an account in the bank into which he deposited the check. He then withdrew the entire amount in cash, handed it to me, and closed the account. Problem solved.

But there were other problems, the most important being that for the first time in my life, I was in a country where I could not even read street names. Going by taxi was comparatively easy. One normally had the address written on a piece of paper in Japanese and one handed this to the driver. But I also like walking around and it was all too easy to get lost, particularly for someone like me who has no sense of direction and no visual memory. I can get lost in my own backyard.

My base was at the British Embassy, and I began every day by going there first to see what arrangements had been made for me. This was done by taxi. I had a slip of paper with the words "British Embassy" in Japanese written on it and each morning I handed this to the driver, who promptly drove me there.

For someone who relishes language as I do I felt I must, at least, learn how to say "British Embassy" in Japanese, so I asked my host how to say it. I wrote it down, memorized it, and the next day when I got into the taxi I asked for the British Embassy in Japanese. He looked bewildered; I tried again; he looked still more bewildered; I tried a third time and he put out his hand with the clear message "Stop the nonsense and give me your piece of paper," which I did.

For one of my temperament this was not only frustrating but humiliating. I asked my Japanese host again to repeat the words for British Embassy in Japanese and this time I realized what I had done wrong. I had got the words right but the not the intonation, which is very important and can vary according to circumstances. The next time I lowered my pitch and had the words come from deep in my throat. How delighted I was to be whisked away to my destination.

I was reminded of a colleague of mine who studied Japanese in England at a time when it was impossible to go to Japan. He did however meet, fall in love with and marry a Japanese girl. They lived happily together in London and he became fluent in Japanese. After the war, he went to Japan for the first time, and wherever he spoke to Japanese they were obviously making great efforts not to laugh at him. Finally he mustered the courage to ask them why and they told him, "You speak Japanese like a young girl."

My program included meetings with dignitaries, visits to institutions, and the usual lectures. It was explained to me that for foreigners like me lecturing in Japan, a common occurrence, there were three possibilities. First, one could lecture in English to a limited invited audience of Japanese with a sufficient knowledge of the language to follow the lecture and participate in a discussion. This was very rare, but when it happened, it worked. Second, one could provide a written text to be duplicated and distributed to the audience so that they could follow the lecture as one read it. And thirdly, the most frequently used, the speaker could lecture in English with an interpreter standing by his side who translated, sentence by sentence. This was generally the most effective method, the one with the greatest level of communication between the lecturer and his audience. I recall one incident when an English lecturer told a rather long and rambling funny story which the translator rendered in one very short sentence followed by laughter from the audience. My escort explained to me that what he had actually said was, "This is a joke; please laugh."

One of my fellow students in Paris before the war was from Kyoto and had since become a professor at the university of Kyoto. I was eager to see him again and renew our acquaintance. We made the necessary arrangements but the simple train journey from one Japanese city to another proved incredibly complicated. I could neither read nor speak and I developed a lively sympathy, which I have retained ever since, for the physically impaired. However, I did manage to get there.

Some years later I went on a second visit to Japan, this time as guest professor at one of the Japanese universities. I had a sort of guide/interpreter permanently attached to me and that certainly made everything a lot easier.

It has apparently long been a tradition of the Japanese royal house that those members not directly engaged in government choose a profession and make a career of their own. Normally, they chose the armed forces. Prince Mikasa, the younger brother of the Mikado of Japan, was different and chose the academy. More specifically, he chose the history and archaeology of the Middle East. He made a deep and extensive academic study of these and eventually was appointed professor at a Japanese college. I met him several times in the Middle East and was his guest on this visit for lunch at the Palace in Tokyo.

My hosts arranged to take me on a trip into the mountains outside Tokyo to visit a sacred shrine and meet the religious leader. The British Embassy had warned me that the Queen was coming on a royal visit to Japan and that there would be a reception at the embassy to which members of the British community would be invited. They told me the day and I made sure that I had no engagements. Sometime later my friend at the embassy telephoned to say that he was sorry but there had been an error; the reception was not on that day but on the following day. I had in the meantime told my Japanese hosts that I was free on that day and they had made all their arrangements for the pilgrimage to the mountain. I explained this to the embassy and said that I could not change my plan at the last minute and would therefore not be able to come to the reception.

Somehow word of this reached my hosts at the university, and on the day we went to the mountain they explained to me how flattered and gratified they were that I "stood up the Queen" to come with them. Not exactly accurate, but not entirely wrong.

Lunch at Buckingham Palace

The one and only time I was invited by Her Majesty the Queen to lunch at Buckingham Palace was sometime in the 1960s. The British government had announced its intention of withdrawing all British troops from the Gulf sheikhdoms in Arabia, and the Gulf sheikhs were scurrying to London one after another to discuss how to deal with the problems that would arise following this precipitous and unexpected withdrawal. Publicly they proclaimed their delight at the British decision to go. Privately they came to express their concerns and to plead for some delay. As they were all heads of state, however small, they were entitled to the appropriate welcome and hospitality, and for several weeks there was a very full program of royal and quasi-royal occasions. The guest lists grew longer and longer, and even reached my level. I was tickled when an invitation with the royal crest arrived, inviting me and my wife to join Her Majesty and Prince Philip at a lunch she was giving in honor of I forget which Gulf sheikh. We accepted with alacrity and were then given further instructions. The appropriate garb was what was known as "morning dress"—a long gray jacket with tails, and a kind of bow tie. I did not of course own these and had no intention of buying them but they were available for hire. I also received a Buckingham Palace parking permit which I would have loved to keep, but I had to surrender it when I used it.

Half a century later, two recollections remain. The first one was the introductions. The guests, about fifteen or twenty, were ushered into a reception hall and arranged in a semicircle. The Queen then arrived, accompanied by the official who had chosen the guest list and made the arrangements. They walked around the semicircle and the official introduced us to Her Majesty, one by one, by name and description. When this was completed, we stood partaking of refreshments for a few minutes, and then the guests of honor arrived—the sheikh with his entourage. They also came around the semicircle but this time with the Queen leading the guests. What really astonished me is that without any written text or any visible prompting, the Queen introduced each one of us to her guests correctly, by name and function. Either she has an excellent memory or a secret device.

While we were having drinks before lunch, a footman suddenly came over to me and said that Prince Philip wanted to talk to me. I went and found that the problem was one of communication. Prince Philip was chatting with the Gulf sheikh. The Prince knew no Arabic and the sheikh knew very little English. They did however have an interpreter and for some reason the interpreter was unable to cope with the situation; either he didn't understand or could not translate the words that were used. The sheikh put his point to me in Arabic and fortunately I was able to understand it and repeat it in English. A moment of immense pride, but unfortunately I haven't the slightest recollection of what it was about.

The lunch itself was less than exciting and was, at best, tepid. My table companion, one of the ladies-in-waiting, explained to me that the food served at Palace banquets is never hot—the distance is too great from the royal kitchens to the royal tables.

History and the Present

The primary concern of the historian is the past—to study it, using whatever evidence he can find, and then to communicate the results of his study to others by means of writing and teaching. For some reason, historians are often asked to say what will happen next. Most of us reply that our business is the past, not the future; that we are historians, not prophets. But that is not usually enough to put off the persistent questioners. I remember a meeting of historians in Rome where we were discussing whether historians should or should not attempt to predict the future. That was when the Soviet Union was still alive and well. A Soviet colleague among us remained silent through the discussion and then we turned to him to ask him what his view was. He said, "In the Soviet Union, the most difficult task of the historian is to predict the past." He was of course referring to the constant rewriting of the past by the Communist hierarchy.

I don't think the historian can reasonably be expected to predict the future but there are certain things that the historian can and should do. He can discern trends. He can look at what has been happening and what is happening and see change developing. From this he can formulate, I will not say predictions, but possibilities, alternative possibilities, things that may happen, things that may go this way or that way, in evolving interactions. It is of course much safer to predict the remote rather than the immediate future. There are occasions, however, when the historian, for one reason or another, becomes involved in the present, not just observing and recording the historical process, but affecting or influencing or even directing it. Most historians have some experience of this. My own work on

His Majesty's service during the war years would I suppose come under this heading. Even after my return to academic life, like most of my colleagues, I had occasional encounters with the historic process through meetings which made policy. Over the years, in my innumerable visits to the Middle East I had meetings with kings, presidents, prime ministers, other high officials, as well as with ambassadors of different states. We talked of various things, and from time to time I gave my opinions—sometimes in response to a request, sometimes not.

I do recall one particular episode when it was precisely my work as a historian, using the technical professional methodology of the historian, which seems to have affected the historical process. On May 27, 1971, Russia and Egypt, known at that time as the Soviet Union and the United Arab Republic, signed, in Cairo, a "Treaty of Friendship and Cooperation." Given the situation in the Middle East at that time, the signing of this treaty was a major event, with considerable impact on the international political process.

Since the treaty was between a Russian and an Arab government, it was drafted, signed and ratified in two languages, Arabic and Russian, both texts being valid. Both the Soviet and Egyptian governments published English translations, one based on the Russian text and the other on the Arabic text. Though these were official, they were nonbinding. Interestingly, both the Soviet and the Egyptian versions in English used British not American spelling, but otherwise differed on a number of points.

I became keenly aware of these differences in a quite accidental way. My copy of the treaty was provided by the Egyptian Embassy, the Arabic text with the Egyptian English translation. It so happened that the next day I was participating in a discussion group on the international situation. At a certain point I wanted to quote the treaty, but had omitted to bring my copy with me. I was sitting next to a colleague who was a specialist in East European affairs and I asked him if by any chance he had his copy of the treaty with him. He did and he very kindly passed it to me for my use. His copy had been published by the Soviet Embassy and contained the Russian text and their English translation. Glancing at it, I saw immediately certain differences between the two versions. I therefore procured a copy of the Soviet handout, and proceeded, in the way of the professional historian, to make a comparative study of the two.

The differences were significant and far-reaching, and led me to some further comparisons—between this treaty and other treaties signed by the Soviet Union, with its allies, its satellites, and neutral powers. I wrote a long article indicating these differences, which eventually appeared in a learned journal.

This lengthy piece, as is normal, had little or no impact outside the academic community. But besides my scholarly article for a learned journal, I also wrote a brief journalistic one, which was published in *The Times* of London on October 8, 1971. This apparently came as a shock to the Egyptian diplomatic establishment, and may even have had some influence on their subsequent dealings with the Soviet Union. The following year, on July 18, 1972, President Sadat ordered the Soviet military to leave Egypt.

There was a moment of anxious concern—would they go, or would they respond as they did in Czechoslovakia and Hungary—move in and take over? The Soviets decided not to risk it and went peacefully. The way was open for a radical change in Egyptian policy.

Passing as a Turk in Algeria

I got to know a Turkish diplomat when he was vice-consul in London and I was assistant lecturer at the university. We were about the same age with similar problems such as career inexperience and young children. We achieved an immediate understanding and developed a friendship which lasted for the rest of his life. At one stage, while I was still in London, I received a letter from him saying that he was now the ambassador in Algiers and would like me to come for a visit and stay with him as his houseguest.

The result was a fascinating visit. I was naturally there when he had guests and the guests usually got the message to include me when they reciprocated. By now, my Turkish had improved. I normally spoke Turkish with him and the embassy staff and I had the impression that I was regarded by the Algerians as just another Turkish official. This meant that people felt free to express opinions and attitudes as they would not have done in the presence of a Western European. It was most enlightening. One example was a conversation I had about the time of the 1967 war. My neighbor at a dinner party noted that in most Arab capitals they had to bring troops in to protect the British and American embassies but Algeria had to protect the Egyptian Embassy. I asked why. He then explained that after their long and bitter struggle for independence, when Algeria had established an independent state, a series of missions, both civil and military, had been sent by the Egyptian government. Their members came with an air of lordly superiority and tried to tell their hosts how to run things. They absolutely infuriated the Algerians—the Egyptians with their undistinguished military record trying to teach the Algerians, who had just won a striking victory over the French. The level of anger was quite remarkable. I was also told that they supported the Palestinian cause because it was a Third World cause against imperialism, not for any other reason. I didn't quite know what to make of that.

At an early stage in my visit I did what I always do when visiting a country for the first time: explore the bookshops to see what is being published and what people are reading. To my surprise, I found that the bookshops had only French books, none in Arabic. I searched and searched in shop after shop and could find none. Eventually I asked a shopkeeper why he had no Arabic books and he replied with a dismissive wave of the hand, "If you want Arabic books, go to the Kasbah. You'll find them there." I went to the Kasbah, the old citadel and covered markets, and I did find bookshops and they did have Arabic books. The problem was that the only Arabic books they had were textbooks.

Sometime later, at a dinner party in Algiers, I found myself sitting next to a librarian. I told him about my unsuccessful attempts to find Arabic books and I asked him why this was. He explained, "When the French were here, we had only French books, no Arabic books and no Arabic culture. When we became independent, we tried to import Arabic books, and a mission came from Egypt bringing books and trying to initiate us into modern Arabic literature and culture. We found it deeply disappointing; after all, under the French, we had become accustomed to a certain cultural and intellectual level."

Turkey

There was in the sixties, and for all I know still may be, a full treaty regulating cultural relations between England and Turkey. Under the terms of this treaty, a six-person commission, three British, three Turkish, met in alternate years in London and Ankara. For a long time the three British members consisted of the representative of the British Council in Ankara, the head of the relevant government department in London, and me. The three Turkish members consisted of the member of the Foreign Ministry concerned with cultural relations, the member of the Ministry of Education concerned with foreign relations, and the professor of English at Ankara University. The four officials were constantly changing; hardly ever were the same ones at two consecutive meetings. The two professors, as is the way of professors, went on forever.

I particularly cherish the memory of one meeting. Meetings were normally conducted in English, but on this occasion one of the two Turkish officials didn't know any English, so we had to use interpreters. We could have used French, because he knew French, but that was against the rules. We were concerned with cultural relations between England and Turkey, so if we couldn't use English, we had to use interpreters. So we had an interpreter who translated what they said in Turkish into English for us and they had an interpreter who translated what we said in English into Turkish for them. As I understood Turkish fairly well, I found this a very interesting experience, listening to what happens to something in translation.

At that time we were giving a number of state-funded, competitive, scholarships to Turkish students to study at British universities. The leader of the Turkish delegation made an eloquent speech in which he was effusive in saying how much he and his country appreciated our making these scholarships available. He elaborated on that for quite a while and went on to say that there were always many more candidates than places and it would greatly help matters if Her Majesty's government could see a way to increase the number of scholarship places made available to Turkish students.

This was all carefully translated into English by our translator and I could say, accurately translated. The leader of our delegation made an equally eloquent reply, saying that we were delighted to hear that these scholarships were appreciated and were valuable, and we were sure that they were of enormous importance in developing the cultural relations between our two countries. We were particularly touched by their feeling that there was a need to increase the number, and although at the present time, for various budgetary reasons, we couldn't make any immediate promises, we would do our best to increase the number in future years. To render all of this, the Turkish translator simply used the one-word negative, *"Yok."*

It was of course a perfectly accurate translation.

Foreign Students and Their Embassies

There are many satisfactions in being a scholar. The most obvious one is that you can earn a living by doing what you would want to do anyway. For the scholar, scholarship is not only a profession and a livelihood; it is a commitment, one might even say a passion. That is probably why many retired scholars live so long after retirement—unlike most other professions, there's very little change in your way of life. You have the possibility of working independently and following your own inclinations and beliefs. You also have the pleasure of having not just students but, shall we say, disciples. One of the great satisfactions of my profession is watching the success of former students becoming themselves independent scholars and teachers and researchers of renown. I have been a "proud papa" many times over.

Though by now many of them are retired, I have had former students teaching in Cairo, Alexandria, Jerusalem, Tel Aviv, Amman, Damascus, Beirut, Baghdad, Basra, Riyad, Tehran, Tabriz and several places in Pakistan. Students came of their own free will and they enjoyed complete freedom of research and expression. Even when the colonial presence was still powerful we had students coming from those areas to do research denouncing the evils of British imperialism. And they did so with British scholarships and got British Ph.D.'s for this. It's what you might call democratic imperialism.

A high percentage of the undergraduate students and the overwhelming majority of the graduate students went into teaching as a career. In the course of time I developed a network of former students all over the Middle East. This provided a useful system of communication. As far as possible, I remained in contact with my former students and used to see them occasionally when I visited their countries.

Their situation generally was very bad. Apart from the wealthy oil states, which had few academic institutions, university teachers were underpaid and overworked. Their teaching load was vastly in excess of anything that would be normal or even acceptable in Western countries. Their salaries were barely enough to keep them and their families for the first ten days of the month. This meant that they had to seek other ways of earning money, and to find time to do so. The result was catastrophic. Time and time again I was devastated when talented and promising students who produced excellent theses went home and never published anything of significance again. Some of them managed to publish their theses, as submitted or revised; many did not even find time for that. I can only describe this waste of talent as tragic.

Of the Middle Eastern officials in London with whom I had to deal it was, generally speaking, the Egyptian officials who were the most concerned and the most sympathetic. They were personally acquainted with their students, aware of their problems, and eager to help in whatever way they could. Some of the others seemed to have regarded students as a nuisance. True, they were responsible for them, more particularly for those, the majority at that time, who held government scholarships and were therefore on the embassy payroll. Many of the students sent to England for higher education were paid by their governments and were looked after by the embassies. The majority of these embassies had an educational attaché whose sole task was to look after the students. Most were fairly decent people with whom one could get on. But not all.

If I had a problem with an Egyptian student I could telephone the educational attaché in the Egyptian Embassy. He would know immediately who the student was, what his problems were and we could have a sensible discussion on how to help the student.

In my entire time at SOAS, I could never do that with the Iraqi Embassy. First of all, they didn't know their students. They were just files, and they would have to send for the file. And second, I would never dare to suggest that there was the slightest difficulty with a student, because their immediate remedy for all problems was to send him back to Baghdad. They had no compassion at all and treated the students like dirt. They were government students, and were entitled to government allowances when they needed to make a trip or needed to get a manuscript copied. They always insisted on a certificate from me that this was for what they needed the money. I once expostulated to the educational attaché that these were scholars and gentlemen, not petty criminals who had to be watched in this way. It didn't have the slightest effect.

There was a problem once with a transfer of registration. All our higher-degree students were registered in the first instance for a master's degree. Nobody could be registered directly for a Ph.D. Depending on their rate of progress they were either examined for an M.A. or allowed to bypass the M.A. and go straight on to a Ph.D. But this took time. There had to be written work and reports, and the transfer had to be approved by various committees.

I remember one extremely good Iraqi student whose transfer, because of some administrative delay in the university which was not his fault, missed the last meeting of the academic year and nothing could be done until the beginning of the new academic year in October. I had a call from the Iraqi Embassy telling me that they had decided to discontinue his scholarship. I asked why. They said because he had not been transferred to Ph.D. registration. They sent him to London for a Ph.D., and if he was not going to get a Ph.D. they had no interest in keeping him there. I said, but he is, and explained the situation to them. They said that was not their affair and as he'd not been transferred they would send him home. We argued and argued, but they were absolutely adamant. I pointed out that this was in no way the student's fault. This was May, and nothing could be done until October. Finally, they recanted to a limited extent and said, "We won't send him back, but we'll discontinue his fellowship." I said, "You mean you'll just leave him stranded, without any funds?" "That's right." I said, "I don't think you'll get good results from students by holding a pistol to their heads." He said, "I resent that expression." "Good, I'll write you a letter containing it," which I did. In the end, they didn't send him back but they did cut off his scholarship. I found some money in the university's coffers to keep him for a few months and his fellow students got together and donated funds from their pittances to help him until October. Actually, more than October, because though in October his registration was changed it took a few weeks to get his fellowship restored.

It's not just that the embassies sent them back, but when they sent them back they held the students liable for all the money that had been spent on them so far. They were sold into a sort of slavery. They and their families were held responsible. This particular student had already been in London for two years, and it had cost the Iraqi government a fair amount. If he had been sent back at that stage, he would have been liable for all the money they had spent on him, fares, fellowship, etc. Everything was refundable. It was very difficult, and often put the school administration in a difficult position. We never dared to fail an Iraqi student in any examination, however trivial, because if we did they were sent back and sold into bondage. We had one Iraqi student who committed suicide. He was not neurotic; he was perfectly normal and a good student, but he failed an examination. It happens. When I say failed an examination what I mean is he didn't reach the required level. He didn't do too badly, but he didn't reach the level needed and was informed by the embassy that his scholarship was terminated. He was to return to Iraq immediately and repay everything. The poor devil shot himself.

Not all my students chose an academic career when they returned home. Some chose government, through either politics or the civil service. But these were definitely a minority. One Palestinian deserves special mention. Musa Abdullah al-Husseini was a member of the famous Husseini family of Jerusalem and, to the best of my recollection, a nephew of the notorious Grand Mufti. He was a member of my first graduating class and received his B.A. with honors in Middle Eastern history in 1940. After graduation he went to neutral Spain allegedly for a holiday before returning to Jerusalem. In fact he proceeded from Spain to Germany where he joined his uncle the Mufti and spent the rest of the war in Germany. There he enrolled in a German university and pursued a doctorate. He was therefore in the rather remarkable position of having an English B.A. dated 1940 and a German Ph.D. dated 1943 or 1944. After the war he came to see me in London. He told me of how he had traveled to Spain, then to Germany, and how he had been arrested by the British after the defeat of the Third Reich and deported to the Seychelles Islands, where there was an internment camp for people like him. He told me that he had a very pleasant and relaxing holiday there, playing tennis and riding horseback for much of the time. Eventually he was released and went back to Jerusalem where he opened a travel bureau in the Old City, then part of the Jordanian kingdom. It was from there that he came to see me for an exchange of recollections of our very different war experiences.

He returned to Jerusalem, and I did not hear about him again until the time of the murder of King Abdullah of Jordan in Jerusalem in 1951. To my utter astonishment, I learned that Musa Abdullah al-Husseini had been arrested and charged with the murder of the King. He had confessed to the crime and had been executed.

A Memorable Interview

One of the jobs we are sometimes required to do in the academic world is interview students who are asking to be accepted for a place at the university. In London I was, for a while, on the committee to interview applicants for undergraduate admission. One of the applicants was a young lady from a school on the Welsh border who said that she wanted to learn Chinese in order to study Chinese history, a rather surprising request coming from that quarter. We asked her why and she said that as far back as she could remember she had been fascinated by China. She had read every book she could lay her hands on about China; she had studied every aspect she could of Chinese history and culture, and now that she was going to university, her dearest wish was to learn Chinese so that she could undertake the serious study of Chinese history.

My colleagues who knew something about Chinese and Chinese history asked her appropriate questions. I know nothing about Chinese or Chinese history and when it was my turn, I asked a sort of routine historian's question. "You say you are interested in Chinese history. Are you mainly interested in ancient, medieval or modern history?"—using the normal classification of Western historians. The young lady hesitated for a perceptible interval and then she said, "Sir, if you could explain to me what these words mean in relation to Chinese history, I will try to answer your question."

This was a remarkably intelligent and, considering the circumstances, a courageous answer. We accepted her but unfortunately she didn't come, presumably because she had a better offer elsewhere—or possibly because she didn't want to go to a school where professors ask such stupid questions. But her answer has remained with me ever since and even helped me to reassess my own approach, not to Chinese history, but to Islamic history where the same considerations might apply.

Leaving London

During my last two years in England, before I left for the United States in 1974, my life was very difficult, perhaps "tormented" would not be too strong a word. My dissolving marriage affected me in every aspect of my daily life. I was still able to discharge my professional duties (teaching courses for undergraduates and supervising dissertations) but I could not muster the energy or the will to undertake any new historical research projects. Both the research and the writing were beyond my capacity at that time.

Salvation came in the form of a letter from an American publisher, Harper & Row, asking me if I would be willing to edit a volume on the history of the medieval Middle East, consisting of excerpts from original sources in English translation. This seemed like just the right thing for me to be doing at that time, and I readily agreed. Reading and editing seemed about as much as I could do, in that state of mind.

The idea was that my contribution, like the others in the series, would consist of excerpts from already published translations, of which a considerable quantity was available in English. There was, my publisher pointed out, a real need for such a book, to give students of history something of the flavor of the original sources. And, as the publisher also pointed out, this was merely a scissors and paste job which could be quickly and easily completed. I began my work with these two assumptions.

The first assumption was no doubt true. The second proved false. There were indeed many translations into English from Arabic and other Middle Eastern languages, but they varied enormously in style, character, interest and, most important of all, accuracy. Inevitably, they reflected the tastes and concerns of the translators, their time, and their intended readers, and therefore omitted much that was of vital concern to the historian. A collection based on existing translations might have been a representative anthology of translators, but not of medieval Islamic history and civilization.

Translation is an art in and of itself and has to be put into a contemporary idiom. Not too contemporary; one doesn't want to make it so modern that it jars, and I wouldn't translate a medieval text into slangy English. But I certainly would not try to reproduce an archaic effect by using archaic English. After all, what they wrote was not archaic. The major problem is understanding what the text means, the first part of any translation job. But a second problem, a much more difficult one, in a text of any literary quality, is trying to preserve that quality, or at least preserve some of it, in an English translation.

I began my work by supplementing my cut and paste collection, and finally decided to scrap it entirely and start afresh. The publishers had asked for one volume; in my enthusiasm I produced enough for two, which they agreed to publish.

The resulting volumes consist of a series of excerpts from Arabic, Persian, Turkish and Hebrew writings, translated into English, and where necessary, with explanatory annotations. Volume I covers politics and war and volume II religion and society, and the whole is entitled *Islam, from the Prophet Muhammad to the Capture of Constantinople.*

Though not a best seller it has maintained a steady level of sales and is available in a paperback edition published by the Oxford University Press. It is probably the most frequently cited and accepted of my various publications. The reason is obvious. It is not often that one has easy and ample access to what the peoples of the Middle East say about themselves and their own history.

Charles Issawi, a friend of mine at Princeton, used to ask from time to time a painful question—which, if any, of your books will still be read a hundred years from now? If any of my publications qualifies, I think this would probably be the one.

In my last year in London, the breakup of my marriage was due in no small degree to a relationship between my wife and one of my colleagues at SOAS. This even appeared as an item in the press. During that year we had a visiting professor from the United States. One day she and I were chatting and she said to me, "You know, your colleagues here really are gentlemen." I replied, "Yes. I assumed that, but what makes you say so?" "I heard about your divorce," she said, "and I tried to talk to your colleagues about it but none of them would say a word. Every time I raised the matter they would change the subject or walk away. They really are gentlemen." I believe this is true and I am most grateful to them for it.

During that last year at the School of Oriental and African Studies we had a visiting professor from Princeton University, Avrom Udovitch, who witnessed the turmoil in my life. It was he who orchestrated that on the day my divorce was final I received three telegrams: one from the chairman of the department of Near Eastern Studies at Princeton University offering me a chair, one from the director of the Institute for Advanced Studies inviting me to be a member and one from the president of the university urging me to accept these concurrent appointments. It was the first and only time the two institutions had collaborated in this way. I should explain that the two institutions are completely independent and the only connection is that they are located in the same town.

In the months preceding my move from London to Princeton in 1974 I spent some time with an old friend and colleague, Taki Vatikiotis, who had just moved from Princeton to London. We were therefore able to exchange useful information and guidance. One of his remarks was very telling. "Here in London," he said, "you have friends. In Princeton you will have colleagues, neighbors and in certain situations, allies, but you will not have friends as you understand and use that word here."

7.

Crossing the Atlantic

1974. A very new year. My devastating divorce was final and I left my country, my job, my life. I arrived in Princeton, New Jersey, a new country, two new jobs, a new life and a new home, with a new woman.

My financial position when I came to Princeton was poor. My lawyer and my ex-wife's lawyer had agreed that it was to our mutual advantage to settle for a lump sum rather than an annuity. I went along with this but had to borrow extensively in order to produce the lump sum. As a result I was penniless and heavily in debt, and when I moved from London to Princeton I did not even have the minuscule amount of money one was allowed to take out of the sterling zone at that time. What saved the day was that Princeton University's financial year starts on the first of July and when I arrived in Princeton at the beginning of the academic year in September I had two months' salary waiting for me. After that my financial position began to improve thanks to lecture fees and book royalties.

One other factor which helped greatly to stabilize my financial position during my early years in Princeton was when, to my utter surprise, I was awarded the Harvey Prize by the Haifa Technion, the Israel Institute of Technology. This consisted of $30,000. I spent one-third on a trip to Mexico, put one-third into the stock market and the final third, which proved far and away the most long lasting and valuable, into an addition to my home. This extension to what had been the master bedroom became my study, replete with bookshelves designed as stacks to hold at least half of my fifteen-thousand-volume library. The rest went into similarly constructed stacks in the basement.

My life, and more specifically my adjustment to this small town, was greatly helped by a relationship which had begun not long before I left England. Early in 1974 I met an aristocratic Turkish lady at a reception in the Iranian Embassy. She was just passing through London at the time but we "clicked" and resumed our relationship when I was in the Middle East later that year. After our divorce my ex-wife tried to suggest that it was because of this woman that our marriage broke up. This is false. We met for the first time when the date for the divorce trial had been set, and the relationship did not develop until after the divorce was final. It then developed rapidly, and by the time I moved to America she was willing to come with me. A house was found by the university and we moved in.

After the shattering breakup of my marriage this woman made an enormous and invaluable contribution to what I might call my reconstruction. She restored my faith in life and in myself. She put me back together and I am most grateful to her. She also provided a very successful beginning to my social life in Princeton by organizing truly magnificent dinners, *alla Turca*. An unexpected bonus was that my Turkish improved dramatically.

Over time it became clear that we had different perceptions of our relationship, and we agreed, after ten years, to end it and she returned to Turkey. We remained friends.

At the time of my divorce my ex-wife and I decided that we would share the house and its contents equally. The house was not a problem as it was heavily mortgaged and what was left after paying off the mortgage was an insignificant amount. More difficult was the division of the contents of the house. Since I was moving to America and she was staying in London it made sense for her to retain most of the furniture and for me to be compensated in other areas. My daughter, who had recently married a physician and migrated to the United States when he took a position at an American hospital, intervened strongly and said that I must keep all the carpets. These were from Turkey, Iran, Afghanistan and other places in the Middle East and Melanie insisted that they were an essential part of "who you are and what you do." My wife agreed to this, but it left some tension between mother and daughter.

This meant that when I came to America and moved into a house I had lots of carpets and pictures, but no furniture. I set out to fill this deficiency.

In this I was helped by a very fortunate accident. A few weeks before moving to Princeton I was there on a short visit during which I was invited to dinner by a colleague and neighbor. I was greatly impressed by the beauty and elegance of the furniture in his home. He told me it was made by a Japanese American, George Nakashima, who had a workshop not very far from Princeton, in New Hope, Pennsylvania. I thought this was something worth pursuing and when I moved to Princeton one of the first things I did was to get in touch with Mr. Nakashima.

His methods were unusual. He only made furniture to order and the procedure was that the prospective customer would visit the workshop and discuss with him what pieces of furniture were wanted. He would make some drawings and then take his guest on a tour of his workshop. After some discussion, the customer and the artist would reach agreement on the shape and size of the furniture and then together choose a slab of wood for each item.

This left the question of price. Nakashima's method was distinctive. He would neither request nor accept any deposit, but waited until he was ready to work on your project. At that point he would provide a figure, and he expected not a deposit but the payment of the entire amount. This was less alarming than one might have thought in that he also agreed that if you did not like the finished product when you saw it he would take it back and refund the entire amount.

I found this unusual but was willing to go along. In due course he called and named an amount, roughly the same as I would have had to pay had I bought these items in a furniture store. I agreed and after a period of weeks the items were delivered. They were gorgeous. Since then Nakashima has become a famous name in the art of furniture making and his works, even the pieces made in his workshop after his death, are highly esteemed and highly priced.

When I was growing up in London my entire family—grandparents on both sides, uncles, aunts, cousins were all within a twenty-minute bus ride. Now my family of children, grandchildren and great grandchildren are scattered across the United States, where eventually my whole family, at different times, by different routes, relocated. We are now an all-American family. It is only on rare and special occasions that I am able to meet them face-to-face. Telephone and e-mails provide some compensation but are a poor substitute for proximity.

Princeton

I have never for one moment regretted moving to Princeton. On the contrary, I think this was one of the best decisions and most creative changes in my life. In Princeton I had both the comfortable quietness and collegiality of a small university town, yet a place within the New York–Washington corridor. The architecture for the most part is pleasant, that is to say, deeply familiar to one newly arrived from England. So often the architecture of higher education facilities in the United States is a mixture of the pseudo-phony and the neo-bogus styles. Princeton, or much of it, is an authentic product of its time, or rather of the various successive periods during which it was built.

After my move I gained several substantial advantages. The first was more free time. Thanks to my joint appointment I had to teach only one semester; the rest of my time was free of teaching responsibilities, except of course for the supervision of graduate students preparing dissertations. For a teacher with a sense of responsibility toward his students, and that means most of us, this is a task that goes on all through the year. A second advantage was that being a newcomer from another country, I was free from the kind of administrative and bureaucratic entanglements that had built up, over decades, in England. This was a most welcome relief. I never had much taste nor, I must confess, aptitude for administrative tasks and responsibilities. Had that been my desire, I would have either gone into business in pursuit of real money or into politics in pursuit of real power. I would not have stayed in the university, where neither the money nor the power is real. The satisfactions that the life of a scholar offers are of quite a different character.

Another advantage is that Princeton is a delightful place in which to live and an excellent university in which to teach, with a very high standard of capacity and accomplishment among the students and agreeable colleagues with whom to work. I did learn that at Princeton I had to change my style of lecturing. In the United States I found that the sort of gentle irony which is a normal component of intellectual discourse in England was either missed entirely or misunderstood. People either didn't see it or they felt obscurely that they were somehow being got at and weren't quite sure why. For me, not being able to use irony is like cooking without using salt or pepper. Finally, at Princeton I was provided with the kind of infrastructure which English universities simply cannot afford, such as hiring student assistants to find and fetch books from the library, instead of having to go and find them myself. Here too, the time-saving was enormous.

There was another important change; I was growing older, at least physically, and I decided that it was time to start closing the files. During the course of my work as a researcher and as a teacher, perhaps most of all simply as a reader, I had built up a series of files on topics which aroused my special interest. Whenever I came across anything relevant, I made a note of it and put it in the appropriate file. What I have been doing since coming to Princeton is taking these accumulations of material built up over the course of decades, and turning them into books. This is the explanation of what might otherwise seem an extraordinary output in my postretirement— fifteen books—as contrasted with a rather small output in the much longer period of my teaching career.

There are two rather different kinds of books that a scholar, and more particularly a historian, may decide to write. One of them is what you might call a monograph. At a certain moment the historian decides to write a book on such and such a subject. He begins to identify, to read and to study all the relevant and available material, and after three, four, five, six or however many years it may take, he sits down and writes his book. A large proportion of historical books and almost all historical articles published in learned journals fall in this category. Like most younger historians, I produced a number of studies in this category; like most older historians, I have tried my hand at the other category of book, one in which the historian's source material is, in a sense, the entire literature of a civilization, or at least of a period. His task here is not simply to collect the relevant material for a book and then write it. His material is the accumulation of a lifetime's reading.

An example of this for me occurred in 1974, when I was invited to deliver the Gottesman Lectures at Yeshiva University in New York City. Given the occasion and the audience, this was an opportunity, indeed an invitation, to go beyond the strict limits of my specialized field of study, and to have a look at the very nature of history, both as a discipline and as a vocation. Most of my illustrative examples were naturally drawn from the field of historical study with which I am most familiar, but I tried to achieve some deeper insights in broader perspectives and reach some more general conclusions. The lectures were first published with the title *History Remembered, Recovered, Invented* by the Princeton University Press in 1975, and reprinted in various editions after that. The book was well received at the time.

Two of the files I took up dealt with the Muslim discovery of Europe and the position of Jews in Muslim lands. Another dealt with the political language of Islam—a semantic and historical study of the terms used in politics and government in the Islamic world over the course of the centuries. Yet another was on race and slavery in the Middle East.

In addition to several monographs on specific topics, I also prepared a collection of odd bits on various subjects, translated from various languages, that didn't fit into any of my major projects. They brought an interesting, and sometimes an amusing, diversity to a volume called *A Middle East Mosaic*. This included such gems as a description of an Italian's first encounter with a banana, a Turkish diplomat in France seeing the Atlantic tide for the first time, and a number of bewildered comments on the treatment and behavior of women in the Western world. This is one of my favorite books which occasioned one of my favorite reviews, thanking me for enabling scholars and others to quote primary sources on a wide range of topics without having to learn the languages or read the books.

The university provided me the stimulation of able and active colleagues and students, and the feeling, at once comforting and invigorating, of being part of a great scholarly environment. It also gave me the opportunity to keep in touch with the real world and real people, more particularly with the rising student generation. The only negative was that as I was half-time, there was no procedure by which I could be kept informed of administrative processes. The grapevine is usually an effective means of communication, but it is subject to both delay and inaccuracy.

One day, while I was working in my office at Princeton, a professor of Chinese history telephoned and asked if I were free and would be willing to come up to his office for a few moments. He wanted me to meet a visitor from the Beijing Academy of Sciences who he thought would interest me. The visitor was a specialist in the Muslim minorities of the western provinces of China, most of whom speak Turkic languages. I was intrigued. As the gentleman knew no English nor any other European language and I knew no Chinese, my colleague said he would act as interpreter, but only as a last resort. He felt that we should be able to establish some form of communication.

An interesting exercise followed. His guest spoke Uighur Turkish and had some slight acquaintance with Central Asian Turkic languages. I spoke Istanbul Turkish, and also had some slight acquaintance with Central Asian Turkic languages. The relations between them can be as close as between Danish and Norwegian, or as distant as between French and Portuguese. We began, as trained scholars would, by trying to determine rules of sound change. We started with numbers, followed by parts of the body, and were then able to establish a fairly basic form of communication on a limited range of topics.

At one point our Chinese visitor mentioned that he was a descendant of the ancient, now extinct community of Chinese Jews of Kaifeng. I asked him what, if anything, he knew of Judaism. He replied in four words, "One God. No pork."

One of my most distinguished colleagues at Princeton was the social historian Lawrence Stone. One day when the staff of the faculty lounge and dining room were on strike the professors were compelled, unless they were willing to go into town to a restaurant, to bring their own lunches. On that day Mrs. Stone brought a chicken for her husband's lunch and the two sat in the faculty lounge to share it. Someone passed by, saw them together, and exclaimed, "Two Stones with one bird."

The Institute for Advanced Study

I first visited the Institute for Advanced Study sometime before I even thought of moving to the United States. On one occasion, while I was still in London, the director of the Institute called and asked if I would be willing to make a short, special, trip to Princeton to help him in a certain matter. He was proposing to elect a scholar in a field previously unrepresented. There was some resistance to this proposal, and he asked if I would come to Princeton to attend a meeting, make a case in favor of this scholar, and then return. I agreed and therefore made a hurried transatlantic round-trip for just two days, to plead the case for this appointment. The gentleman was duly appointed. He did not, of course, know of the circumstances.

In 1974, when I returned to Princeton with a joint full-time appointment shared between the university and the Institute for Advanced Study, I had a chance to gain a better understanding of its curious structure. It consisted of two major groups, on one side mathematicians and physicists, on the other side historians, later expanded to include social scientists. Each scholar was provided with an office including ample space for a library, with an assistant if one were required and a generous stipend. The Institute also had its own apartments for scholars within easy reach of the office and with very favorable terms. The arrangement normally continued after retirement, but not always. Fortunately my home in Princeton was a university house, not an Institute house, and therefore I was not in danger of eviction on retirement.

I'm told that my appointment, half-time university and half-time Institute, was the first and last of its kind. Thanks to the dual appointment I had the time and the setting in which to be quite productive. For my part, I found it an excellent arrangement—the Institute gave me leisure, space and privacy, all three of them, especially the latter, in ample measure. The obverse of the value of privacy was that there was not the cross-fertilization among disciplines that was envisaged when the Institute was created. But this I managed to find at the university.

A footnote to this is that on my retirement in 1986, the university very kindly allowed me to retain an office on the campus and something even more rare and precious, a parking permit. I would have preferred at the same time to keep an office at the Institute since it was there that I had stored my entire library and where I did most of my work, but one member of the faculty was insistent that my appointment to the Institute had terminated and I must therefore vacate the office which I had been using. This caused considerable inconvenience. For one thing I had to cancel a lecture tour in France which had been arranged sometime earlier. For another, it meant building an addition to my house in which to store my fifteen-thousand-volume library and papers which I had to transfer from the Institute library where I had hitherto had my own section. The person in question was the one for whom I had made that special trip, though I never told him, so he could be invited to join the Institute.

Politics

My connection to political Washington goes back to when I was still living in England and had not even thought about migrating to the United States. It began during one of my lecture tours in America when I spoke to a small invited audience in Washington about the situation in the Middle East and the policies of the outside powers. In the audience was a young man who at that time was an assistant to Senator Henry M. "Scoop" Jackson, Richard Perle. Hearing my lecture, he felt it would be a good thing if the Senator could meet me and hear my views directly. He arranged a meeting and in due course

Senator Jackson and I met and chatted, the first of many conversations and the start of a close personal relationship which continued until his untimely death in 1983 at age seventy-one.

He was a truly great man and I feel it was a privilege to have known him personally. He was one of the few politicians of whom you could really use the word statesman, a man of total and unswerving integrity, a patriot and a gentleman. Among my many meetings with him my most vivid recollection is of an incident which occurred during the primaries for the presidential election of 1976. Scoop was running for the Democratic nomination and had already carried Massachusetts and New York triumphantly. When we met and talked in New York he had just reached the painful conclusion that, despite these successes, he would have to withdraw from the race for the simple reason that he had run out of funds. For a man of Scoop's meticulous integrity, funding was always a problem since he was not willing even to consider the kind of deals on which political campaigning was and is so often based. The next contest was in Pennsylvania for which he had already made media buys. He transferred them to his chief rival, Jimmy Carter, whose campaign was amply funded. Imagine how different the course of history would have been if Scoop Jackson had been the Democratic candidate and had been elected President!

An example of Scoop's scrupulousness in financial matters which impressed me occurred when it was decided that senators should be required to notify the Senate of fees received for lectures. At this point Scoop revealed that over the years he had deposited all honoraria into a fund which he had established to help needy students. Two things are notable about this; first, he felt long before the Senate reached any such conclusion that receiving fees for lectures was exploiting his status as a senator, and therefore, improper. He made no personal use of these funds. The second even more remarkable point, is that he did not disclose this fact until required to do so by Senate regulations.

Senator Jackson was sufficiently impressed by my views to invite me several times to testify before Senate committees. The proceedings of the meetings, my statements and the question and answer sessions, were published in the Senate proceedings. My connection with the Senate continued after his death in 1983 and I was invited to give testimony on several occasions and to meet with groups of senators for private discussions.

In the late 1970s Scoop was very concerned about the possible loss of the presidency to the Republicans and felt that the Democrats must make a special effort to retain or recover it. He decided that although Senator Edward Kennedy was not a strong candidate he was all there was and we should do what we could to educate and prepare him. With Kennedy's permission Scoop set up an evening meeting at the Kennedy residence to which he came with several specialist advisers, I among them. This was to be an informal dinner, completely off-the-record, to discuss questions of foreign policy. We sat around the table with Senator Kennedy presiding and carried on a lively conversation, in which, for the most part, our host was silent. A few days later I was startled to receive questions from the press about some remarks I was alleged to have made concerning Iran in general, and the role of the Shah in particular. I made inquiries and found that the remarks in question had been made by Senator Kennedy during a visit to the West Coast. When challenged, he said he had been told this by me. This was doubly improper—first, quoting a conversation from a private, off-the-record meeting, and second, far worse, misquoting it to the point of absurdity. I called Scoop immediately and he shared my outrage. He got in touch with Kennedy's office and the best he was able to get was a rather lame, ambiguous retraction. Fortunately, no one else seems to have taken any notice of it.

Oddly enough, the only other occasion when Senator Kennedy's path and mine crossed was in Iran, at a dinner. Sometime in the early 1970s at a time when I was in Tehran, Senator Kennedy suddenly arrived, unannounced and unexpected. The Shah was angry. He felt that a visit by a U.S. senator, particularly one with the dynastic name of Kennedy, was a state occasion and that he should therefore have been notified in advance so that appropriate arrangements could be made. Despite his annoyance, however, the Shah felt that he had to go ahead and do something to honor so distinguished a visitor. He dealt with this problem by finding a subtle Iranian way of honoring and rebuking Senator Kennedy at the same time. The Palace gave a formal dinner at which the Senator was the guest of honor. However, the Shah himself did not participate in this dinner, but instead left the task of presiding to his teenage granddaughter. From an Iranian point of view, this conveyed a clear message. The Senator however was delighted and I have no doubt that he enjoyed his dinner with the teenage girl much more than he would have enjoyed it with His Imperial Majesty.

I was invited to this dinner, and the Palace staff very kindly provided a car and driver to take me there and back. These two drives, in a Palace car with a Palace driver, were a nerve-racking experience. For such an august conveyance the rules of the road simply did not exist; the driver was free to go whichever way seemed convenient for him—on the wrong side of the road, through traffic lights, across intersections, and without any regard for speed limits. They were alarming journeys but were safely accomplished. The Senator obviously enjoyed his evening, and was, I am told, quite unaware of the fact that he was being subtly rebuked. On the contrary, he took it as a compliment.

The Shah of Iran

In October 1971, I was delighted to receive an invitation from the Iranian Embassy in London to attend the Shah's elaborate and luxurious ceremony celebrating the twenty-five-hundredth anniversary of the founding of the Persian Empire by Cyrus, the largest the world had yet seen. I vividly remember the climax. The Shah arrived at Persepolis by helicopter, stood on a raised platform in front of his assembled guests, a global Who's Who, and facing the tomb of Cyrus the Great concluded his remarks by saying, "Oh mighty Cyrus, you may sleep in peace, for we are awake!"

A year before the 1979 Revolution, I saw the Shah again at his palace, where he had a very large study with his desk at the far end. I think that was a trick he picked up from Mussolini, making a visitor walk down a long room in order to get to the royal desk. When I came in, the first thing he said was, "Why do they keep attacking me?" I hadn't a clue what he was talking about. So I said very politely, "Who, Your Majesty?" And he ticked them off, "*The New York Times, The Washington Post, The* London *Times, The Manchester Guardian,* and *Le Monde.* The five weird sisters dancing around the doom of the West. Don't you all realize that I'm the best friend you have in this part of the world? Why all the criticism?"

I said, my sense of mischief welling up, "Well, Your Majesty, you must remember that Western foreign policy is conducted on Marxist principles." He was very startled at that. Then I said, "I don't mean Karl, I mean Groucho. You have seen the Marx Brothers films?" He said, "Yes, of course," and I continued, "Do you remember a moment when Groucho says I wouldn't want to be a member of any club that would have me as a member? A principle of Western foreign policies is that we do not worry about the friendship of any government that would seek our friendship. It's only our enemies in whom we are interested." He said he understood perfectly.

The day before this interview with the Shah I was having lunch with some Iranian friends when my host said that he understood that His Majesty's granddaughter was an undergraduate at Princeton and asked how she was doing. I said, "I haven't the slightest idea; she has never taken any of my courses. As far as I know she's never come near our department, and I don't know what happens to all the students at Princeton." My host commented that he knew I had an audience with His Majesty the next morning and that since I was from Princeton it was very likely that His Majesty would ask how his granddaughter was doing. "If you answer him as you have just answered me, it will not be good." I countered, "There is no other way I can answer him. I don't know how she is doing, I've never seen her." So he waved his hand to his telephone and said that thanks to the wisdom and foresight of His Majesty, we now have direct dialing to the United States. "Why don't you call Princeton and find out?"

It so happened that the adviser to foreign students was the wife of a good friend of mine, so I not only knew to whom to speak; I even knew the telephone number. This was Janina Issawi, the wife of the great economic historian Charles Issawi. I dialed the number and Janina answered the telephone. We chatted for a moment. She was having breakfast, I had finished lunch. I said casually, "By the way, I am calling from Tehran." When she had recovered from her shock, she asked if I were calling for some particular reason. I said, "Yes."

I wanted to be very careful, because I thought it likely that telephone calls were monitored, so I said, "I'm seeing someone rather important tomorrow who has a close relative at our place." And bless her Polish heart, she understood immediately. If I had been talking to a normal American, they would have said, "Who do you mean? What are you talking about?" They don't have the conspiratorial approach to things she had by birthright, but she understood. "Well, how is she doing?" I asked. She replied, "Oh, hopeless. We decided to throw her out." "What?" I sputtered. Apparently, this girl never got up until midday so any courses in the morning she missed automatically. For the rest of the day she regarded her courses as something to be fitted into her program of social engagements. She had been warned several times but it didn't have the slightest effect. So they had decided to throw her out.

I said, "Couldn't you get her an extension, just one more semester, until I get back to Princeton?" She said, "This is a decision that has already been made. It's very difficult to change." I pleaded with her to try. She asked me to call her back in an hour, which I did. She explained that she had taken it up with her department and spoken with the chairman who referred her to the dean who referred her to the president. Everyone said he didn't want to countermand somebody else's decision, but Janina said she was working on it and to give her another half hour and call again. I did. With exaltation in her voice she told me it was okay. The girl would get one more semester but if she didn't pull her socks up, she would be out. I was greatly relieved and expressed my thanks. The next day I saw His Majesty. I was with him the whole morning, almost three hours. He never once asked about his granddaughter, possibly because he didn't care, more probably because he'd already had a transcript of this conversation and knew what it was about.

The sequel, which is a nice one, is that she was given a really severe warning and was told that if she didn't mend her ways she would be out. She turned herself around, stayed on, took her degree, and did well. So the story has a happy ending. The following year was the Revolution. If she had been thrown out she would have been sent back to Iran and would have been in real trouble. As it is, she was at Princeton, which was bad enough because suddenly she lost her escort, and her status; she was the devil's granddaughter because the Shah was very unpopular in liberal and enlightened circles. Everybody was in favor of the Revolution, not realizing that Iran's new rulers were much worse than anything that the Shah could ever have thought of. She showed great courage and dignity and really stood up to it extremely well.

The other consequence was that her father sent me a large tin of caviar.

A Near Defection

In 1972, when my son Michael was graduating from high school I received a letter from some old friends in Jerusalem saying that their son had just gone into the army to do his military service and they "had a vacancy in their home." As the long vacation was just beginning, would Michael like to stay with them for a month as their houseguest? Michael agreed, and off he went. Toward the end of that month I received a letter from him saying he would like to stay longer, but as he did not feel he could ask his hosts to extend their hospitality, he was going to spend a little while on a kibbutz. He explained that the shortest period for which the kibbutz would accept a temporary member was three months, and he had agreed to that condition. There then was a series of postponements of his return to England until it began to look as though he were going to stay permanently in Kibbutz Kfar Blum. In the kibbutz he met a summer volunteer from Cleveland, Jessica, whom he married. It was she who persuaded him that it would be a good idea to go to the United States and, more specifically, to university. He agreed, and chose Rutgers, the State University of New Jersey. His reason for choosing Rutgers was very simple. He had learned that since he was the son of a New Jersey resident and taxpayer (myself) the university's fees were minimal. With a kibbutz mentality, he did not want me to be burdened by tuition fees. Michael and Jessica both graduated from Rutgers; Michael emerged as a Phi Beta Kappa and went on to do graduate work in politics at Princeton. While they were at Princeton, they presented me with my first grandson, Zachary.

In accordance with Jewish custom, the newborn boy had to be circumcised on the eighth day after his birth. It was therefore necessary to find a *mohel,* a ritual circumciser. There wasn't one in Princeton but I found one in New Brunswick who agreed to come and perform the ceremony. As is usual on such occasions we had a little party to which Michael and Jessica invited their friends and I invited mine. One of my friends, Harry Wolf, the director of the Institute for Advanced Study, was a very busy man. At one point he went up to the *mohel* and said, "Excuse me, but how long is this going to take?" The *mohel* looked at him and asked, "Sir! Are you asking me to cut it short?"

I discovered later that the *mohel* in question was a brother of the comedian Jackie Mason. It obviously runs in the family.

Identity and Citizenship

During the war I attended a dinner party in London when suddenly we heard the sound of aircraft approaching from the distance, and the usual anxious question immediately arose—were they British or German, ours or theirs? One of my fellow guests, a colleague at the university, said he was pretty sure they were ours. I should mention that he had come to Britain as a Jewish refugee from Germany, had been a resident for eight years and was a naturalized British citizen. Our hostess looked at him coldly and said, "No, they are ours." What she meant of course was that he was right in thinking that they were British, but wrong in using the word "ours" to convey that. I must confess that I felt a similar irritation myself, and this was then the normal response. In Britain, as in the United States, naturalization is possible after five years' residence, and in principle brought with it all, or almost all, the rights of citizenship. But the reality was different, and most people in Britain felt at least a mild irritation when naturalized citizens, especially with foreign accents, used such words as "we" or "ours."

When I came to America I found that the exact opposite was the case—that the naturalized citizen was expected to think of America as "we" and could sometimes be reprimanded if he failed to do so. The difference was more than one of just social usage. In Britain as elsewhere in Europe, naturalized citizens could achieve great success in scholarship, in science, in business, in sports and in other fields, but not in politics or government. Such figures as Henry Kissinger or Zbigniew Brzezinski would have been, and indeed probably still are, impossible in Britain. The same is true in Europe generally.

The difference lies in the very nature of those societies. To become a Frenchman or a German is a change of ethnic identity, a difficult process that can take several generations. To become an American is a change of political allegiance, a much less difficult and complex matter. In Britain, as so often, we had it both ways. The naturalized foreigner becomes British. He does not become English, still less Scottish or Welsh.

The process of acquiring citizenship differs from country to country. In England, since time immemorial, the rule has been clear and simple. Anyone born under British rule was British by birth, even if the birth took place in the transit lounge at Heathrow Airport. This centuries-old rule was changed, amid general applause, by the government headed by Prime Minister Margaret Thatcher, and the law now reads, "Born in Britain to legally resident parents." The parents do not have to be British, but they do have to be legally resident. I understand that there are some who would favor a similar change in the United States.

Sometime in the 1970s, not long after my move to Princeton, I was invited to participate in a seminar in Berlin on the new Muslim—primarily Turkish—minority in Germany. This sounded interesting and I was very happy to accept. The organizers of the conference were very liberal, very open-minded; painfully aware of their country's history in the matter of racism and intolerance and desperately anxious in no way to repeat it. While I was in Berlin I was approached by a Turk who asked me if I would like to meet some members of the local Turkish community. I said that I would be delighted and was invited to dinner the same evening with a group of Turkish residents of Berlin. The picture I got from them was completely different. The

Germans were making every effort to be tolerant, accepting, even welcoming; the Turks felt themselves to be the victims of prejudice, discrimination and even hostility. I was stunned by a parting remark by my Turkish host who, speaking of the Germans, said, "In a thousand years they couldn't accept six hundred thousand Jews. What hope is there that they will accept two million Turks?" Since then the number, and with it the tension, has increased considerably. The district of Kreuzberg, a suburb of Berlin that is now overwhelmingly Turkish, is sometimes known as Klein-Kleinasien, little Asia Minor.

By now, the whole question of the Muslim presence in Europe has assumed a new aspect. Thanks to migration and demography on the one hand and a dwindling European birthrate on the other, the Muslim proportion of the population is increasing steadily. The Syrian scholar Sadiq al-'Azm remarked in an essay that the only question that remains regarding the future of Europe is, "Will it be an Islamized Europe or a Europeanized Islam?" That question is very close to being answered.

A Difference of Degree

The fact that I came to the United States from England gave me some significant advantages over other foreigners—the most important being the English language. But I soon found that apparent resemblances could conceal real differences, not only in syntax but in university practice. An English poet I knew was invited to take the chair of poetry at Cornell University. He had a fellowship at an Oxford college but as the professor of poetry at Cornell he really had a sinecure. He was only required to give an occasional public lecture on a subject of his own choice and to be available to students who wanted to come and talk to him. And he had what by English standards was a princely salary. The last time I went to Cornell I met him again. To my surprise he told me he had decided to go back to England. I asked why, since he seemed to be having a marvelous time in the United States. He said that he was a poet and could only live where his language was spoken. I said I was under the impression that they spoke English at Cornell. And he said, "Yes, but not my kind of English." I understood what he meant—a framework of allusion and reference which comes from a common background, common education, a common set of traditions and jokes and stories and so on. A poet needs that. The university teacher would like it, but it's not absolutely indispensable.

Good undergraduate teaching is possible only if the students arrive knowing something. If you have to spend the first two years of undergraduate education teaching them what they should have known by the time they were fourteen, they aren't going to get very far. Both in high school and at college, American students are no longer required to do history, not even general history. They do "social studies" which may include some history, but that can often be very specialized. A student may take a course on the history of France from 1789 to 1815. He will be extremely well informed on the revolutionary and Napoleonic period and have only the vaguest ideas about what happened before and perhaps none at all about what happened after.

Heinrich von Sybel, the German historian, said a long time ago that students should arrive at the university knowing their centuries. I think that puts it well. If you say fourteenth century or seventeenth century, this should immediately evoke something in the mind of a reasonably cultivated man or woman. When you say seventeenth century, an educated person will think of baroque buildings and Vivaldi or the wars of religion.

Over the years I have seen a decline of scholarly standards in my own field as well; nowadays people even undertake learned and synoptic projects, or efforts meant to be that way, without knowing the relevant language. Previously the study of Middle Eastern history was

cultivated by very few teachers teaching very few students, and therefore reasonably high standards were maintained. In the fifties and
sixties, there was an enormous growth of interest in the region for
political reasons, military reasons, and commercial reasons, and the
development of these studies was liberally irrigated with oil and other
money. If there is a greater need for books than there are people who
are capable of writing them, more appointments to be filled than
people capable of filling them, then there will be a deterioration. It's
inevitable. You get a kind of Gresham's law of scholarship, the bad
driving out the good. But there are some very good young people
writing in the field today and we can hope for some improvement.

In this country there is a great dichotomy in that we educate a
few very well from the beginning, but we educate a lot of youngsters
very poorly. I think we are moving toward a kind of mandarin class
which is highly educated, sophisticated, capable of high-level interaction in ways that are unintelligible to others. Then there is a mass of
semiliterates whose highest aesthetic appreciation is a good commercial on television. I think that is a very dangerous development.

I have often been asked what differences I have found in the general intellectual climate, in the scholarly community, between England and the United States. That is a difficult question to answer. In
England I was teaching at the University of London, a big university
in the capital. In the United States I was teaching at Princeton, a
small university in a small town. It is difficult to say whether the differences I observed should be attributed to the difference in size or the
differences between England and North America. Another factor is
the time period. It has been remarked that in the United States, one
hundred years is a long time and in England one hundred miles is a
long way. So much has happened since I moved. Now when I go to
England, I find a good deal of what struck me as typically American
is now also typically English.

And yet there are some points which are striking and they arise from differences in the systems of education. Much greater stress is laid in England on the last two years of high school, and therefore at university specialization occurs almost immediately. American universities reject this model and want students to have a more general education in the first two years of college with specialization occurring only in the last two years. Even at Princeton, which lays special stress on undergraduate education as compared with other American universities, the undergraduate years are seen as a period of general liberal education rather than professional training. That is why American graduate studies are much more complex than English graduate studies. In an English university, if you have a good B.A. honors degree, it is assumed that you are ready to write a thesis; whereas in an American university you still have a lot to go through before you can start writing a thesis.

The best way to get a really good education is to take a B.A. degree in an English university and then do a Ph.D. in an American university. Unfortunately what many people do is the other way around—they take an American B.A. and an English Ph.D., thereby getting the worst of both systems.

In the early 1960s an honors student at SOAS came to see me and said that she had decided to give up her course and leave school but didn't feel that she should just disappear. She thought it a matter of courtesy to let me know. When she asked for an appointment I looked up her record and found she was one of our best undergraduates that year. Usually if students say they have to leave it's for financial reasons. English rules say you don't ask personal questions but I managed to indicate that if it were a financial matter, we might be able to help. She said it was nothing like that and explained that she had fallen in love with a young man and they were about to get married. The young man had so poor a high school record that he had not been able to get admitted to any university in the country. So at the age of eighteen he had to go to work.

I vividly remember this young woman. She, who must have been about nineteen, maybe twenty, said, "I don't think it would make for a happy marriage if the wife were educated to a higher level than the husband." I was shocked at this and wanted to say to her—if you happened to fall in love with a man with one eye would you feel obliged to poke out one of your eyes? I didn't, of course, but I remember thinking that. There was nothing I could do. She left and I've never heard of her since. That unmistakably was the point at which I became a feminist. It made me acutely conscious, in a way that otherwise probably would never have happened, of some of the difficulties of female students, first admitted to Princeton in 1969, and the challenges they face.

When I came to America, this intensified, because the position of women in the universities was far worse in the United States than it was in England at that time. We had women students and even women professors at Oxford and Cambridge before there were women students at Harvard, Yale and Princeton. When I was a beginner at the University of London, the vice chancellor, the head of an English university, was a woman. My very first article was published in 1937 thanks to a woman editor, the professor of medieval economic history at Cambridge University and the editor of one of the major journals.

In my early years at Princeton I found that women students had a feeling—how shall I put it?—of persecution, of discrimination, which on the whole I must say was not without reason. I always did what I could to help them. When I retired at age seventy, I had seven students preparing theses, six of whom were women. Apparently the word got around that I was sympathetic to women students. All six of them finished their Ph.D.'s and went into academic careers. The situation now is very much better than it was when I came to America, but there are still problems for women in the academic world.

America is a free society in which you can publish anything you like if you can find a publisher, and you can usually do that if you try hard enough. There are constraints, however, in the way in which one can discuss certain topics. This particularly affects university teaching. When I taught in England I could express myself on any subject and give expression to any opinion. In the United States one has to be more careful. There is a series of sensitivities which one must take care not to offend. One sometimes gets the impression that one is walking around in a room full of sensitive toes and that one must step warily not to tread on them.

There are many taboos. There have always been taboos, of course. For example, in the eighteenth century and the early nineteenth century, there was the taboo of the church. It was simply not permissible to question or even raise questions about the basic dogmas of the Christian church. In the nineteenth century it was sex. The eighteenth century was fairly free and easy on the subject of sex but in Victorian England it became a taboo subject to such a degree that one couldn't even use the word "leg," not to speak of other more directly involved parts of the body. We got over the sexual taboo and we got over the religious taboo. But other taboos have taken their place. Like earlier taboos, they are strictly enforced. If you violate a taboo, you will suffer penalties in terms of professional advancement. As in the past, there are inquisitors who endeavor to detect heresy and punish it. Because these are taboo subjects, I won't go into details.

My mother, age eighteen.

My beloved maternal
grandmother, Annie, age thirty-
seven, 1914.

Grandfather Joseph, my father, my mother's younger
sister Betty, my mother, and her mother (left to
right) on my parents' wedding day, 1915.

Me, about eighteen months, 1917.

Dressed in a borrowed outfit in Syria in 1938 while I was a graduate student working on my thesis on the Isma'ilis.

With my mother and a fellow soldier in 1944. During the war I served in British intelligence and spent much of my time decrypting messages in London.

With my parents in London in 1944.

With Melanie in 1955 in the park outside our flat in London.

My children, Melanie (five) and Michael (three), in the Swiss Cottage neighborhood of London where we lived for thirteen years.

With Senator Henry "Scoop" Jackson in his office on one of my first forays to Washington. The inscription reads, "With appreciation for your superb testimony before my committee. Sincerely, Henry M. Jackson, March 17, 1971."

Greeting the Shah of Iran in the early 1970s. The Shah expressed his frustration at how he was treated by the Western press.

With King Hussein of Jordan in the desert in the 1970s. I was already acquainted with his brother, Prince Hassan, whom I had met at a conference of historians in Amman and who introduced me to King Hussein.

With Crown Prince Hassan of Jordan in the mid-1970s on one of my annual trips to Jordan.

A portrait from 1973, shortly before my move from SOAS to Princeton.

With Teddy Kollek (far right), who would become the longest serving mayor of Jerusalem and who would become a good friend in the late 1970s.

During an Iraqi scud missile attack on Tel Aviv in 1991.

BELOW: With Turgut Özal (right), president of Turkey, in 1992. I first met Özal when he was a young parliamentarian and he came to visit me once at Princeton. Like many Turks, he was intensely interested in history.

One of the small gatherings at Castel Gandolfo to which I was invited by Pope John Paul II (left) in the mid-1990s. I'm on the far right.

With Pope John Paul II
at the Vatican in 1996. He
was one of the finest people
I have met in my long life.

With Israeli Prime
Minister Yitzhak
Rabin in 1995,
shortly before he
was assassinated.

With Buntzie
after I received an
honorary doctorate
from Princeton in
2002.

With Vice President Dick Cheney in his office in 2003.

Buntzie and I had a wonderful time at the Allen & Company conference in Sun Valley, Idaho, in 2004. It's an annual retreat for Hollywood moguls and Wall Street tycoons.

8.

The Neighborhood

From the time when I began to read classical Arabic and later other Islamic texts, I was struck, and fascinated, by the rich vein of humor in Islamic civilization. I suppose that most if not all civilizations have their own distinctive form of humor but I cannot think of any other remotely comparable with the centrality and antiquity of humor in Islam. From the time of the Prophet in the seventh century to the present day Muslims have been telling, and recording, jokes about themselves, their rulers, their societies, their customs, even their sanctities. There are jokes about muftis and qadis, about imams and dervishes, and about every aspect of Muslim life, not excluding religious life. What is somewhat remarkable is that this humor is richly and amply documented in literary and even religious writings, in Arabic, Persian, Turkish and no doubt other Muslim languages, from the earliest times to the present day. The tradition continues to our own time notably in the form of the political joke. Political humor flourishes in every society but particularly in those that are repressive. There are no other outlets for frustration. In the Middle East, Egypt has perhaps the richest tradition of all.

A sample joke from the Nasser era, when there was a shortage of everything in Egypt: A man living by the Nile bank, desperately hungry, went fishing and managed to catch a fish in the Nile. He brought it triumphantly to his wife and said, "Here's a fish, this should provide us with one meal." And his wife said, "Only if you are prepared to eat it raw. We have no oil, no butter, no power; there is

no way I can cook it." And the man said in disgust, "I don't eat raw
fish," and he threw it back in the river and the fish rose above the
waters and yelled, "Long live President Nasser."

A friend relayed to me that Ethiopian Emperor Haile Selassie,
who was on friendly terms with President Nasser, told him that
Nasser was a keen collector of Egyptian jokes about himself and was
even willing to share them with suitable companions. (As a curious
aside SOAS decided to confer an honorary fellowship on Haile Selassie; as I was acting dean at the time it fell upon me to make the
formal presentation. I greeted His Imperial Majesty with the appropriate formulae and placed the diploma of his appointment in his
hands. He thanked me and then asked, "Do you also have problems
with students?")

There is even a joke about Nasser's collection of Nasser jokes. As
the Egyptians tell the story, Nasser decided one day that enough was
enough. He summoned his chief of police and ordered him to find
and arrest the man who was inventing and circulating all these jokes.
A week later the chief of police reappeared at the presidential palace
bringing with him a man whom he had arrested. "This," he said, "is
the man who has invented all these jokes about you, Mr. President."
Nasser turned to the man and said, "Are you indeed the man who has
been inventing and circulating jokes about me?" "Yes," said the man.

As they tell the story, Nasser then tells one joke after another, as
many as the audience can stand, and at the end of each one he asks
the man, "Did you invent this story?" And the man says, "Yes, I did."
Finally Nasser says to him, "You are an Egyptian as I am. I presume
that you love our country as I do. Why do you do this? You know
that I have made Egypt great and free and respected." To this the
man says, "That joke I didn't invent."

Egyptian Identity and the 1967 War

I developed fairly good relations with people in Pakistan after my trip there for the opening of the University of Punjab in 1957 and was informed, probably improperly and inappropriately, of a very interesting development after the six-day 1967 war. After that war Nasser was naturally devastated by what had happened and believed the Egyptian armed forces were in urgent need of reconstitution and redevelopment. He felt he couldn't turn to the West since they were not on his side and he did not want to turn to the Soviets since he felt that they had let him down rather badly. Pakistan had done rather well in its recent war with India, a much larger and stronger country. Nasser decided therefore to turn to Pakistan and ask for its help in reorganizing the Egyptian armed forces. The government of Pakistan was willing, but on condition that it be permitted to send a small feasibility mission to examine the situation and then advise on what, if anything, Pakistan could do. It told Nasser that the mission must be allowed to go wherever it wanted, and its questions must be answered truthfully and honestly. Nasser agreed, saying that there would be no point otherwise.

A small group of Pakistani officers was then sent to Egypt. They toured the country, spoke to many people and reported that they were not told the truth. The reason that they were not told the truth is that nobody knew the truth. In the Egyptian armed forces, they said, "The corporal lies to the sergeant, the sergeant lies to the lieutenant, the lieutenant lies to the captain, the captain lies to the major and so on all the way up the chain of command. By the time it reaches the high command or the Ministry of Defense, they haven't a clue what is going on." The Pakistani general heading the mission concluded that the high command in Cairo was sitting on the top of a pyramid of lies. The Pakistani government therefore declined and said it was sorry but it could not help.

By the late 1960s Egypt was becoming a Soviet dependency, almost a colony. I remember traveling in Upper Egypt and chatting
with a shopkeeper who was lamenting the difficult times. "The tourists have stopped coming—the English, the French, the Americans
and the rest—and business is terrible," he said. To which I remarked,
"But you have plenty of Russians." At this he spat eloquently into the
gutter and said, "The Russians! They won't buy a pack of cigarettes
and they won't even give you a cigarette." I saw his point. Russians
bought only from their own stores and were not sociable.

Another Egyptian remarked that both the British and the Russians had regarded Egypt as a cow, to be used for their own convenience. "The difference," he said, "is that the British wanted milk,
while the Russians want beef."

I met an Egyptian friend and colleague in Mexico not long after
that at an international congress of Orientalists. He had gone there
somewhat earlier in order to take advantage of the opportunity to
acquaint himself with the country. He was stunned by what he found.
The Spaniards had conquered Mexico and imposed their language
and their religion, just as the Arabs had conquered Egypt and imposed Arabic and Islam. Mexico remains a Spanish-speaking, Catholic country. But it would not occur to any Mexican to call himself a
Spaniard. On the contrary, they are proudly aware of the history of
Mexican civilization from ancient times. "Why is it that the Mexi-
cans were able to preserve their memory and their identity while we
Egyptians completely lost ours until it was restored to us by modern,
mainly Western, scholarship?" he asked.

I was struck by this observation and tried to answer his question.
I pointed to two important differences. One was that the Arabs had
come from next door, and remained next door, while the Spaniards
were thousands of miles away. The second was that by the time the
Arabs arrived in Egypt in the seventh century, the ancient civilization
had already been to a large extent obliterated by the successive phases

of Hellenization, Romanization, and Christianization. Mexican identity and its awareness of that identity were still current and vivid.

He saw my point, but wasn't satisfied. He said, "After all, in Egypt we had a great and glorious civilization of which many major monuments remain. The Mexican heritage is comparatively trivial by comparison."

I think that did less than justice to the Mexican heritage, but the larger question remains. It is not just Mexico and Spanish. Americans call the language they speak English, but they do not therefore call themselves Englishmen.

The Yom Kippur War

In October 1973, Sadat launched his famous attack on Israeli occupying forces on Yom Kippur. The opening phase of the war was successful. The Israelis were taken completely by surprise when Egyptian forces crossed cease-fire lines to enter the Israeli-held Sinai Peninsula, and at the same time, Syrian forces entered the Golan Heights. Both areas had been occupied since the 1967 Six Day War. But an Israeli counterattack speedily restored and indeed aggravated the previous situation. Israeli troops, well ensconced in the Sinai Peninsula, now crossed the Canal and soon established what came to be known as a "pocket" on the Egyptian side of the Canal. A cease-fire was agreed and negotiations followed which eventually led, six years later, to the first peace treaty between Israel and one of its Arab neighbors.

I was in Egypt at the time and shortly after and have vivid recollections of the Egyptian mood. This is perhaps best exemplified by the Egyptian sense of humor, notable at all times and especially remarkable at this difficult moment in their nation's history. I spent an evening at a dinner party in Cairo where a number of professors were present from both religious and secular universities, and before very long, as almost always happened in Egypt, they started telling jokes.

"Have you heard about the conversations between Golda Meir and Anwar Sadat?" one began. "In the morning she said to him, *'Bonjour,'* and he replied, *'Ubūr'* " (in Arabic, "crossing." The term applied to the crossing of the Suez Canal by the Egyptian forces at the beginning of the war. Note that the words rhyme). In the evening he said to her, *"Bonsoir,"* and she replied, *"Deversoir"* (the name of the dam where the Israeli forces crossed the Canal into Egypt proper).

Israeli forces advanced as far as Kilometer 101, east from Cairo, which they had reached when the cease-fire was agreed. The Israeli negotiator, General Arele Yariv, set up his headquarters in a tent at Kilometer 101 and waited for the Egyptian representative to arrive. Sadat summoned his defense minister, General Mohamed Abdel-Ghani al-Gamasi and told him he must go to Kilometer 101 to meet with the Israeli and negotiate the Egyptian surrender.

It was not long after this that I met Gamasi's deputy who told me this story. He said, as one can readily understand, that Gamasi was devastated. The defeat was unequivocal and he was sure that he would be utterly humiliated. But there was nothing he could do about it. He was the minister of defense and the head of his government had ordered him to go and discharge this painful duty. He went to General Yariv's tent, and entered it in a state of utter devastation.

This changed totally when General Yariv spoke his opening words, "Would you like tea or coffee?" This brought a feeling of immense relief to Gamasi and led to a relaxed and more or less friendly conversation between equals. They even started talking about their personal lives which led to the one bad moment. Gamasi was speaking of his wife's illness which apparently was quite serious. Yariv at once responded, "We have excellent doctors in Israel including specialists on this. Would you like me to arrange to send some to help you?" Gamasi was insulted at the implication that Israeli doctors were better than Egyptian doctors and could succeed where the latter would fail. Yariv was able to soothe him and the discussion continued on a friendly basis.

I knew Yariv quite well and was able to compare the account received from Gamasi's deputy with his. They tallied.

In spite of their final victory, the Israelis were not happy about the way in which the war had been conducted and were especially aggrieved by the opening victories won by the Egyptian forces. The public debate reflected these concerns.

At about the same time President Sadat in Egypt, latching on to the initial Egyptian success in crossing the Canal, started talking about "our victory in the recent war." The rejoinder was memorable. Some Egyptians, in astonishment, looked at Sadat and said, "Our victory?" to which President Sadat replied, "If you don't believe me, listen to what the Israelis are saying."

Golda Meir and Peace with Egypt

The students of Princeton University have a very well-endowed debating society—well-endowed because the university is two and a half centuries old and so too is the debating society, and many Princeton alumni have done well in the world and generously remembered their alma mater. It had become the custom that from time to time the society would invite a distinguished person to come to Princeton as their guest. In 1975 they invited Golda Meir, who had just ceased to be the Prime Minister of Israel. She accepted and had a very lively visit with many events. At one point an earnest student admonished her that she shouldn't smoke so much as it was bad for her health. "Well," replied the seventy-seven-year-old "I'm not going to die young, am I?"

During the several days she was on campus the female students, who were still a novelty at Princeton and quite defensive, put up a poster with her photo on it and the caption, "But can she type?" The high spot, in this as in similar visits, was a public address in the largest lecture hall of the university. The auditorium overflowed. The chairman, a senior university dignitary, made the appropriate speech introducing our distinguished guest and called on Golda Meir to speak.

She went to the lectern and said, "I think you will agree with me that on occasions like this the speech is usually a bore. What is interesting is the question and answer period. If the chairman will agree, I would suggest that we skip the speech. You know who I am, you know where I come from, you know what I am likely to say, so let's eliminate the speech and get straight down to the questions." The audience loved it. The chairman was more than a little startled but agreed and we had a remarkable question and answer session.

At that time, UNESCO had refused to admit Israel but had admitted the Palestine Liberation Organization. A student asked, "Why did UNESCO reject Israel and admit the PLO?" and Golda Meir said, quite correctly, "That is a question that should be addressed to UNESCO, not to me." And the student followed up, "You are right, but it would be interesting to know why, in your opinion, UNESCO made those decisions." She, with a perfectly straight face, said, "As you know, UNESCO stands for United Nations Educational, Scientific and Cultural Organization, and one must assume that these gentlemen, after due and careful consideration, decided that the PLO has more to contribute to education, science and culture than Israel has." It brought the house down.

Golda Meir was very tough, very committed. Particularly in that generation, but still today, for a woman to succeed in politics she has to be tough. Golda was fitted with a kind of personal filtration system—she only heard what she wanted to hear. If she picked up anything in what I was saying to her that fit within her pattern of thought, she would immediately grasp and use it. Anything that didn't fit just went straight past her as, for example, when I came to

her in 1969 with my story of Egypt being ready for peace negotiations. It is noteworthy that what she was actually doing while we
discussed this was giving me a cup of tea and a piece of cake in her
kitchen.

I had met her a number of times in Tel Aviv but I particularly
recall that conversation: I'd been in Egypt for a while and I had come
away with a very firm, clear belief that Egypt was ready for peace
negotiations with Israel. I was sure of it. I had no doubts whatsoever.

During my occasional visits to Egypt I used to see more or less
the same people every time. If you go to a country at intervals and
talk to the same people you have an opportunity to measure changes
in mood and changes in attitude. It gives you a cross-section of opinion, using the same samples. After an absence of several years I had
gone back to Egypt in 1969. Nasser was still alive and in control.
Although I did meet Nasser I had no serious conversation with him,
but I saw a lot of people, including old friends, and I was very much
struck by the change in mood. I came away with a very clear impression that Egypt was ready for peace. I even wrote an article, published
in *Encounter,* in which I said that. I didn't use my own name because
I didn't want to get my Egyptian friends into trouble. (Egypt was
under a ruthless dictatorial regime; as a foreign, particularly Jewish,
visitor I must have been carefully observed by the police and they
would have known whom I had seen and with whom I had talked.)
So as not to endanger my Egyptian friends, I used a pseudonym. I
said that I thought Egypt was ready for peace and that negotiations
could really lead to a treaty between Egypt and Israel. That was almost ten years before it happened.

I went to Egypt again several times after that, in 1970, 1971,
1974, both before Nasser's death in 1973 and after the Yom Kippur
War. I did not meet Sadat, who took over the presidency on Nasser's
death in 1970 but I met some of his close advisers and was absolutely
convinced that a direct approach to Egypt would produce results.

At the first opportunity after my return from my trip in 1969 I went to Israel, sought out Golda and tried to convince her that the Egyptians were ready, and that a direct approach would almost certainly produce results. She didn't believe me. She indicated that I had allowed myself to be duped by the Egyptians and that it was all nonsense. I tried the same on Moshe Dayan. I think he did believe me, but he didn't like it. He just didn't want to negotiate. He said, "If we talk we'll have to give them something. What else would we talk about?" He thought at the time that Israel could still hold on to half of Sinai.

I put this to Golda, I put it to Dayan, I also put it to Rabin. I even wrote Rabin a letter to that effect. But it fell on deaf ears; they didn't believe me or didn't want to believe me. Menachem Begin did.

The Egypt/Israel Peace Treaty

The Israel/Egypt peace process took a long time, and it would take a change of government for Israel to reconsider its position. This happened when Menachem Begin took over as Prime Minister in 1977. The paradox is that Begin was an ultranationalist rightist in his party, the Likud. He was always taking the strong, hard line. But the Likud were the ones who were ready to make peace with Egypt, not the Labor Party. Rabin, a Laborite, was asked about it later, and he said, "When I was Prime Minister I had to worry about Begin. Begin didn't have to worry about Begin." There was something to that. It was de Gaulle who gave away Algeria; it was Nixon who opened a line to China. There are things that right-wing patriots can do which liberal politicians cannot because they will be attacked by the right. Some people express such hopes about Netanyahu. Nixon made peace with China, de Gaulle made peace in Algeria, Begin in Sinai. Why shouldn't Netanyahu be able to do what Peres couldn't do and make peace with the Palestinians? But that's a different ball game.

In the end Anwar Sadat, not unreasonably, decided that on the best estimate of Israel's power and the worst estimate of Israel's intentions, Israel was less of a danger to Egypt than was the Soviet Union. I was told that when Sadat finally went on his trip to Jerusalem in November 1977, he was received by the Prime Minister and then was introduced to dignitaries, both of the government and of the opposition. I don't know if it's true but the story is that when he came to Golda Meir and shook her hand she said to him, "What took you so long?"

When Sadat went to Jerusalem and addressed the Knesset he had two Egyptian guards with him and an Israeli interpreter, who was my informant on this story. He went in with his guards to address the Knesset and when he spoke the Knesset was completely silent; you could have heard a pin drop. They listened in total silence and respect until he finished his speech. When Begin stood up to reply, the Knesset reverted to its normal behavior—people coming and going, members talking to each other, interruptions and the like. The two Egyptian guards looked at this in utter amazement and one said to the other, "What is this?" The second one replied, "This is democracy." And the first one shook his head and said, "By Allah, a very sweet thing."

The Israel/Egypt peace worked. A lot of people were dubious. The pessimists said it will end when Egypt gets back Sinai. Some said it will end when Sadat dies—it's his personal thing. Some people said it would not stand up if there was a conflict between Israel and another Arab state. All those things happened. The Egyptians recovered the whole of Sinai, and the treaty stood. Sadat was murdered, and the treaty stood. And then there was the 1982 war in Lebanon. The Egyptians were miffed, but the treaty stood. The Egypt/Israel peace has survived a number of major shocks but it still stands.

The term "separate peace" was used by many Arab states to condemn the Egyptian/Israeli peace treaty. They said that Egypt was letting down the Arab cause, that by making a separate peace with Israel, they were leaving the other Arabs in the lurch.

In the preliminary agreement between Sadat and Begin, Sadat wanted to include a clause according to which Israel would recognize "the legitimate rights of the Palestinians." Begin, the small-town lawyer, immediately wanted to know what these "legitimate rights" were. Sadat reassured him. He explained that he could not simply abandon the Palestinians. What he wanted was to be able to say to them that he, as ruler of Egypt, could only negotiate for Egypt. The Palestinians must do their own negotiations and he had eased their path by getting Israel to agree to their "legitimate rights." It was now up to them to negotiate with the Israelis on the definition and application of those rights.

I was told by someone who was at Camp David that President Carter raised the same question about "the legitimate rights of the Palestinians" and Sadat gave him the same answer, at which President Carter exclaimed in horror, "You mean you are prepared to abandon the Palestinians?"

The peace with Egypt had a profound impact on the balance of power in the Middle East and secured for the first time some measure of recognition for Israel among its neighbors. But any hope that it would pave the way to a more comprehensive peace remains unfulfilled. The Palestinians didn't negotiate, not for a very long time. And when they did, at Oslo in 1993, it was due to quite other causes, mainly the end of the Cold War and the collapse of the Soviet Union. It is significant that these were bilateral negotiations between the two parties without any outside intermediaries except the Norwegians, who provided a place to meet and some practical help. The United States was brought in at a later stage.

In the Egyptian-Israeli negotiations, the United States wasn't brought in until the treaty was made public. I was visiting the White House at the time, and when the news broke that Sadat had made a speech declaring his willingness to go to Israel in order to make peace, it came as a total shock. The political establishment was even alarmed. I remember Zbigniew Brzezinski, then National Security Advisor, whom I was visiting in his office, saying, "It will be a disaster. Sadat will fall flat on his face, Begin will give him nothing." My connections with Washington at that time were limited but I had a slight acquaintance with Brzezinski as an academic colleague with some coinciding interests. I asked why he was so sure that Begin would give him nothing. He went to his desk and picked up a letter he had from Nahum Goldmann, founder and longtime president of the World Jewish Congress, who had said just that. I said, "Do you really think that Begin would confide his plans to Nahum Goldmann?" "Well," he said, "I know they are not on good terms, but even so."

What neither Brzezinski nor I knew was that when Sadat made his famous speech he had been in secret negotiations with Begin for quite a long time and they had worked out the main points in advance. When Sadat made his speech he wasn't taking a shot in the dark. The process began with a very secret approach from Begin to Sadat. It was conducted through two channels, the King of Morocco and Nicolae Ceaușescu of Romania. Extremely hush-hush meetings were held between Israeli and Egyptian negotiators in Morocco and in Romania. The advantage of these two places was their locations. They were under authoritarian governments and there was no danger of journalists snooping around and picking up the story. Journalists who tried snooping in Romania got short shrift.

On the White House Lawn

In 1993, hosted by President Clinton, Prime Minister of Israel Yitzhak Rabin and PLO leader Yassir Arafat shook hands before cheering crowds on the White House lawn in Washington. The handshake, the first ever in public between the two former archenemies, marked the signing of a Declaration of Principles for peace between the Arabs and Israelis. This event made worldwide headlines.

On TV it looks so smooth and coordinated. In fact, the arrangements were chaotic. The sun was blazing; there was no shade, no shelter and I didn't have a hat. I had brought *The Washington Post* because I thought that there would probably be long periods of waiting and wanted to have something to read. I was sitting next to the Turkish ambassador and his wife. He asked if I could let him have part of my *Washington Post*. I assumed he wanted to read it and I gave him a section. He proceeded to fold the paper into two paper hats which he and his wife donned. I wished he had made me one as my efforts to hold the paper over my bald head didn't work very well.

We waited and waited and waited. Eventually the proceedings began and they were very moving. The sight of these people who had been at war with each other for a century, and these individuals for decades, shaking hands and talking peace and mutual recognition and coexistence was something I thought would come, but I never thought it would come in my lifetime. They rose to the occasion and this culmination of the occasion, the handshake, was truly wonderful.

Norway is not an authoritarian country but it managed to keep the Oslo negotiations secret all the same. There's a remarkable similarity between the negotiations preceding the Egyptian/Israeli treaty and the negotiations preceding the agreement with the PLO. Once the Israelis had signed the Oslo agreement, the PLO had in effect recognized Israel. That let a lot of others off the hook. It made it possible for the Jordanians to sign a full-fledged peace treaty with Israel and for many other Arab states—Morocco, Tunisia and several of the Gulf states, Oman and Qatar, for example—to enter into direct contact with Israel. When the peace process breaks down, those other links are endangered or broken. In regard to Syria, various Israeli governments, first that of Rabin and then of Peres, were willing to make territorial concessions to Hafiz al-Assad; but he wasn't willing to give them anything in return. He was virtually offered the Golan Heights on a plate; the Israelis didn't ask for any major concession other than making peace. He refused. Peace and normalization he refused also. That contributed quite considerably to Netanyahu's victory in 1996.

Sadat didn't need to convince his people that it was the right move; they were ready for it. He was following rather than leading them in this. Later, the Egyptians were able to persuade themselves that they'd won a great victory in the 1973 war, but that was not their initial reaction. The war was in October and I was in Egypt two months later, in December and early January. At that time there wasn't the slightest doubt among Egyptians that they had been badly beaten and there was a feeling of great resentment. I remember an Egyptian friend, a prominent journalist, saying, "For long enough Egypt has been the blood bank of the Arab world." There was a feeling that the Egyptians were suffering for a cause which was not theirs. Another man I knew who had always been actively pro-Arab said, "Enough of this 'Arab' stuff. We have to think about Egypt." There were many such incidents, even before the 1973 war, and many more after. So Sadat did not have to persuade his people of the need for peace; they were well aware of it. They were thoroughly war-weary, particularly after the humiliation of 1973.

That Sadat was able to persuade Egyptians that they had won a victory in 1973 made it much easier for him to approach Israel. In a sense they did win a victory as in the opening phase they succeeded in crossing the Canal under fire and seizing the other side. But having done that, they weren't able to follow up their advantage. In the weeks that followed, the Israelis crossed back onto the west bank of the Canal and entered the Nile valley. Nevertheless, there was this very considerable achievement at the beginning which restored a sense of Egyptian national pride, badly damaged by the Six Day War in 1967.

There was no real problem when it came to negotiating the terms of the peace because nobody seriously questioned that Sinai was Egyptian. There was some niggling over a very small piece of territory called Taba, but that was of minor importance. For a while some Israelis, notably Moshe Dayan, thought they could hold at least part of Sinai. Dayan once said he'd rather have Sharm el-Sheikh without peace than peace without Sharm el-Sheikh, but the Israelis in general did not hold that view. The Egyptians made it clear—and I had said this myself when I spoke to Golda Meir, Moshe Dayan and others—that Israel could not have peace with Egypt while holding Egyptian territory. The starting point had to be to assure the Egyptian government that Israel had no claims on its territory. With that, there was no real difficulty on either side. The Egyptians didn't want Israel, and the Israelis didn't want Egypt, which makes it much easier for them to live side by side.

Territory is a bargaining chip. If you have something that the other side wants, then you have something to talk about. The Israelis were in possession of the greater part of Egyptian Sinai. The Egyptians wanted it back. And the Israelis said in effect, yes, we'll give it back to you, but we want a proper peace treaty in return. The Egyptians were quite ready for that. The same thing happened with Jordan. There were some very minor territorial adjustments between Israel and Jordan and a peace treaty was finally agreed, right after Oslo in 1994.

Palestine

The conflict between the Israelis and the Palestinians is of quite a different nature. Israel and Egypt are two neighboring countries and, as is not unusual in human history, there can be long and serious disagreements between neighboring countries about where the frontier lies. The same may be said about the conflict between Israel on the one hand and Syria and Lebanon on the other. Israel and Palestine are not two countries, but two different names for the same country, representing different perceptions, held by different people and transformed in various ways in the course of the centuries.

The name Palestine was first applied to the country by the Romans, after the suppression of the Bar-Kokhba Revolt in the second century. The Romans decided that they had had enough of these troublesome people, and that the only way to deal with them was to eliminate them. Most of the Jewish people were removed elsewhere; their capital city, Jerusalem, was renamed Aelia, and the country was renamed Palestina or Syria-Palestina—that part of Syria which had centuries earlier been inhabited by the long extinct Philistines. It was hoped by these means to obliterate any connection between the Jewish people and their ancient homeland.

The name Palestina was retained for the remaining centuries of Roman and then Byzantine rule, and, for a while, by the Arab conquerors. Before long however it was forgotten, and the country had no separate name, being seen simply as part of some larger entity. In Christian Europe, where the country was usually known by the name of "The Holy Land," the Roman name Palestina reappeared with the classical Renaissance, and became a common term to designate the country. From Europe it was brought again to the Middle East, but was used almost exclusively by Europeans and other Westerners, and not by Jews or Arabs. The former preferred to use the biblical names; the latter had no need for a special name for what was simply part of a larger whole of the Arab world, or at least of Syria. With one brief interlude, that of the Crusader states in the Middle Ages, this remained the situation of the country for almost two millennia, from the triumph of Rome to the fall of the Ottomans.

It was with the British conquest of the country in World War I that Palestine for the first time since remote antiquity became a separate entity, this time in a mandate held by the British Empire and approved by the League of Nations. The name adopted to designate this entity was "Palestine," resuscitated from an almost forgotten antiquity. Interestingly, during the period of the British Mandate, that is, until 1948, the terms "Palestine" and "Palestinian" were primarily used by Jews, not by Arabs. They were not happy with these terms, but at least they designated the country as a historically separate entity. Overwhelmingly the Arabs rejected this name which they saw, not unreasonably, as a British imperialist device, with Zionist collusion, to slice off a part of the greater Arab homeland.

After the war which followed the termination of the British Mandate in 1948, much of mandatory Palestine was held by the Jews, who decided to adopt the ancient name Israel. The remainder, a not insignificant part, was held by the neighboring Arab powers—Egypt, Syria and most importantly Jordan. In none of these did the new rulers take any steps to create a Palestinian entity. The Syrians simply annexed the occupied area, regarding it as part of historic Syria. The Egyptians, more cautiously, retained it as occupied territory, and even experimented briefly with a local authority, but abandoned the attempt. Most importantly, the Jordanians simply annexed the whole area under their rule, declaring it part of the Kingdom of Jordan and extending Jordanian citizenship to all its inhabitants "other than Jews." In later wars, when the Israelis conquered and occupied these territories, the Jordanians withdrew their claims and it was then that, for the first time in history, the notion began to develop of a distinctive Arab national entity in this region. To designate this entity, the name Palestine was adopted.

This gave a peculiar complexity and difficulty to the ensuing conflict between the Israelis and the Palestinians. This was not, as in the case of Egypt and Syria or Lebanon, a quarrel over a disputed frontier. It was a conflict over the very nature and identity of a country to which both contenders had strong historic claims, deriving from different periods of history. Extremists on both sides, both Jewish and

Arab, claim the whole country as their historic national heritage, both with evidence and plausibility although from different periods of history. More recently, the idea has emerged of two separate states, one Israel, the other Palestine, in the territory previously historically claimed by both. But this kind of solution is difficult to formulate let alone to accept.

Ralph Bunche, an American mediator, presided over the first negotiations between Israelis and Palestinians on the island of Rhodes in 1949–50. Despite long and difficult arguments, they eventually achieved an armistice agreement, and Ralph Bunche's contribution to this was recognized by a Nobel Peace Prize. A story current at the time was that at one moment when both sides were being difficult, one of the mediators, forgetting that he was speaking to Jews and Muslims, exclaimed, "Why can't you settle this like good Christians?" Many years later, I was surprised to hear this remark quoted again, in what turned out to be a rather amusing context. It was at a meeting at the University of Toronto and one of the professors, discussing the ongoing Arab-Israeli conflict, quoted this remark, "Why can't you settle this like good Christians?" There was the usual laughter, and then a member of the audience said, "He shouldn't have told them that! That's what they've been doing ever since."

Arafat

In the 1970s I was in Tunis as a guest of the university to give a public lecture and attended a dinner at which my host told me a remarkable story. Yassir Arafat had passed through Tunis on his way to his memorable, gun-toting, 1974 appearance at the General Assembly of the United Nations. Habib Bourguiba, the ruler of Tunisia, gave a dinner in his honor. In the course of the evening Bourguiba told his guest that he had to decide whether he wished to be a revolutionary leader or a statesman. Arafat replied that of course he wanted to be a statesman but in order to obtain a state he had to be a revolutionary leader. Right, said Bourguiba, but there is a way in which you can get your state immediately. How so? asked Arafat in astonishment. Bourguiba advised that when he appeared before the General Assembly he should tell them that he is now prepared to accept Resolution 181 (which recommends the establishment of a Jewish state and an Arab state in Palestine; it was on the basis of this resolution that the state of Israel was proclaimed and accepted by the UN). By accepting that resolution, the legality of the Palestinian state would be on the same basis as that of Israel. The UN would have to accept it, the Americans would have to accept it, and even the Israelis would have to accept it. There would be a Palestinian state in Palestine.

Arafat was appalled, as that would mean he would have to renounce the rest of Palestine. Bourguiba explained that it would only be for the time being. The rest of Palestine won't go away, he said. It'll still be there. And when the time is ripe, raise the matter again and prepare for the next step. In the meantime, Palestine will have a seat and a voice in the United Nations and you will have a state at least in part of Palestine. Arafat shook his head and declared he could not stand up before the world assembly and renounce the rest of Palestine, not even as a tactic.

Jordan

For many years I traveled almost every year to Jordan, where I had a personal relationship with the royal family. This helped me keep in touch with what was going on in the Arab world. I also paid frequent visits to Turkey, Egypt, and when possible, Lebanon. I have not been to Iran since the Revolution, though I did once, to my surprise, receive an invitation to participate in a conference on religious dialogue there. The subject is a very interesting and important one, but I did not feel inclined to discuss it under the auspices of the current regime.

In the early 1970s I was invited to participate in a congress of historians of the region held in Amman. The meeting was convened and presided over by Prince Hassan, the younger brother of Jordan's ruling monarch King Hussein and heir to the throne, or Crown Prince. To Westerners it may seem odd that a younger brother should be the heir to the throne. In Middle Eastern monarchies it was the norm. Dynastic succession was well established in the Islamic lands, as everywhere else in the world, but succession was by some form of nomination or selection. The usual practice was for the ruling monarch to nominate a member of his family as being most ready and most competent to succeed him when the necessity arose. Normally, this was a younger brother, and succession by brothers and sometimes by nephews was normal. If one looks at the two most important dynasties in Islamic history, the caliphs in Baghdad and the Ottoman sultans, one sees long series of brothers succeeding one after another. It was therefore perfectly natural that King Hussein should appoint his younger brother as heir to the throne. But Prince Hassan was more than just heir; he was an active participant in the government of the country, playing an important part in almost every aspect of domestic and foreign policy. During the King's frequent travels abroad he was not only heir but viceroy. During his last years, when he was frequently incapacitated by illness or out of the country for medical treatment, Prince Hassan ran the show.

In the mid-1970s I was a guest of King Hussein and his brothers Prince Hassan and Prince Mohammad at a gathering of the loyal Bedouin tribes, great numbers of them, at a very elaborate tribal get-together in the Eastern Desert of Jordan. We sat in a large and rather well-upholstered tent and consumed endless cups of tea and coffee and sweet things until lunch was ready. Lunch was served with the guests standing around huge cauldrons and a large metal tray covered with a mound of rice, on top of which was mutton.

It was challenging to eat because there were no utensils. You can only use your right hand to eat in Muslim culture as the left hand is by tradition reserved for unclean purposes. So I had to eat standing, with one hand, and at the same time carry on polite conversation with my neighbors. In this instance my neighbors happened to be the King and the Crown Prince. Since I was their guest I had to maintain royal etiquette and elegant conversation while trying to eat bits of meat with very greasy fingers. Difficult!

For entertainment the host tribe had invited a tribal poet who declaimed a long ode in honor of the King, a traditional Arab eulogy. The King was sitting cross-legged on a piece of canvas on the sand as he listened to the poet recite at some length about the greatness of the King—the usual sort of fulsome eloquence. And then he stopped. The King thought he had finished and stood up. He started to say thank you but the poet cried out, "Wait a minute! I haven't finished yet!" And the King immediately sat down and let him go on, and on, and on, as it turned out.

Chairs are not part of Middle Eastern tradition or culture. There are very few trees in the region and therefore wood is rare and precious; it is used by artists for carvings but furnishings are made of wool and leather. (Plenty of animals produce wool and leather.) You sit on carpets on cushions or hassocks and eat off metal trays. When brought to Europe the hassock was transformed into an "ottoman." One of my favorite *New Yorker* cartoons shows a mound of hassocks, eight or ten of them, and the caption reads, "The Ottoman Empire." With a large number of people such as you would have at a Bedouin feast there is nowhere to sit. You can't sit on the desert floor and as there are no tables and chairs you gather around strategically placed stands.

The idea of serving meals in courses—appetizer, entrée, salad, dessert, brandy—is basically a Western concept though it is becoming more and more prevalent around the world. The Middle Eastern custom is to serve everything on the table at the same time, and to have more than one main dish. You can help yourself to the dishes in any order that you please. In a home it would be considered inhospitable to have just one main course, but among the Bedouin there is only one kind of meat. In general they slaughter a whole sheep, or as many sheep as may be needed.

I have been told that the eyeball is a particular delicacy and people are said to pop eyeballs into their mouths. All I can say is it never happened to me and I've never seen it. I have had a host pick out a particularly juicy piece of meat for me and pop that into my mouth, but never an eyeball.

An interesting thing about the Muslims and particularly, but not exclusively, the Bedouin, is the high respect for bread. If a piece of bread is dropped on the floor I've seen people pick it up and kiss it. Bread is God's greatest gift by way of food, and it has to be treated accordingly. It is considered very bad to put anything other than food on bread. Disrespect to bread is disrespect to God, who gave us this precious gift.

King Hussein was married four times and had four sons. His last wife, Lisa Halaby, the American daughter of Najeeb Halaby, who was then president of Pan American Airways, was working in the Pan Am office in Amman when they met. After she converted to Islam her name became Noor. Although she was his fourth wife he decided to confer upon her the title of Queen. In the past, Muslim monarchies did not usually have queens, neither as reigning monarch nor as the wife of a reigning King. Noor was the first Queen of Jordan. The principle of primogeniture, the right of succession of the eldest son of the monarch, is European and has only very recently been introduced into the Middle East; it is unfortunately more prevalent in republics than in monarchies.

In the late 1990s I attended a lecture given by Prince Hassan at the University of Amman in which he spoke about the possibility of outreach toward Israel, a strange idea at that time, and expressed the hope that this might occur. "But," he said, "the Israelis would also have to do something to acclimatize themselves, to really become part of the region and not be an alien body." I was there with an Iraqi friend, who like me was a guest of Prince Hassan. At this remark he turned to me and said, "What do you say to that?" To which I replied, referring to the recent assassination of Prime Minister Rabin, "The Israelis have already made a start. They've murdered a Prime Minister." My Iraqi friend was greatly amused at this wisecrack. When the meeting was over we joined our host Prince Hassan in his car, to travel with him back to the palace. To my acute embarrassment my Iraqi friend said to the Prince, "Bernard made an interesting comment about your suggestion that the Israelis should acclimatize themselves to the region. I think you ought to hear it." There was no escape. The Prince looked at me and asked for my comment, and I had to give it to him. He responded with one word, "Touché."

The story of Prince Hassan's supersession as heir to the throne is a sad one.

I attended the King's funeral in February 1999 and at that time Prince Hassan shared with me his experience of the King's final scenes. King Hussein had called Hassan and asked him to nominate Queen Noor's eighteen-year-old son, Hamza, as his heir. Hassan was not happy with this request and raised two issues which he saw as problems. The first was that it would be rather odd, to say the least, for him to nominate and appoint an heir while he himself was only heir. One is heir to the throne, not heir to the heir. His second point was more serious, that Noor's son Hamza was the fourth son of the King and he had three elder brothers. To set aside the others and nominate the fourth son might start a crisis. If the King was determined to do this, as apparently he was, Hassan suggested that a family council be called to discuss it. This would have been a more or less normal procedure in an Arab tribal situation, and the Jordanian monarchy was, to no small extent, a tribal institution.

The King was furious at his response. A written statement from the King then removed Prince Hassan from the succession and appointed the King's eldest son, Abdullah, in his place.

The King died not long after. Abdullah succeed to the throne and among his first acts were to confer the title of Queen on King Hussein's widow, who had lost the title when her husband ceased to be King by death, and to install formally her eighteen-year-old son, Hamza, as heir to the throne. This clearly was what his father had asked him to do and he was willing to accept. Everything seemed to be going Noor's way, but not for long.

Later, when he was firmly installed, King Abdullah took some further steps. One was to confer the title of Queen on his wife, Rania, unusual by Middle Eastern standards but normal by Western, and by now international, standards. His second step was to appoint his own five-year-old son, Prince Hussein, as heir to the throne, nullifying the previous nomination of Prince Hamza. This is what Prince Hassan could have done. But that was not his way.

Hamza was now out of the line of succession and dowager Queen Noor returned to the United States.

King Abdullah followed exactly in the footsteps of his father by removing his brother from the succession and appointing his own eldest son as heir.

I went to Jordan to attend King Hussein's funeral and on one or two subsequent occasions to attend meetings. I have not been there since.

A Concert in Jerusalem

Over the years when I went to Jerusalem I often stayed as a guest in one of the small apartments of the Jerusalem Foundation. Their lovely

facility is called Mishkenot Sha'ananim. *Mishkenot* means "dwell-
ings." *Sha'anan* (plural *sha'ananim*) in biblical Hebrew means "tran-
quil." In modern Hebrew it has acquired the connotation of
"complacent." I'm sure that in using this name the Foundation had
only the biblical meaning in mind.

One afternoon I was in my apartment in Mishkenot when suddenly there was a knock at the door. I answered it. A man with a
vaguely familiar face said, "I hope my practicing the violin doesn't
disturb you. I am afraid you can hear it in your flat." I said: "No, not
at all, not at all." He said, "You see I am giving a concert tonight, so
I feel I have to get myself into shape." I said, "I am delighted to listen." I had realized in the meantime that this was none other than the
world-renowned violinist Isaac Stern. Oh, you're interested!" he exclaimed, "Why not come to the concert tonight? I'll get you in as my
guest." I said I would be honored and delighted to do so, but that
unfortunately I had an engagement. I was taking two ladies, an old
friend and her daughter, out to dinner. "Bring them along," he said.
"I'll make arrangements for all three of you." So I did. It was a wonderful concert and, more importantly, the beginning of a long and
cherished friendship.

My eightieth birthday was celebrated by my colleagues at Princeton in the traditional scholarly way by producing a Festschrift, a volume of studies contributed by colleagues, friends and others in honor
of the occasion. My family celebrated with a party at my home for
about fifty guests. I was very touched by some of the comments made
by former students and friends. My daughter, going through my address book, invited Isaac Stern. Unfortunately he was unable to come
as he was scheduled to give some concerts in Europe that week. He
did, however, find a substitute; he sent a tape recording with his personal greetings and his rendition, on the fiddle, of "Happy Birthday
to You."

There were many different kinds of visitors at Mishkenot: academics like myself who were there to give a lecture or two, musicians there to give a performance, archaeologists who had come to help and advise on a dig and so on. One morning, I was having breakfast with a visiting violinist in the Foundation breakfast room. Normally we transacted our business with the waitress in English but this time the waitress on duty knew no English, so I did the honors in Hebrew and ordered breakfast for myself and for the violinist. He looked at me in surprise and said, "You speak Hebrew?" I said, "Yes," and he said, "In that case, why are you giving your lectures in English? Why don't you give them in Hebrew?"

"Can you play the piano?" I responded. And he said, "Of course, every professional musician can handle a keyboard." "Well," I said, "why don't you give concerts on the piano?" "Ahhhh," he muttered, and he instantly understood. The English language is my instrument. I can speak other languages, but I can't perform in them.

The one exception, when I had to perform in another language, was when I received an honorary doctorate in 1996 from the University of Ankara. Normally, honorary doctorates are given in batches and one of the recipients, by previous arrangement, is called upon to reply on behalf of the honorees. Since the correspondence regarding my award made no reference to this, I assumed that someone else would be making the appropriate speech, and there was no need for me to do anything.

I was wrong. When I arrived in Turkey, my host arranged to meet me and accommodate me overnight in Istanbul so that I could rest and recover before continuing on my way to Ankara the following day. And by the way, he said in passing, there will be just two recipients, you and Prime Minister Süleyman Demirel. We were each expected to make a short speech in response, and, of course, that speech would be in Turkish.

I now faced a really difficult problem. I was exhausted after the long transatlantic, trans-European journey and the last thing I wanted to do was to prepare a speech, more particularly a speech in a language other than my own. But there was no way of avoiding it. So I set to work and prepared a more or less autobiographical speech, starting with my first encounter with the Turkish language as a student and the first time I set foot in Turkey. I delivered the speech the following day at the university and breathed a sigh of relief. My hosts either liked it or were polite, I'm still not sure which. The two are, of course, not mutually exclusive.

Teddy Kollek

One of my oldest and most interesting friendships in Israel was with Teddy Kollek. I remember when he was first elected mayor of Jerusalem in 1965, which at that time meant West Jerusalem because East Jerusalem was still ruled by the Jordanians. (This was before the Six Day War, during which the Israelis captured East Jerusalem.) Between 1948 and 1967, when the Old City was under Jordanian control, Jews were not allowed to enter the Old City, let alone to live in it. The inhabitants of the ancient Jewish Quarter were evicted, and even dead Jews were removed from their graves in the ancient cemeteries. The tombstones were used for a variety of practical, mostly unclean purposes.

At the time the Jordanians would not admit anyone of whom they disapproved to the holy places in East Jerusalem or indeed to East Jerusalem in general. Jews of all nationalities and Israelis of all religions were barred. Israeli Muslims and Israeli Christians as well as Israeli Jews were not allowed to go into the holy places of the Old City with one exception. That was on Christmas Day—the Western Christmas Day not the Orthodox Christmas, so it was clearly intended for Western impact. On Christmas Day the Jordanians allowed Christian Israelis to cross into the Old City for the day, spend a few hours there, visit the Church of the Holy Sepulchre, and then return.

I was in Jerusalem on a very cold, blustery Christmas and Teddy had had a refreshment counter set up just near the crossing point. Coffee, tea and snacks were dispensed free to the Christians who were going and then coming back. I was enormously impressed because there was absolutely no political mileage in this. Many of these people were not from Jerusalem but from other parts of the country so they couldn't vote for him and there was certainly no political gain from his constituents in Jerusalem. It was simply an act of human compassion at a time of bitter conflict. That told me something of the character of the man and everything that happened afterward confirmed it.

Teddy Kollek was a great man who did great things for the city. I said to him once that there must be many people all over the world who could tell you the name of the mayor of Jerusalem but couldn't tell you the name of their own mayor. He said he didn't think so. I said, "Well, me for one." I didn't know the name of the mayor of Princeton. He laughed and he said, "If you'd had the same mayor for twenty-five years, you would know his name." That is probably true. Normally in democracies politicians work mainly with a view to pleasing the people who elect them. But Teddy thought in global terms and in human terms, not just about how to get reelected but how to do a good job for the people of Jerusalem and for all those countless millions of other people for whom Jerusalem matters. That is a quality of greatness.

Teddy and I met many times and developed a close friendship, which continued until his sadly lamented death in 2007. One of my most treasured possessions is a mezuzah, a sacred text in a case attached by Jews to their doorpost, given to me by Teddy when I rented an apartment in Tel Aviv. It's inscribed, "To show that I forgive you for choosing Tel Aviv, not Jerusalem."

To be perfectly honest, Tel Aviv had actually chosen me. In 1980 I received a most attractive invitation from Tel Aviv University, proposing that I should become a Visiting Fellow on a continuing annual basis. My only obligation would be to deliver two public lectures at the university and to meet with students who wanted to talk to me. As my schedule at Princeton was quite light, I was happy to accept. Of the many lectures I delivered there over the years, some were revised and published as articles in journals; some became chapters in my books. The greater majority remain unpublished but are accessible on the Tel Aviv University Web site. For many years these lectures attracted large audiences filling the main university auditorium and often an overflow in adjoining rooms outfitted with loudspeakers. Laterally, as both the members of the audience and I have aged, the numbers have diminished to about two hundred.

This relationship provided me with the convenience of an office and a base from which I could visit other countries in the region quickly, easily, and without jet lag. This last point was an important one, as with increasing age I find long-distance travel more and more difficult.

A Brit Looks at Golan

In the late 1940s I became acquainted with Geoffrey Arthur, a leading Foreign Office Arab expert, with whom I remained in close touch for many years. He had a good knowledge of Arabic, served in a number of posts in a number of Arab countries and eventually became head of the Foreign Office department dealing with the Middle East, North Africa and the United Nations. (A rather interesting combination I thought.) We used to meet once or twice a month for lunch or dinner at his club or mine and exchange news and views. Normally, he provided the news and I provided the views, though sometimes it was the other way around. Our conversation after his first visit to Israel in the early 1970s was memorable.

He had gone there in his official capacity and met a number of senior Israeli politicians and diplomatic officials. He said that it had been a rare pleasure in that part of the world to be able to converse with politicians as rational adults and not have to watch his words as if he were talking with neurotic children. I asked him if he had told them that. He said, "Yes, I did and they were rather flattered, but then one of them said, 'If that's how you feel about us why aren't you nicer to us?'" I asked how he had answered that. He said he told them his job was to look after British interests and there were many more Arabs than there were Israelis in this part of the world so Britain had to shape her policies accordingly.

The Israelis took him for a tour of Israel which included a flight over the Golan Heights, which the Israelis captured in the 1967 war. He told me that while they were flying over the Golan Heights, whose possession by Syria had been a major threat to the northern part of the country, he looked down and the words slipped out before he could stop himself. He blurted out, "You can't give this back!"

During my travels in Arab countries I heard again and again the line of argument: "We have time, we have patience, history is on our side. We got rid of the Crusaders; we got rid of the Turks; we got rid of the British. We'll get rid of the Jews in due course." Finally, I heard it once too often and sitting with a group of friends, I think it was in Jordan, I said: "Excuse me, but you've got it wrong." They said, "What do you mean? That's what happened." I said, "Not quite. The Turks got rid of the Crusaders. The British got rid of the Turks. The Jews got rid of the British. I wonder who's coming here next?"

9.

The Clash of Civilizations

There have been many civilizations in human history, shaped and guided by many different systems of religious belief. Most religions have a "relativist" approach, to use a term invoked by the Catholic church to indicate disapproval, though I use it approvingly. Others, again to use the term applied by its detractors, are "triumphalist." The relativist view would be something like this: Just as men have invented different languages to talk to each other, so they have invented different religions to talk to God, and God understands all of them. Perhaps not all equally well, but he understands all of them. Followers of triumphalist religions, in contrast, believe they are the fortunate recipients of God's final message to humanity, which it is their duty not to keep selfishly to themselves, like the Jews or Buddhists, but to bring to the rest of humanity, removing whatever obstacles there may be in the way. There are two such religions, Christianity and Islam. Their shared attitude has been summed up in the formula: "I'm right. You're wrong. Go to hell." Both have played a global role, and remain in competition to the present day.

The ancient civilizations of Asia, notably of China and India, were rich and creative and made an enormous contribution to human development but they never claimed exclusive or global truth. Their religious systems sometimes exercised considerable influence, but it was indirect, for the most part unintentional, and limited. Christianity and Islam are different. Between two such religions, related in

228

their historic past, almost identical in their self-perceived mission, conflict was inevitable.

In one of his sermons Saint John of Capistrano, a Franciscan whose name, along with those of other Franciscans, graces the map of California, accuses the Jews of propagating the monstrous and absurd idea that everyone can be saved in his own religion. Saint John of Capistrano said many things about the Jews and the Muslims, both of whom he disliked intensely (recommending pogroms on the one and crusades against the other) but on this particular point he was right. The Talmud says that the righteous of all faiths have a place in heaven.

That is not the Christian or the Muslim point of view. Their message is that only their religion can save you. If you accept it, you will be saved. If you don't accept it, then your religion is either incomplete and superseded, or false—incomplete and superseded if it is previous, false if it is subsequent. For those who believe they are the fortunate recipients of God's final revelation to mankind, followers of a previous religion have a faith that is outdated. It can however contain elements of truth. This was the classical Christian perception of the Jews; it remains the orthodox Muslim perception of both Jews and Christians. In the foundation narrative of Islam, in the Koran and the biography of the Prophet, Christians are viewed more favorably than Jews, since the Prophet had no direct and hostile encounters with them. In subsequent stages of Islam, these attitudes were reversed. For one thing, Jews did not embrace the Trinity, seen by Muslims as a form of polytheism; nor did they accept the divinity of Jesus, seen by Muslims as a form of idolatry. More important, unlike the Christians, they did not constitute a global rival and were even, at various times and in various ways, useful. More recent developments changed these attitudes dramatically.

There is a long history of Muslims and Christians attacking each other, and invading one another's territory. At first clashes arose from their resemblances more than from their differences. Christians and Muslims could argue meaningfully. They did so right through the Middle Ages in areas where they met, notably Spain and Sicily. When a Christian said to a Muslim or a Muslim said to a Christian, "You are an infidel and you will burn in hell," each understood exactly what the other meant because they meant the same thing. Their heavens are somewhat different, but their hells are the same. Saying that to a Buddhist or a Hindu or a Confucian would not convey much meaning. When you have two religions making the same claim with the same self-perception and in the same geographical area, you are bound to have trouble.

According to the Muslim narrative the Prophet Muhammad, during his lifetime, sent messages to the emperors of Byzantium, Iran and Ethiopia, telling them of his mission and urging them to accept this final version of the true faith. Iran was conquered and Islamized. Christianity, despite many defeats and losses, survived both in Byzantium and in Ethiopia, as well as beyond in Europe, and the long struggle continued between the two rival claimants to the mission—that is, the custodianship and spread of God's final message to humanity.

The followers of the Prophet conquered the hitherto Christian countries of Iraq, Syria, Palestine, Egypt, and North Africa, and invaded Europe, conquering Sicily, Spain, and Portugal and invading France. After some hundreds of years Christians were able to reconquer Spain and Portugal and Sicily but they could not reconquer North Africa, and failed in their attempt, known as the Crusades, to recover the lost Holy Land of Christianity.

The second Muslim attack came when the Ottomans created a new empire in the Middle East. They conquered the ancient Christian city of Constantinople, and invaded Europe. Their allies, the Barbary Corsairs—we might call them privateers—operating from the North African coast, raided the shores of Christendom as far away as Iceland, and seized hundreds of thousands of Christians to be sold in the slave markets of Algiers and elsewhere in North Africa.

That phase too ended in defeat. The decline and collapse of the Ottoman Empire during World War I was followed by the expansion of the European imperial powers, Britain, France, Russia and to a lesser extent the Netherlands and Italy, into the lands of Islam. That domination was ended after World War II, and what is happening at the present time is seen by some as the third attempt by Muslims to fulfill their divinely appointed mission of bringing God's truth and final revelation to all humanity. This time it is not by invasion and conquest, but by migration and demography.

In the past one might have said that the clashes between Islam and Christendom arose less from their differences than their resemblances; the same global view, the same historic background, the same self-perceived sense of mission. But the growth of secularism in the Western world has brought a radical change. Far from sharing the Muslim self-perception, most people in the West are unable even to understand that perception, and react with bafflement and incomprehension to the challenges that it presents.

Politics and Islam

All history, as the great German historian Leopold von Ranke remarked, is contemporary. This applies no less to the Islamic than to the Western world—indeed, perhaps more so, since the Islamic world is only now beginning to traverse the great sequence of social, cultural, economic, and religious changes which transformed Europe from the world of medieval Christendom to that of the modern secular, industrial states. Religion still has a public and social significance in the Islamic world—as the source of authority, the focus of loyalty, the definition of identity—which it has not known in Europe since the changes resulting from the Renaissance, the Discoveries, the Reformation, the Enlightenment, and the Industrial Revolution.

But beyond that there is, in a more profound sense, a link between religion and politics in Islam which has never existed in the Christian religion. The founder of Christianity bade his followers render unto Caesar that which is Caesar's and unto God that which is God's. For more than three hundred years, Christians were a minority, deprived of power, and often subject to violent persecution. It was not until the conversion of Constantine that Christianity became the religion of the state, and by that time it had formed its own institution, the church, which had its own laws, its own courts, and its own administering hierarchy. Throughout Christian history, and in virtually all Christian societies, it has been accepted that there are two authorities, dealing with two different matters—God and Caesar, church and state, religious and secular affairs. These two have sometimes been associated, sometimes separated, sometimes in harmony, sometimes in conflict, sometimes one dominant, sometimes the other, but always two.

In premodern Islam, in contrast, there was only one. The founder of Islam was not forbidden, like Moses, to enter his promised land, still less did he suffer martyrdom. On the contrary, he achieved military and political success during his lifetime. After his migration from Mecca, his birthplace, to Medina, he created a new state and was ultimately able to conquer and rule Mecca itself. Muhammad became a sovereign—commanding armies, making war and peace, levying taxes, dispensing justice; in a word, performing all the acts of sovereignty in which, in the Muslim perception, he set a model for generations to come.

There is thus in Islamic history, and more specifically in the early formative events which are the common possession of Muslims everywhere and which shape their corporate awareness, an interpenetration of creed and power, of correct belief and worldly dominance, that has no parallel in Christianity, and that has had no parallel in Judaism since the earliest books of the Old Testament. "Islam," said the late Ayatollah Khomeini, "is politics or it is nothing." Not all Muslims would go that far, but there is no doubt that the Ayatollah was putting his finger on an important element in the relationship between religion and politics, as conceived by Muslims and as manifested in Islamic history.

This does not mean, as some have assumed, that the activities of those who present themselves as terrorists in the name of Islam are in any sense encouraged, or even condoned, by Islamic doctrine, tradition, or law. Far from permitting such practices as the indiscriminate murder of noncombatants or the taking of hostages for blackmail, Islamic law expressly forbids them. No man, says the Koran in several places, shall bear another's burden. Islamic law does indeed regulate the giving and taking of hostages, but this is on a voluntary basis, when hostages are exchanged between parties to an agreement, as pledges for the fulfillment of their obligations. Such practices were at one time very common and have nothing whatever to do with the modern practices of kidnapping and blackmail. Similarly, while Islamic law enjoins holy war, that is to say, warfare for the faith against infidels and apostates, it lays down certain rules of warfare, including respect for noncombatants. The earliest formulations of these rules of warfare go back almost to the beginning of the Islamic era.

In the past, the Muslim world was perhaps unique in its sense of history and of its mission, constantly renewed by the annual pilgrimage to the holy cities of Mecca and Medina, which brought millions of Muslims from all over the world to share in common rites and rituals. Today modern communications and the media have given the Western world a similar opportunity, but for the most part that opportunity is not exploited as both our historical knowledge and historical awareness remain extraordinarily deficient. The Islamic world still defines itself in terms of its religion and its religious civilization.

Such terms as "the Middle East," and even "Europe" and "Asia" are comparatively recent innovations in Islamic usage. In contrast, the West no longer defines itself as Christendom; indeed, to do so would be seen as both misleading and offensive. Such terms as "the West" obviously lack the resonance and power of the word "Islam."

In my work I was constantly reminded of these significant differences between the Islamic and the Western worlds. I also became aware, from the late 1950s, of the changing mood among Muslims. This awareness came and grew in a number of ways: by reading or hearing what was written and said in Muslim countries, by talking to Muslim students, and by traveling in Muslim countries. In all these cases being able to follow what Muslims said and wrote among themselves in their own languages was crucially important. To understand what is going on a knowledge of the languages of the region is essential. But it is not in itself sufficient. In this society appeals to the past, sometimes no more than a name, a date, or a place, are common.

For a while it seemed that the Islamic world, even in its opposition to the West, was becoming Westernized, perceiving its identity and loyalty, its grievances and ambitions, in Western terms. But in the course of the twentieth century this began to change, and there were increasing signs of Islamic identity and loyalty. One of the most notable was the development of the organization known as the Muslim Brothers, founded in Egypt by a religious teacher, Hassan al-Banna.

The Muslim Brothers began with social, religious and educational work and extended that first into economic and then into political activity. They actively protested the Anglo-Egyptian Treaty of 1936, which legitimized the British military presence in Egypt, and later took up the cause of the Palestinian Arabs against both British and Zionist rule. In 1948 they sent volunteers to fight with the Arab armies against Israel and from that time onward they have played some role in public affairs. The then Egyptian Prime Minister,

Nuqrashi Pasha, dissolved the organization and confiscated its property. He was assassinated by one of them in 1948 and shortly after that the leader of the Brothers was himself murdered in circumstances that remain obscure. For a while the Brothers functioned as a secret organization. In April 1951 they were again legalized in Egypt, though not officially permitted to engage in any clandestine or military activities. They took part in the actions against British troops in the Suez Canal zone and seem to have had links with the so-called "Free Officers" who seized power in Egypt in 1952. Thereafter their relationships with the rulers of Egypt have gone through different phases, sometimes openly hostile.

The Muslim Brothers and related organizations operated in the main in the Arabic-speaking countries, but there were parallel movements in Iran, in Turkey, and in the predominantly Muslim republics of the Soviet Union. The Brothers were also active among the Palestinians and for a while had links with Fatah, the largest and most important of the Palestinian guerrilla organizations.

Muslim Identity and the Eclipse of Secularism

My earliest recorded reference to the much-discussed "clash of civilizations" occurred at a conference held at the School of Advanced International Studies of the Johns Hopkins University in Washington, D.C., in the last week of August 1957.* In this I tried to answer a question of agonizing concern to Americans at that time, "Why should the United States, which has never annexed or occupied an inch of territory in the Middle East, which on the contrary has shown a generosity without precedent in history toward the states of the Middle East, be included in this generalized hostility to the West?"

*The proceedings of the conference were published in a volume entitled *Tensions in the Middle East,* edited by Philip W. Thayer, Baltimore: Johns Hopkins Press, 1958, pp. 50–60. My talk was reprinted in *From Babel to Dragomans,* pp. 232–39.

In response to this very natural, indeed obvious, question, I tried to explain that for the vast majority of the Muslim peoples of the Middle East, country and ethnicity, the main determinants of identity and therefore of loyalty in Christian Europe, were of secondary and usually of minor importance. Both patriotism and nationalism, identity and loyalty by country and nation, were new and imperfectly assimilated concepts. The basic identity and therefore loyalty was religion. In the West we think of a nation subdivided into religions. In the Islamic world, they think rather of a religion subdivided into nations, subdivisions which, though locally important, are globally secondary. In the Middle East the Western nations, primarily seen as Christendom, are often perceived as one group, sometimes, though not usually, including Russia.

When I was working in the Turkish Archives in the 1950s, I stayed in Turkey rather longer than would be possible with a normal visitor's visa. I therefore had to apply for a temporary residence permit. There was no difficulty. I filled in the form, handed it in to the office and called a couple of days later to collect my permit. As I was walking away, I noticed that under the identity line, they had written the word "Protestant." I went back and said, "There's some mistake, you have written me down as a Protestant. I am not a Protestant, I am Jewish." The official said, "Well, you must have written 'Protestant' on your application form, otherwise we wouldn't have put it in." I said, "I most certainly didn't. I know what I am." So they looked and said, "You wrote 'English' and English means Protestant, everybody knows that." It took lengthy explanations and an appeal to a higher authority before I could get my residence permit corrected. A similar incident occurred in Tehran where an English colleague and I went together to get our residence permits. There, more explicitly than in Turkey, was a line for religion. My case presented no difficulty. I filled in my religion and received my permit. My friend had a problem. He had written down "Christian," and for the Iranian authorities this was insufficient. "We need to know what kind of Christian you are," they said. "Are you Greek, Armenian, Catholic, Orthodox or what?" He tried to explain that he came from a secular family and did not participate in any kind of worship but this was not acceptable and he finally had to chose one specific denomination. This enabled him to get a temporary residence permit.

By the mid-twentieth century there were already numerous indications of a growing awareness in the Islamic world of a common Muslim identity and of a common shared enemy in the global world of the unbelievers. Some examples: in November 1945 demonstrations were held in Egypt on the anniversary of the British publication of the Balfour Declaration. The organizers of the demonstration intended this as a protest against the British government and its Zionist protégés. It soon developed into an anti-Jewish riot and, more remarkably, into a more general anti-non-Muslim outbreak in the course of which several Catholic, Armenian and Greek Orthodox churches were attacked and damaged. A similar expansion of the enemy occurred in January 1952, when demonstrations were organized in Suez against the continuing British occupation of the Suez Canal. The anti-British demonstrators also looted and set fire to a Coptic church and killed a number of local Christians of various denominations. The Copts, with a history going back to antiquity, are surely the most authentically Egyptian of all the inhabitants of that country. As I write this book in late 2011, events have forced almost a hundred thousand Copts to leave Egypt. In the moments of passion, they have been seen as part of the enemy and treated accordingly. According to a saying attributed, probably falsely, to the Prophet, "Unbelief is one nation." That is to say, the world is divided basically into two, on the one hand the community of the true believers, on the other hand the world of the unbelievers, the subdivisions of which are small and of diminishing importance.

This religious perception was increased by such events as the Lebanese civil war of 1958 and the struggle in Iraq the following year between the nationalists and the communists. On March 17, 1959, a prayer was recited in Egyptian mosques and published on the front pages of the Egyptian papers for those who had been killed in Mosul. It included the following passage: "Oh God Almighty . . . strengthen the community of Thy Prophet with Thy favor and disdain for their enemy . . . in sincerity we call upon Thee, the blood of our martyrs we entrust to Thee . . . for the glory of Thy religion they shed their blood and died as martyrs: believing in Thee, they greeted the day of sacrifice blissfully. Therefore place them, O God, as companions with the upright and the martyrs and the righteous." The religious passion and fervor caused growing alarm among Christian minorities in Lebanon and elsewhere.

In the spring of 1967 a dramatic example of this new religious fervor occurred in Syria, at that time governed by a very secular military regime. On April 25 a young officer published an article in the army magazine setting forth a secularist, even in a sense an antireligious, view. Syria was and had been for some time ruled by a ruthless dictatorship in which the suppression of free speech, the confiscation of property and other misdeeds evoked no response. But the denial of God and religion in an officially sponsored journal revealed the limits of acquiescence, the point at which Muslim people were ready to stand up and resist. Protests erupted across the country. The government responded in various ways. The first was to arrest a number of religious leaders. That didn't help. They then proceeded to confiscate copies of the magazine containing the offending article and to arrest the author and the members of the editorial board. Finally, they resorted to what became in time the standard solution to all such difficulties. On May 7 Radio Damascus announced that "the sinful and insidious article published in the magazine *Jaysh al-Sha'b* came as a link in the chain of an American-Israeli reactionary conspiracy . . . investigation by the authorities has proved that the article and its author were merely tools of the CIA which has been able to infiltrate most basely and squalidly and to attain its sinful aims of creating confusion among the ranks of the citizens." Later, additional, equally authentic, details were provided. During the three years following this incident, more mosques were built in Syria than in the previous thirty years. The plot, they said, had been concerted with the Americans, the British, the Jordanians, the Saudis, the Zionists and a Druze opponent of the regime. On May 11 the author and editors were sentenced by a military court to life imprisonment.

From this time onward public expression of secularism of this kind virtually disappears. Even in Egypt, where the regime had its own problems with the militant religious opposition, Islam continued to serve as a main focus of identity and loyalty. Thus for example in a manual issued by the supreme command of the Egyptian forces in 1965, the wars against Israel and, surprisingly, in Yemen, are presented as a jihad, a holy war for God against the unbelievers. In reply to questions from the troops as to whether the classical Islamic obligation of jihad has lapsed or is still in force, orientation officers were instructed in the manual to reply that the jihad for God is still in force at the present time and is to be interpreted in our own day in terms of a striving for social justice and human betterment. The enemies against whom the jihad is to be waged are those who oppose or resist the achievement of these aims, that is to say, imperialism, Zionism, and the Arab reactionaries. "In accordance with this interpretation of the mission of Islam and in accordance with this understanding of the jihad, we must always maintain that our military duty in Yemen is a jihad and our military duty against Israel is a jihad for God. And for those who fight in this war there is the reward of fighters in the holy war for God . . . Our duty is the holy war for God. 'Kill them wherever you come upon them and drive them from the places from which they drove you' " (Koran 2:191). Similar ideas were found in the manual of orientation issued to Egyptian troops in

June 1973 and it is surely significant that the code name for the military operation of crossing the Canal was Badr, the name of one of the battles fought by the Prophet Muhammad against his infidel enemies. Curiously, the enemy named in the manual is not Zionism or Israel, but simply "the Jews."

Islam and Anti-Semitism

As I was born to a Jewish family in England, I was brought up in what has come to be known as the "Judeo-Christian tradition" of civilization. The term is a modern one; in earlier times it would have been equally resented on both sides of the hyphen. But the reality is an ancient one, going back to the first appearance of Christianity as a Jewish sect in the Holy Land. Though Christianity parted from Judaism and was often involved in bitter conflicts with its parent religion, the two nevertheless retained much in common, notably the Hebrew Bible which Christians renamed the Old Testament and to which they added a New Testament embodying their own revelations and doctrines.

Though the term is not commonly used, one might also speak of a Judeo-Islamic tradition of civilization. From the destruction of the ancient Jewish state to the creation of the modern Jewish state Jews have everywhere been a minority, principally, indeed overwhelmingly, among Christians and Muslims. There have been Jewish communities elsewhere, for example in India and China, but it is surely significant that they appear to have played no role of any importance in the history or culture of those countries or of the Jewish people. Perhaps this is because those communities were small or perhaps because for Jewishness to flourish it needs to receive some attention, some recognition.

The Judeo-Islamic tradition differs from the Judeo-Christian tradition in several important respects. The Muslims, of course, retain neither the Old nor the New Testament, regarding both as super-seded by their own final revelation, the Koran. But the Muslims have much in common with the Jews that Christians either neglected or rejected. Notable among these is the idea of a holy law regulating every aspect of public and personal life. Some of the regulations are indeed strikingly similar, for example, the rejection by both Judaism and Islam of pork.

Both Jews and Muslims were aware of these and other affinities. In the Middle Ages, when Jews in both the Islamic and Christian worlds were sometimes persecuted to the point of martyrdom, a rabbi decreed that it was permissible to feign conversion to Islam in order to survive, but not to Christianity. Believing neither, it was less blas-phemous to say that Muhammad was a prophet of God than to say that Jesus was the son of God. On another level, when the first Mus-lim students were sent by their governments to Europe at the begin-ning of the nineteenth century, they were told that they might eat Jewish, but not Christian, food. Jews observe the same basic rules as Muslims; Christians will eat anything.

These affinities, and my growing awareness of them, certainly helped me to achieve some understanding, even a sympathetic under-standing, of Islam, despite the growing tension between Jews and Muslims over the issue of Palestine. It has helped me within my stud-ies of Islamic literature and history and my personal dealings with Muslims, both at home and abroad. Unfortunately, it does not seem to have had much effect in creating better relations between Israelis and Palestinians. One may still hope that it may do so at some time in the future.

The Jewish population of Israel and indeed of the world is tradi-tionally divided into main groups, Ashkenazi and Sefardi. Ashkenaz and Sefarad are two place-names mentioned in the Bible, but of un-certain identity. I am inclined to think that the biblical Ashkenaz refers to the Black Sea region, and may be related to the Greek name

Euxinos. But conventionally, from the early Middle Ages, Jewish usage identified these names with Germany and Spain, the two most important Jewish communities in Europe. The Jews of Spain, after a period of persecution, were finally expelled in 1492, and the great majority of them found refuge in the Ottoman Empire. The Jews of Ashkenaz migrated eastward, and formed what later became the large and important Jewish communities of Poland, Lithuania and Russia. In Israel at the present time the term Ashkenazi is applied principally to Jews of European origin, whether from eastern or western Europe or beyond. The term Sefardic is applied not only to the descendants of the émigrés of Spain, but also to the native Jews of Egypt, Syria, Iraq, Iran, Afghanistan and Yemen, whose ancestors had never been anywhere near Spain.

Looking at both groups, at the differences and encounters between them, and at the traditions and attitudes they had brought with them from their countries of origin, I came to realize that the real division was not geographic or sectarian or communal; it was a meeting, and resulting clash of civilizations between what one might call the Christian Jews and the Muslim Jews.

This is obviously an absurd statement, so let me explain what I mean. Judaism is a religion, a culture, a way of life. It is not a civilization; Jews never had either the numbers or the freedom to create a civilization of their own. But they were an important component in two other civilizations, the one Christian, the other Islamic. Christians and Jews share many things, starting with the Old Testament, and the whole religious culture that is based on it. Even when outlawed and persecuted, Jews were an important part of Western civilization to which they made a significant contribution.

There has been quite a lot of argument of late about whether or not there is a tradition of anti-Semitism in the Islamic Middle East. Some say it is there, right from the beginnings of Islam; others say that it is a modern innovation introduced from the West, more specifically from Christendom. In discussing this it might be useful to begin with a definition of anti-Semitism. It is not sufficient to define anti-Semitism as hating Jews. Hating people who are different is normal. Hating and, where convenient, persecuting people who are different is the normal pattern of human nature and behavior. We find it in every society and every place. Some historians talk for example about anti-Semitism in the Greco-Roman world, and adduce various Greek and Roman texts attacking Jews. I do not think one can call that anti-Semitism. They are no different and in some respects not as bad as some of the texts in Latin and Greek attacking other groups of people who are different. A choice example is when the historian Ammianus Marcellinus remarked about the Saracens that they are desirable neither as friends nor as enemies. I do not recall any classical remark about Jews as nasty as that. Anti-Semitism is a different hostility. It is one which attributes a quality of innate and cosmic evil to the Jews.

That is distinctively Christian, and is obviously connected with the narrative of the crucifixion. This approach developed in medieval Christian Europe and went through a number of transformations, the most notable one being in the late Middle Ages, when numbers of Jews were converted or pretended to be converted and the Inquisition was set up to detect false converts. That introduced a racial element, examining a convert's ancestors in order to determine whether he was or was not Jewish, even if he claimed to be Christian. That was again transformed in nineteenth-century Germany, when the term anti-Semitism was first used and the attack on Jews was defined quite explicitly in racial terms.

In the Muslim world, and more specifically in the Arab world, the history is quite different. Obviously Jews were not the equals of Muslims; they were regarded, as were Christians, as inferiors to the true believers, and the holy law of Islam discriminates against Jews and Christians in various ways. In most of medieval and early modern Islamic history, Jews seemed to have fared rather better than Christians. It is true that in the Koran and in the narrative of the life of the Prophet, the tone is more favorable to Christians than to Jews. That's because the Prophet had few if any dealings with Christians, but did have a number of quarrels with Jews. In the subsequent development of Islam, after the death of the Prophet, Christendom was the main rival and enemy, and Jews were unimportant and at times even useful. So the attitude to Jews was different. I wouldn't say it was friendly but it was more tolerant than toward Christians. This continued into the Ottoman period, when Jews were found to be extremely useful—a valuable, revenue-producing asset.

The change came in phases. One was the introduction of European-style anti-Semitism into the Middle East, mainly by Arab Christians who translated anti-Semitic texts, especially from French, and distributed them. This happened particularly at the time of the Dreyfus affair in the 1870s, though there are signs of it earlier, and of course it continued after.

This process was enormously accelerated after the accession to power of the Nazis, who won considerable support among the Arabs and were able to disseminate the Nazi version of anti-Semitism very widely in the Arab world. The third phase came with what one might call the Islamization of anti-Semitism. In the second phase it was more or less secular, national, or perhaps what we nowadays call "racist." In this latest phase, it is given a religious coloration and the attempt is made to justify it in terms of Islam, the Prophet, and the sacred writings and traditions.

For many years Jews could not visit most Arab countries. An amusing story is that in the early 1970s Henry Kissinger, as part of his shuttle diplomacy, went to Saudi Arabia. Of course they knew he was Jewish but he was the Secretary of State of the United States and they had to let him in to see the King. King Faisal just could not let it pass that a Jew came to Saudi Arabia and his welcoming sentence to Kissinger was, "Secretary Kissinger, we receive you here as a human being." Kissinger, never short of a response, said, "Some of my best friends are human beings."

The Return of Islam

In the early 1970s I was in India as a visiting professor when I was informed by the University of London that a decision had been made to appoint me as its representative to a conference in Australia. The reason I was chosen was very simple: I was in India. It would cost less to send me from India than to send someone from home. I looked into the ways of getting from India to Australia, and found that the most convenient way was to change flights in Singapore, where I had never been. I decided to spend several days there. A former student from SOAS was teaching at the University of Singapore. I got in touch with him, told him I'd be stopping in Singapore and asked that he book a hotel room for me. He replied that he had booked a room and would meet me at my flight. I thought that was very nice of him.

On the day of my arrival he picked me up, took me to the hotel and said, "By the way, you have an appointment at ten o'clock tomorrow morning with the Prime Minister, Lee Kwan Yew." You can imagine that I was more than a little startled. I asked, "But why?" "We thought he'd be interested to meet you," he said. "We asked him, and he was."

The next morning, with some apprehension, I turned up at Lee Kwan Yew's office at ten o'clock and he got straight down to business, without any ceremonies or politeness. He said, "I understand you're a specialist on Islam. We have a problem. In Singapore we have a Muslim minority, partly Malay, partly from South Asia. We do everything we can to help them. We give them preferential treatment in school and in the university, in government employment, and for businesspeople in the awarding of government contracts. We do everything we can to help them. Don't misunderstand me. I'm no bleeding-heart liberal, but the last thing we need here, between two large Muslim countries, Indonesia and Malaysia, is a discontented Muslim minority. Now," he said, "despite everything we do to help them, they keep sinking to the bottom of the pile. I have two questions for you, Why are they like that, and what can we do about it?" I provided an inadequate answer to the first question and none at all to the second.

From the 1970s onward, to anyone following events in the Muslim world and reading or listening to what Muslims were saying in their own languages, the surge in religious passion was increasingly obvious. In January 1976 I tried to draw attention to this in an article entitled "The Return of Islam," published in the monthly magazine *Commentary*. I shall take the liberty of quoting from it at some length here, as it has held up to the test of time:

> If . . . we are to understand anything at all about what is happening in the Muslim world at the present time and what has happened in the past, there are two essential points which need to be grasped. One is the universality of religion as a factor in the lives of the Muslim peoples, and the other is its centrality . . . For the Muslim, religion traditionally was not only universal but also central in the sense that it constituted the essential basis and focus of identity and loyalty. It was religion which distinguished those who belonged to the group and marked them off from those outside the group. A Muslim Iraqi would feel far closer bonds with a non-Iraqi Muslim than with a non-Muslim Iraqi . . .
>
> Islam from its inception is a religion of power, and in the Muslim world view it is right and proper that power should be wielded by Muslims and Muslims alone. Others may receive the tolerance, even the benevolence, of the Muslim state, provided that they clearly recognize Muslim supremacy. That Muslims

should rule over non-Muslims is right and normal. That non-Muslims should rule over Muslims is an offense against the laws of God and nature, and this is true whether in Kashmir, Palestine, Lebanon, or Cyprus. Here again, it must be recalled that Islam is not conceived as a religion in the limited Western sense, but as a community, a loyalty, and a way of life—and that the Islamic community is still recovering from the traumatic era when Muslim governments and empires were overthrown and Muslim peoples forcibly subjected to alien, infidel rule. Both the Saturday people and the Sunday people are now suffering the consequences.

In the late 1970s I visited Córdoba, in Spain, to attend a conference of Islamic studies. A number of my Turkish colleagues and friends attended the same conference. I was delighted to see them and was standing and chatting with them, in Turkish, when someone came and said he would like to speak to us. He explained that he was from the local Islamic center and would like to invite us, if we were willing, to visit that center. His invitation included me, obviously on the mistaken assumption that I also was a Turk. This seemed too good an opportunity to miss. I went along with my Turkish colleagues and we had an extremely interesting visit. At the Islamic center our hosts explained their perception of the situation and their own role in dealing with it. This place (i.e., Spain), they said with some passion, was for centuries part of the lands of Islam. It is an ancient Islamic country but it was captured by the infidels and its people forcibly converted to Christianity. All these people around us, they said, are the descendants of Muslims whom they conquered and forced to betray their faith. It is now our duty to restore these people to the true faith and to bring this country back into the House of Islam where it belongs.

They were not alone in this perception. When I was working on my book *The Muslim Discovery of Europe* I read a number of Moroccan Embassy reports from Spain, mainly from the eighteenth century. When the Moroccans mentioned the name of a place, a city or district, they usually added the formula, "May God speedily restore it to Islam."

In Córdoba, with my Turkish colleagues, I visited the famous cathedral which in earlier times had been a mosque, the Mesquita. One of the Turks who was moderately religious said, "When I come into this ancient shrine, this former mosque, I feel that I should recite the afternoon prayer." His friends were horrified, and tried to persuade him not to do it. "Don't make a scandal," they said. "That's the last thing we need." But the more they pressed him not to, the more eager he became to do just that. "We must be proud, not afraid, of our heritage," he insisted. Suddenly one of them had an idea and said, "If some Greek were to come into Hagia Sofia [a former Greek church, then a Turkish mosque, then a museum in Istanbul] and start celebrating Mass, how would you feel?" He immediately saw the point, and desisted.

I had in the course of my travels come to appreciate a subtle distinction in Muslim countries in the relationship between identity and group affiliation. In most Western countries, when you drink with somebody, you drink to their health. In Turkey you drink to someone's honor. This raises interesting reflections regarding the general position and meaning of honor in different societies. Western society is sometimes called a duty/guilt society, in which you are impelled by duty and feel guilt if you fail in that duty. In contrast, Islamic society has been described as an honor/shame society. What really matters is honor, and if your honor is violated the result is shame. Duty/guilt is obviously personal. Honor/shame affects one's family and one's group. One might distinguish it this way: duty/guilt is subjective and personal, in other words it is internal; honor/shame reflects how you are perceived by others, your reputation, your standing in the society to which you belong or of which you are a part. It is external. So-called "honor killings" are part of the Middle Eastern tradition. Far from being approved by Islam, they are condemned and forbidden by Islamic law, but with limited effect.

Three years after my article appeared in *Commentary*, Americans and Europeans in general would find themselves suddenly far more keenly interested in the subject of political Islam.

The Iranian Revolution

In 1979 a major change took place in the Middle East, the Revolution in Iran. The terms "revolution" and "revolutionary" have been much used in the modern Middle East. Indeed, revolution nowadays is the only generally accepted title to legitimacy and has been claimed and used by a variety of personal, sectional, regional and tribal ruling cliques. But the Iranian Revolution was a genuine revolution in the sense in which we use that word when we speak of the French and Russian revolutions. It signaled a major shift of power, with a major ideological basis and argument. Like the French and Russian revolutions, it had an immense impact in the whole region with which Iran shared a common universe of discourse, namely, the world of Islam. I was on a lecture tour in Indonesia not long after the Iranian Revolution and was surprised to find portraits of Khomeini proudly posted in student dormitories. I am told that there were similar responses as far away as Morocco and Central Asia.

The rise and spread of anti-Americanism, which was such an important feature of the Iranian Revolution, were not the result of specific American policies or actions. They derived from Soviet propaganda and followed from the perception that America was now the leading power of the Western world, or more specifically, of Christendom—the historic rival and adversary of Islam.

One of the more striking features of the fallout from the Iranian Revolution was what has been called the "meek" American response to the seizure of the American Embassy. For a long time, no attempt was made to rescue the beleaguered American diplomats who were held hostage in the embassy for over a year. When finally an attempt was made, it was a ludicrous failure.

The Iranian hostage crisis and the reactions of the various parties to that crisis provide an instructive lesson on the different attitudes of different societies to problems. It seems clear from what we know now from Iranian memoirs and other sources that when the American Embassy was first seized there was no intention of keeping the hostages for any length of time, and apparently the seizure of the embassy did not even have the approval of the Supreme Chief Khomeini. But the meek response of Washington rapidly convinced Khomeini and the hostage takers that they were onto a good thing and that they could do very much better by continuing to keep the hostages, as indeed they did.

President Jimmy Carter's letter appealing to Khomeini as one believer to another, the American rejection of the Shah, and the unwillingness to help a former friend, all helped to convince people in Iran, and elsewhere in the Middle East, that it was safer and more profitable to be an enemy rather than a friend of the United States. It had already become known during the Cold War that if you said or did anything to annoy the Russians, punishment would be swift and dire. If you said or did anything against the Americans, not only would there be no punishment, but there might even be some reward, as a procession of diplomats, congressmen, journalists, and alas I must add professors came with the anxious inquiry, "Oh, what have we done to offend you? What can we do to put it right?"

The Iranian crisis had further consequences. It convinced the Russians that they could proceed with the invasion of Afghanistan and not worry about any Muslim or American reaction. In this they were right, but they underrated the Afghan reaction. The ending of the Tehran crisis was also instructive. It followed the election of Ronald Reagan, about whom the Iranians knew nothing, but whom they perceived as a cowboy who would come out of his corner with his six-shooters drawn, and was ready to use them. They immediately released the hostages and ended the crisis on his Inauguration Day.

The Iranian Revolution made Washington pay attention to political Islam and that attention grew during the 1980s and 1990s. My historical studies suddenly became relevant and I was called to Washington more frequently to participate in conferences and speak at think tanks. Over the course of my life I have watched the world of Islam shift from the realm of musty archives and academic conferences to the evening news.

At Castel Gandolfo with Pope John Paul II

When the Polish Cardinal Vojtyla was elected Pope John Paul II in 1978, this marked a major event not only in the Roman Catholic Church but more broadly in Europe and indeed, in a sense, in the whole world. Cardinal Vojtyla was the first non-Italian to be elected to the papacy in many centuries. More importantly, he was the first ever to be elected from that profoundly and strongly Catholic country Poland, and this at a time when Poland, along with most of the rest of Eastern Europe, was subject to a Communist dictatorship, imposed and maintained by a superpower, the Soviet Union. The election of a Pole to probably the most important position in all Christendom seems to have caused some concern to the Communist authorities. It also brought a wave of hope to the Polish people.

From the beginning of his tenure, Pope John Paul II was determined to do something to help his fellow countrymen and other victims of the Communist dictatorships in Eastern Europe. But this was not easy. The trade union strikes led by Lech Walesa in Gdańsk had already shown both the possibilities and the difficulties of such action. After careful consideration and consultation, Pope John Paul decided that even the Communist masters of Poland could hardly object to his inviting several of his compatriots to spend a few days as his guests in the papal summer residence at Castel Gandolfo, in the hills not far from Rome. In the 1980s he began, tentatively, to invite small groups of Polish friends and colleagues to spend a little while, during the summer, as his houseguests. Polish authorities kept this under careful supervision but did not forbid or obstruct it. At the same time he invited groups of other guests from the West—carefully chosen people with shared professions, interests and concerns with the Polish guests, who were thereby given the chance to have free, unobstructed conversations with their Western colleagues.

In choosing his Western guests, the Pope sought the advice and help of his compatriot Krysztof Michalski, a Polish social scientist who had lived for some time in Vienna, and who was the founder and director of the Institute for the Human Sciences in that city. The institute granted fellowships of varying duration, arranged conferences, and sponsored publications. It was particularly concerned with promoting dialogue between East and West. I had for some time been a fairly frequent visitor at the institute, where, as guest of Krysztof Michalski, I was able to play some small part in this dialogue.

It was to Michalski that the Pope went for advice on whom to invite from the Western world, and it was, I must assume, on Michalski's advice that I was invited. From 1987 to 1998 he convened a series of meetings, in most of which I participated. The meetings were held at two- or three-year intervals, each devoted to one overarching theme with participants from both sides. Papers were submitted for discussion, and these were published in a series of volumes, both in Polish and in German. Papers of mine were published in five of these volumes.

Apart from, and perhaps more important than, the formal meetings were the informal contacts and associations between the Pope's two groups of guests, a unique and invaluable experience for both groups. We were guests of the Pope and he was at all times a gracious and interesting host.

He used to give three dinner parties arranged by language. On one occasion there were simply not enough French speakers or Italian speakers to justify an evening to themselves. They were forced to fit in with the English or German speakers. The Pope spoke English very well but he didn't understand it as well as he spoke. I've been a teacher all my life and I know when people understand me and when they don't. They say, "Oh yes. Really. Is that so?" but I am not deceived. Sometimes the difficulties in understanding created a little awkwardness. At one dinner the question of Islam came up and he remarked that the theology of Islam is very simple. I responded that it was to start with but then the theologians came and they complicated it. The others at the table, the British and Americans, laughed, a small, polite laugh. The Pope did not understand and he asked that I repeat the silly little quip three or four times by which time I just wished I could disappear under the table.

On my last visit the Pope was obviously in deteriorating health and his English wasn't as good as it had been. That doesn't surprise me because I need help myself, too, as I grow older and become less inclined, and also less able, to speak foreign languages. Perhaps it's laziness but it is a disinclination to make the extra effort that is needed to talk in a foreign language. I still recall a few of his remarks, which I feel free to repeat. In 1998, it will be recalled, the Pope, to everyone's surprise, went at the invitation of Fidel Castro on a visit to Cuba. At the dinner table after his return one of his American guests asked him whether this meant that Castro was preparing to rejoin the church. The Pope hesitated a moment and then said, "I wouldn't put it that way. I think that Señor Castro is looking for what I believe you call in English 'a soft landing.'" On another occasion he was asked by one of his Jewish guests what his attitude was, as Pope, to Jews and Judaism. His reply was truly memorable, "As to an elder brother." The profundity of this remark grows on you.

I was invited to a meeting in Vienna in the 1980s which was hosted by the Cardinal Archbishop of Vienna, Franz Koenig, a very fine man. It was a meeting of Christians and Jews. The Archbishop of York was there and dignitaries of both religions and a number of what you might call unattached intellectuals, unattached in the sense of not having any formal religious position. The Cardinal Archbishop welcomed us and spoke of the importance of tolerance. When it was my turn to speak I quoted a letter of George Washington in which he said, "Let us no more speak of tolerance as if it were by the indulgence of one class of people that others enjoy the exercise of their inherent natural rights." To my surprise and delight the Cardinal Archbishop responded by saying I was quite right and he would no longer speak of tolerance but of mutual respect. That enormously increased my already considerable respect for Koenig. It takes a great man to respond so forthrightly. It would have been so easy to just pass my comment off or ignore it.

When the intellectual arm of the Christian Democratic Party in Italy held a colloquium not long after that on what is called in Italian *alterità,* or "otherness," I was asked to give a talk on the Islamic view of the other, a subject which has always interested me. When I got to Rome I was told that there were three panels, one on religious otherness, one on ethnic otherness and mine, which grouped together various elements—social, economic and so on. I asked if they meant other otherness and they said they hadn't put it that way but that's about what they meant.

When I went to my panel I saw there were three talks on the agenda, one on the Jewish attitude, one on the Christian attitude and one on the Muslim attitude toward the other, more or less what I expected. What I did not expect, and found very disconcerting, was that the Jewish attitude was presented by a rabbi, the Christian attitude by a Catholic priest and the Muslim attitude toward the other was presented by me, putting me in something of a false position. It's true that there was some concession to otherness in that the rabbi was the former chief rabbi of Ireland and the Catholic priest was an Israeli Arab so they were, in a sense, "other" in their own communities. Nevertheless, the rabbi was a genuine rabbi and the priest was a genuine priest. I began my remarks by saying, "Far be it from me to criticize the organizers of the colloquium who did me the honor of inviting me, but I am in no sense a representative or spokesman for Islam. I am not a mullah." The priest sitting next to me said, "No, you're a mufti," which didn't help. A mufti is of higher rank and is one who is authorized to issue a fatwa, a ruling on some point of theology or law.

Shortly after this the rabbi from Ireland played an important role. He was one of the two intermediaries who negotiated the agreement between the Vatican and the government of Israel to establish diplomatic relations. I found it amusing that when Rome and Jerusalem finally decided to talk to each other, it was a rabbi from Dublin who helped bring them together.

The Roots of Muslim Rage and the Clash of Civilizations

In May 1990 I was selected by the National Endowment for the Humanities to receive the annual Jefferson Award. This involved giving a major lecture and delivering it in Washington and again on the West Coast. The subject I chose was "Western Civilization: A View from the East." A slightly shortened version was published in the *Atlantic Monthly* in September 1990, called "The Roots of Muslim Rage: Why so many Muslims deeply resent the West, and why their bitterness will not easily be mollified." I endeavored to draw attention to the growing anger in the Muslim world, and to the forms and direction in which this anger was expressed.

By then it had become popular to refer to the hard-line elements in political Islam as "Islamic Fundamentalism." I tried in the article to point out why this was misleading. Fundamentalism is a much misused word. It dates back to about 1910, when certain Protestant churches who wished to differentiate themselves from the mainstream churches published a series of pamphlets called *The Fundamentals,* in which they took up positions strongly and sharply different from those of the Presbyterians and the Episcopalians and the other main-line Protestant churches. There were two things to which they objected: one was liberal theology, and the other was Bible criticism. They insisted on the literal divinity and inerrancy of the Bible. At some point in the 1980s it became customary to use this same word, fundamentalism, of certain Muslim groups. It was unfortunate because these groups did not in the least bit resemble American Protestant Fundamentalists. They had different issues and certainly different tactics. I objected to the term, but we are now stuck with it. The word is now used principally of the Muslim Fundamentalists, and secondarily of the American Protestants. In fact it is now used universally and not only in English: the French talk about *"les fondamentalistes"* and the Germans talk about *"die Fundamentalisten."*

It is rather like the word "ghetto," which has been re-semanticized, so to speak. Originally ghetto was a neighborhood in a European city to which Jews were confined by law. Now, it is no longer European, it no longer concerns Jews, and it's no longer defined by law. The word "ghetto" in modern American usage has a completely different meaning, which has in effect supplanted the older one. I think this is true of "fundamentalist." Today, when we talk about fundamentalists, we are thinking of Muslims, not of the ones who originally took out the patent on the name.

Muslim Fundamentalists are not worried about liberal theology because there isn't any, and they are not worried about criticism of the Koran because that has not been an issue. Muslims believe in the literal divinity and inerrancy of the Koran text. But that's not the point. The Fundamentalists are concerned about something quite different, which is what they see as the de-Islamization of Islamic countries. What they want is to restore the Holy Law of Islam (Shari'a), to remove legal codes which have been imported from abroad, and to restore the full panoply of Islamic Law. They have an encyclopedia of grievances, the most important of which is the emancipation of women. In the speeches of Khomeini and the writings of the other Fundamentalists, that outranks all the other grievances by far.

I believe that the repression of women has caused enormous damage to Islamic society. Not only is it depriving itself of the talents and services of half the population; it is also entrusting the nurture of much of the other half to uneducated and downtrodden mothers. At the present time there is a very interesting shift in emphasis from class to sex, and a new tendency in historical studies to consider the role of women. I see this as the major change in our times in the perception of what happened, and, more particularly, of what went wrong in Middle Eastern society. Women are after all half the population, and in many ways a much more important group than any religious, ethnic or economically defined entity.

Atatürk, the first president and founder of the Turkish Republic, saw this. He began to campaign for the emancipation of women back in the 1920s. In a series of speeches, his recurring theme was: "Our most urgent task at the present time is to modernize, to catch up with the modern world. We shall not succeed in catching up with the modern world if we only modernize half the population." Others have seen that since. Over the course of the last sixty years I have seen Atatürk's efforts to transform women into equal participants in the professional and political life of their country reversed, both in Turkey and in other countries in the region which were for a time in thrall to the Soviets.

"The Roots of Muslim Rage" was a cover story in the *Atlantic*, and provoked significant interest in the wider media. I was asked to appear on various television and radio shows, and invitations to conferences and study groups in Washington proliferated. In 1993 Samuel P. Huntington wrote an article in *Foreign Affairs* offering an alternative vision of post–Cold War geopolitics to the influential end-of-history thesis advocated by Francis Fukuyama. Huntington graciously acknowledged that he had borrowed the phrase which he used as the title of his article from my *Atlantic Monthly* article, in which I referred to a "clash between civilizations." Huntington developed the theme in his book *The Clash of Civilizations,* which was deservedly a best seller and has become a fixture in many college courses. I think he made a real contribution to our better understanding of one of the great problems of our time.

Anti-Americanism

Since the Iranian Revolution, a common refrain in the writings of Muslim political agitators (including Osama bin Ladin) is that the Americans, because of their depraved and self-indulgent way of life, have become soft and cannot take casualties. The message, as perceived, was clear: "Hit them and they will run." This view is supported by the same narrative of events:

- abandonment of Vietnam

- impotence during the 444 days of the Iranian hostage crisis in 1979

- 1983 attacks in Beirut at the U.S. Embassy and the U.S. Marine Corps HQ

- the withdrawal from Beirut in 1984 and Somalia in 1993, after being attacked

- 1993 attack on the World Trade Center in New York

- attack on an American military mission in Riyad in 1995

- the Khobar Towers, a U.S. barracks in Saudi Arabia destroyed by a bomb in 1996

- coordinated attacks on U.S. embassies in Kenya and Tanzania in 1998

All told, hundreds were killed in these attacks and thousands were injured. This brought angry words from the U.S. government and, at most, a few misdirected missiles. The conclusion that Muslim extremists drew from all this, which they clearly stated, was that the United States had become feeble and frightened, incapable of responding to attack.

On February 23, 1998, an Arabic newspaper in London printed the full text of a "Declaration of the world Islamic front for jihad against the Jews and the Crusaders," faxed to them over the signature of Osama bin Ladin. He blamed the United States for masterminding the bombing of the American embassies in East Africa in August. The document made it clear that its author, a Saudi, was much more concerned with the Crusaders than with the Jews, who receive only brief mention, and that by "the Crusaders" he means, primarily, the United States. Later, when he realized that attacking Israel was very effective in rallying support, he realigned his priorities and put greater emphasis on demonizing the Jewish state.

> Since God laid down the Arabian peninsula, created its deserts, and surrounded it with its seas, no calamity has ever befallen it like these Crusader hosts that have spread in it like locusts, crowding its soil, eating its fruits, and destroying its verdure; and this at a time when the nations contend against the Muslims like diners jostling around a bowl of food.
>
> First—for more than seven years the United States is oc-

cupying the lands of Islam in the holiest of its territories, Arabia, plundering its riches, overwhelming its rulers, humiliating its people, threatening its neighbors, and using its bases in the peninsula to fight against the neighboring Islamic peoples . . . [An odd way of describing American help in response to Arabia's appeal.]

By God's leave we call on every Muslim who believes in God and hopes for reward to obey God's command to kill the Americans and plunder their possessions wherever he finds them and wherever he can. Likewise we call on the Muslim ulema and leaders and youth and soldiers to launch attacks against the armies of the American devils and those who are allied with them from among the helpers of Satan . . .

The importance, indeed the major importance, of this document was obvious to anyone who could read and understand Arabic. But those were few, and of the few many, for obvious reasons, preferred to be silent. I felt it necessary to break this silence and make the document known, and published a description and abridged translation in the November/December 1998 issue of *Foreign Affairs,* under the title "License to Kill."

Osama bin Ladin's Declaration of War demanded a new perspective, one in which movements in the Middle East were no longer seen in traditional terms as local, national, regional or as anti-imperial. The new militant Islamic global struggle was a renewal of a conflict that began with the advent of Islam in the seventh century.

As a close watcher of both events and discourse in the Muslim world, I was appalled but not surprised by the events and attacks of 9/11. As the militants saw it, they had completed the first phase on the path toward Muslim domination—the expulsion of the infidels and their armies from the lands of Islam. The next and final step was to carry the battle into the enemy's homeland to inaugurate the final global struggle between the true believers and the unbelievers for the mastery of the world and bring about the final universal triumph of their cause.

Americans had many questions about who these attackers were and why this happened.

It so happened that the September 11 attacks coincided with the publication of one of my books, *What Went Wrong? Western Impact and Middle Eastern Response,* which appeared in stores weeks later, and to everyone's surprise, not least to that of the publishers, it became an instant best seller. This is not a common experience in the world of academic publishing, for authors or publishers, and this instant success brought a mixture of joy and bewilderment. A second book, *The Crisis of Islam: Holy War and Unholy Terror,* appeared a year later, and that also became a best seller. I thus had the unique experience of having two best sellers concurrently. My son gave me a delightful present at the time, a beautifully laminated plaque showing the best-seller lists from the Sunday *New York Times* of April 27, 2003. *What Went Wrong* was number one on the paperback list and *The Crisis of Islam* was number one on the hardcover list.

Osama bin Ladin made me famous. I was interviewed, quoted, filmed and I even made the front page of *The Wall Street Journal.* I remember remarking at the time that if bin Ladin claimed a percentage of my royalties for promoting the book, I would have to admit there was some justice in his claim. Two simultaneous best sellers brought other consequences—translations into many languages, lecture invitations, unending requests for interviews and the like. And it brought a significant, albeit temporary, improvement in my financial status.

A number of my books have been translated into many languages*

---

*The languages: EUROPE: Albanian, Bulgarian, Czech, Danish, Dutch, French, German, Greek, Hungarian, Italian, Macedonian, Norwegian, Polish, Portuguese, Romanian, Russian, Serbo-Croat, Spanish, Swedish. MIDDLE EAST: Arabic, Hebrew, Persian, Turkish. ASIA: Chinese, Indonesian, Japanese, Korean, Malay, Urdu.

and usually the translation has had more or less the same title as the original. But *What Went Wrong?* seems to have caused trouble to many translators. In some languages, for example in Danish, they found an exact equivalent of the English phrase. But in many languages, including the most widely used, they apparently found no way of rendering this simple, everyday English phrase into their language. The French translation was called *Que c'est-il passé?* When I was informed of this by the French publisher, I pointed out that in French that simply means "What happened?" which is not the same as "What went wrong?" to which the French publisher replied rather coldly, "If something goes wrong, that is what a Frenchman would ask." The Italian translation was more imaginative; the book was entitled *The Suicide of Islam.* The German translation evoked the memory of a famous book by Oswald Spengler, *The Decline of the West,* or literally *The Decline of the Evening Land.* The German translation of my book was entitled *The Decline of the Morning Land,* i.e., the decline of the East—an excellent title. I have no idea what my publishers did with the translations into Chinese, Japanese and other languages that I don't know.

The prompt response against Al-Qaida bases in Afghanistan no doubt came as a shock to the terrorist organizations and obliged them to revise some of their earlier assessments. But the general perception of American weakness and demoralization remains, and is encouraged by the processes, wholly unfamiliar and therefore incomprehensible to them, in which a democratic society discusses and debates its problems.

The Media

The Western media mostly "get" the Middle East wrong. I would divide the errors or misrepresentations into two categories—honest ignorance and dishonest bias. Two familiar American phrases are often turned on their heads. "No news is good news" has been re-versed to "Good news is no news." The other, "My country, right or wrong," has become "My country, wrong."

In all my travels in the Middle East I have met many correspon-dents and only two really had a mastery of Arabic language and culture—one was American and the other Japanese. Both were good Arabic scholars and both had done their Arabic studies in the United States. But they were exceptional in having done their homework.

I have been interviewed many times, by journalists and others, in many countries. These interviews fall broadly into two distinct cate-gories. In the first the interviewer comes with his list of questions, prepared in advance. He may or may not listen to your answers; there is no clear evidence one way or the other. When you finish your an-swer, or are interrupted, the interviewer proceeds to his second ques-tion, irrespective of where you are in the narrative. There is no follow-up. The same thing happens with his third, fourth and any subsequent questions that he may have.

The other kind of interview, very much rarer, is one in which the interviewer actually listens. In effect he comes only with an outline and a first question, listens to what you have to say until you finish your remarks, and then poses a second question arising from your answer to his first. In the same way his third question often arises from the second and so on.

In my experience, the first kind of interview is usually a bore, for the participants as well as for the audience. The second is far more interesting and can even be of value. I suppose, applying economic principles, one might say that its value is increased by its rarity. In my experience I have had many examples of the first kind, very few of the second.

A few years ago I was interviewed by a German journalist on my views on the general situation in Europe and I drew attention to the growing Muslim presence due to immigration, conversion and demography and remarked that if this continued unabated probably by the end of the twenty-first century Europe would have a Muslim majority population. The interview was published in a German newspaper and surprisingly attracted enormous worldwide attention, both positive and negative. As far as I can make out, this was the first occasion in which anyone actually drew attention to this possibility. Not long after this I had a telephone call from an Italian journalist asking to interview me. I said, "What about?" He said, "About the growing Muslim presence in Europe and especially in Italy and how can we defend ourselves and our identity?" "The answer is simple," I said. "Marry young and have children." That was not what he wanted to hear. He slammed down the receiver and I never heard from him again.

Since then this issue has attracted increasing attention from quarters all over Europe.

Right after September 11, I published a fourteen-page article called "The Revolt of Islam" in *The New Yorker* (November 19, 2001). The content is indicated by the subtitle, "A new turn in a long war with the West." I was surprised and delighted that this article was selected for the George Polk Award for magazine reporting, which was duly presented to me and to representatives of *The New Yorker* at a quite elaborate ceremony in New York.

The reason I was surprised is that I am by profession a historian; that is to say, I deal with the past. Not only that; I am a retired historian so even my past is, so to speak, passé. It was therefore with surprise bordering on bewilderment that I found myself the recipient of an award for reporting. Among journalists, it has long been the custom, if you wish to describe a colleague's work as obscure and irrelevant, to call it academic; similarly, in academic circles, when we wish to criticize a colleague's work as glib and superficial, we call it journalistic. But I have learned over the years that behind this reciprocal exchange of insults between our professions, there is a hidden urge toward emulation, with a corresponding desire for recognition. It was for this reason that my initial feelings of surprise were soon overwhelmed in the flood of gratification and gratitude.

Interestingly, *The New Yorker* did not ask me to write for them again; this article was obviously not in accord with their worldview. They did however publish a not very attractive portrait of me in an article on the great photographer Richard Avedon and his work in November 2004. Somewhat mysteriously, I am preceded by some union leaders and followed by Bill O'Reilly and James Carville. Avedon and I each found the other surprisingly interesting and we had an unusually long conversation over a wide range of topics.

10.

Orientalism and
the Cult of Right Thinking

Anyone who studies the evolution of a civilization must, in the course of time, devote some thought to the broader and more general aspects of his topic, as distinct from the more specific objects of his immediate research. Any writer or teacher of history must periodically mentally explore the larger implications of the historic process. And, on a more mundane level, any professional scholar must at times pause and consider the state and needs of the field of scholarship in which he works, more especially when, as now, this field, and indeed scholarship itself, are under attack.

There is a current school of thought which says that history can only be written by insiders—that Arab history must be written by Arabs and no one else, and that Muslim history can only be written by Muslims and Patagonian history can only be written by Patagonians and so on. This has had some echo on the American campus, for example, in various kinds of ethnic studies. This is a dangerous trend because it leads to a kind of intellectual protectionism and limits the free circulation of ideas.

Obviously there are ways in which a Swede can study Swedish history as only a Swede can do. A Swede can know Sweden and Swedish in a way that no non-Swede could ever hope to know it. But nevertheless I don't think any Swede would claim that Swedish history or Swedish literature should be a closed preserve in which only Swedes are allowed to hunt. Some who are not Swedes, from outside, may achieve certain insights, may see things in a perspective different from that of the Swedes and have a useful contribution to make. Sweden is a free country and Swedes can take any line that they wish. Many countries are not free and those of us who live in free countries have a duty to our colleagues in unfree countries to do what they are not permitted to do, and that is to write an honest and objective history of their country.

A relevant example. There were many in Western Europe and the United States who dealt with Soviet history during the Soviet era. Some of them were acclaimed by the Soviets as seeing things in the right light and writing the right kind of history. Others were denounced by the Soviets as enemies of the Soviet people. After the fall of the Soviet Union, the ones who were denounced as enemies were welcomed in Russia, translated into Russian, invited to lecture and generally acclaimed. Those who were previously praised as good friends of the Soviets were dismissed with contempt as either hirelings or dupes of the Soviets. I haven't the slightest doubt that sooner or later the same thing will happen in other parts of the world, including much of the Middle East, when the autocratic regimes which continue even now to rule most of them will be overthrown. Much will depend on the nature of the regime that comes next.

In 1978 an event occurred which affected my life and more particularly my role in academic and in public affairs. This was the publication of *Orientalism* by Edward Said, professor of English and comparative literature at Columbia University, in which he imputed to Orientalists a sinister role as part of the imperialist domination and exploitation of the Islamic world by the West. In particular, he imputed to me an especially sinister role as what he called the leader of the Orientalists.

Scholars engaged in the study of the civilizations of the East came to be known in Europe by the term "Orientalist." The term was coined on the analogy of the Hellenists who studied Greek, the Latinists who studied Latin and the Hebraists who studied Hebrew, the language of the Old Testament. The first two were also known as Classicists; the third came to be called Orientalists. In time they extended their attention beyond Hebrew, initially to other ancient Middle Eastern languages and cultures, and then to the remoter civilizations of Asia. Among those to whom it was applied, the term "Orientalist" has long since fallen out of use. For one thing, the word "Orient" is so vague and variable as to be useless—what, after all, do students of Arabic and of Japanese have in common that sets them apart from the Western humanities? At one time Orientalist, like Classicist, designated a basically philological method, but that too is out of date in this age of greater specialization, when the study of the Middle East, as of any other culture in the world, must draw on many different disciplines. The Orientalists have gone; their successors are historians, sociologists, political scientists, linguists, literary scholars and others dealing with the civilizations of the Middle East in a common intellectual effort with scholars of Middle Eastern origin. The term "Orientalist," abandoned by its practitioners as obsolete and inaccurate, was scavenged by Said and others and recycled as a term of abuse.

Edward Said's thesis is just plain wrong. His linking European Orientalist scholarship to European imperial expansion in the Islamic world is an absurdity. The beginning of "Orientalism"—the study of Arabic and Islam in Europe—occurred at a time not, as he maintains, of European imperial expansion among the Muslims, but of Muslim imperial expansion in Europe. Arab expansion began in the eighth century and extended into Spain, Sicily, Portugal and even southern France. The last Muslim foothold in Spain (Granada) fell in 1492 and thus ended the first Muslim expansion. In the meantime, the second Islamic advance had already begun with the Turkish advance and their capture of the Christian city of Constantinople in 1453, followed by the conquest of southeastern Europe and even part of central Europe and Corsair raids as far as the British Isles and

Iceland. It was during this period, in the early sixteenth century, that the first chair of Arabic was established in France, and in the seventeenth century, the chairs of Arabic at Oxford and Cambridge were created.

The first thing that struck me when I read Said's book was his ignorance, not only of the history of the Middle East but also of Europe. Some of his misstatements serve no polemical purpose and must be ascribed to straightforward honest ignorance. One egregious example is his statement that the Muslim armies conquered Turkey before they conquered North Africa. In fact, the conquest of North Africa preceded the conquest of Turkey by four centuries. Such errors do not inspire confidence in the writer's knowledge of the subject on which he writes. Said's ignorance extends from history to philology. For example he criticizes the German philosopher Friedrich Schlegel because even after "He had practically renounced his Orientalism, he still held that Sanskrit and Persian on the one hand and Greek and German on the other had more affinities with each other than with the Semitic, Chinese, American or African languages." Schlegel's statement is a simple truth, well known to anyone with even a minimal knowledge of philology. In another passage, Said mentions that Egypt was "annexed" by Britain, a statement which reveals ignorance of either Egyptian history or English lexicography. Egypt was indeed occupied by British forces for a long time, but it was never, in any sense, "annexed."

The gap between facts and their interpretation is so wide that I often found myself wondering where ignorance ended and deceit began. Robert Irwin, a self-described Orientalist and the Middle East editor of the *Times Literary Supplement,* called Said's book "A work of malignant charlatanry in which it is difficult to distinguish honest mistakes from willful misinterpretations."

Despite the historical absurdity and bewildering inaccuracy of most of his statements about Orientalism and its role in Western history, his thesis has received not just wide acceptance but has become the enforced orthodoxy in most departments devoted to colonial studies and literature of "the other" in American universities. In spite of, or perhaps because of, Said's popularity, there are, increasingly, books and articles criticizing his ideas, his scholarship and his veracity.

In a piece perfectly entitled "Enough Said," published in *The New Criterion* in January 2008, David Pryce-Jones describes at some length the context in which *Orientalism* was published and thrives.

> Edward Said was an outstanding example of an intellectual who condemned the West root and branch while taking every advantage of the privileges and rewards it has to offer. In its dishonesty and exercise of double standards, his was truly a cautionary tale of our times . . .
>
> The thesis was that every Westerner who had ever studied or written about the Middle East had done so in bad faith. From ancient Greece through the medieval era to the present, the work of historians, grammarians, linguists, and even epigraphists had been "a rationalization of colonial rule." There was no colonial rule in the lifetimes of the majority of these scholars, so they must have been "projecting" what was to come. For Said, these highly eclectic individuals were all engaged in a long-drawn conspiracy, international but invisible, to establish the supremacy of the West by depicting an East not only inferior but static and incapable of change. At bottom, here was the vulgar Marxist concept that knowledge serves only the interest of the ruling class. Said had also latched on to Michel Foucault, with his proposition—modishly avant-garde at the time—that there is no such thing as truth, but only "narratives" whose inventor is putting across his point of view. This reduces facts to whatever anyone wishes to make of them.
>
> Omitting whatever did not fit, misrepresenting evidence, and making unwarranted generalizations, Said committed the very sin for which he was accusing Westerners—concocting a

"narrative" to serve his purposes. As he summed up: "Every European, in what he could say about the Orient, was consequently a racist, an imperialist." . . . Orientalist, the portmanteau term for every Westerner with a scholarly, literary, or artistic interest in the East, is now firmly in the almanac of curse-words . . . .

The interest of Westerners in the East from classical antiquity onwards was motivated by intellectual curiosity. . . . To seek knowledge for its own sake is the special and wholly beneficial contribution the West has made to mankind. . . . Rationalism, universalism, and self-inspection are Western traits which expand civilization. Said's cultural relativism leads only to a dead end.

What motivated Said? I think I have found the explanation.

We all tend to judge others by ourselves. Said grew up in Egypt. As an Arab professor of English, he must have assumed that an English professor of Arabic studies would have the same attitude to his subject as Said had to his. (It may be recalled that Said was able to find imperialism even in the novels of Jane Austen.)

Although I personally was not affected in my career by these insults, many younger people in the earlier stages of their careers have suffered serious damage. They find themselves in a position where they have either to conform or get out. The Saidians now control appointments, promotions, publications and even book reviews with a degree of enforcement unknown in the Western universities since the eighteenth century. The situation in Near East studies is a great detriment to the state of scholarship in the field. This is a part of a general change, a political correctness, in which Islam now enjoys a level of immunity from comment or criticism in the Western world that Christianity has lost and Judaism has never had.

Every civilization, in every era, has had its orthodoxies, a Greek term meaning right ideas. At least some outward conformity to these has usually been necessary, in the more open societies, to succeed; in the more repressive, to survive. Reciting the magic words could open doors and lead to treasures. After all, even magic will sometimes lead to science, to some practical benefits.

A Crisis in Middle Eastern Studies

There are two well-established traditions of studying the Middle East. One is what one might call the classical tradition, which is primarily philological and to some extent theological. It is a tradition of European scholarship developed originally mostly by Christian monks to study Christian holy texts and then applied by extension to other scriptures in other languages. The classical Orientalist literature is mostly of that school. A good many of the scholars were churchmen, not by any means all, but they followed broadly the same methods. And that method, and that kind of scholarship, is still very much in existence and in some places, flourishing. It has, of course, its value; it also has its limitations.

The other approach is what, for want of a better term, I would call the disciplinary approach—people using one or another discipline, historians, sociologists, political scientists, etc. This is more recent, but has already been going for quite a long time. It was once remarked that the history of the Arabs in the Western world was written either by historians who knew no Arabic or by Arabists who understood no history. That is, perhaps, slightly overstated, but not entirely wrong. History was regarded as of marginal importance by classical Orientalists. Its only use was to help in identifying texts, identifying authors, choosing versions and so on. The history of the Arabs as such received very little attention.

Over the years this has changed but a gulf has opened up in the field. We now have historians and Arabists, of whom I won't say that they don't meet but they pass each other with averted eyes. This is a genuine difficulty. History departments tend to mistrust people who have a philological training in an exotic language. Some Middle Eastern language departments brush aside history as of secondary importance. It's a real difficulty, but there are some signs of hope. There are actually some writers of history who are historians by training and know something of the languages. In this particular area I think people coming out of the region can make the best contribution. Indeed some of them have already done so. Middle Eastern studies at the present time are beset by difficulties; on the one hand, the clash of disciplines and lack of mutual recognition between them; and on the other, the deadly hand of political correctness.

Unfortunately, the merits of a scholar are measured by publications, and the merits of these publications are measured by their bulk. This is perhaps inevitable when decisions are made by committees of experts who do not read, or if they read, do not understand, the works of those who come before them for judgment. This development has coincided—I think coincided is the right word—with the neocolonial expansion of the social sciences into whole areas, indeed continents, which were once peacefully cultivated by philologists and historians, and with the increasing use of techniques of research and exposition which are at once extravagant and arcane. This has often meant that works are unread because they are unreadable, uncomprehended because they are incomprehensible. Both qualities are believed to conceal vast learning and great profundity.

There are doctrines that are alleged to hold the key to understanding historical processes. Marxism is one such. I had my phase of Marxist influence years ago. If one looks at what I was writing in the forties and early fifties one will see that while I never became a full-fledged Marxist, I was very much aware of Marxist thought and categories. My book *The Arabs in History* was somewhat influenced by Marxist ways of thought and Marxist approaches to history. Rather more so was my doctoral thesis, *The Origins of Isma'ilism*. Quasi-Marxism was my measles or chicken pox, which I got over at the age when one recovers from these ailments. Some younger people presumably find it necessary to go through the same phase now but I don't think one should make an intellectual virtue of childhood infections.

One of the main reasons I abandoned it was finding in the course of the decades that it was simply inadequate. The Marxist method evolved from the study of European history and it has a certain limited relevance for European history. But if you try to apply it to non-European societies, it breaks down. Marx himself, in a rare moment of intellectual humility, showed awareness that it doesn't apply to non-Europeans societies, and that's why he and Engels mentioned, without actually developing, the notion of the "Asiatic Mode of Production." This was really no more than an idea off the top of the head which they batted back and forth in their correspondence and used occasionally in their writings. But, they didn't develop it. It was left as an issue for debate and sometimes even conflict and repression among later Marxists.

If you try to apply the Marxist sequence to non-European societies you're likely to go badly wrong. In the Middle East, for example, at least since Islam and probably a lot longer than that, the effect of political power, the importance of political power, the way in which economic and every other kind of power flows from political power, makes nonsense of the idea that the state is the executive instrument of this or that class. Obvious examples are the extreme insecurity of property and the difficulty of identifying classes in terms of relationship to means of production. If you really know anything about Middle Eastern history, Marxist analysis just doesn't work.

It's not all nonsense and useless. The Marxists have alerted us to the importance of certain aspects of history which might previously have been overlooked, just as the liberal nationalists of the nineteenth century alerted us to the importance of aspects of history which had previously been underrated. Each of these vogues adds something.

But the serious historian doesn't go by vogues. He will be open to any kind of intellectual approach from wherever it comes and use it as far as it is useful—and no further.

Some people think that if you want to study Ottoman history, it's enough to know this or that and you don't need to be able to read an Ottoman text. This is nonsense. There are people now who write Ottoman history who literally do not know the alphabet, who cannot read an Ottoman text. They think that their Marxist or other ideologically defined method gives them an intellectual sword and buckler with which they can confront every danger.

Acknowledgments

In the course of an academic career one is often asked for help or advice by students and colleagues in one's own or other universities, as well as by others engaged in projects of research and writing. In my profession, if you take your job seriously, you try to help people. Your students are your students in a very personal sense, particularly those who do graduate work. It's not just a case of their attending a course and getting a mark—you try to help them with their work and encourage them in various ways. It often sets up a relationship which continues and some of my students have been extremely grateful and have made a point of thanking me profusely in their prefaces. Others prefer not to acknowledge me because I am not a popular figure among the ruling establishment in my field and the Middle Eastern studies industry has been for long dominated by followers of Edward Said.

Two examples may illustrate the extreme limits. One of them occurred when I was young and inexperienced. A student in another university came to seek help and advice. I helped the student choose and define a subject; I read some drafts, and later, advised on publication. I was, I must confess, somewhat peeved at receiving no mention in the preface or even a complimentary copy.

A much worse case was that of a gentleman from outside the university who came to see me just once about some work in progress, and asked for my help and advice on various points. In due course he sent me a copy of his book, in which he thanked me profusely in his preface for reading his draft and making many valuable suggestions. I had indeed read his draft, and had made many suggestions, which may or may not have been valuable. Since he had not followed a single one of these suggestions, I was not entirely pleased with his acknowledgment of my help. An even worse example is when, as has happened on occasion, one is used in this way to promote some dubious political agenda.

Between these two extremes of ingratitude and name-dropping, there is a wide spectrum of forms of acknowledgment, in which the writer expresses appreciation for services rendered. Among the more meticulous scholars of the old school, this may even include footnotes to the effect that "My thanks are due to Professor So-and-So for drawing my attention to this document." The more usual form is the blanket acknowledgment in the preface of doctoral dissertations. In these, the candidate thanks his supervisor and his other teachers. Sometimes the list is extended to include almost the whole academic community with whom the candidate had contact.

Some acknowledgments, by accident or design, implicate the person thanked in the writer's work. Others meticulously exonerate him, with a formula along the lines that "any faults or errors that remain are entirely my own" or something to that effect. This has become increasingly necessary at a time when much writing and criticism on Middle Eastern matters is affected or even dominated by political and ideological differences. Some reviewers for example proceed on the assumption that anyone thanked in the preface of a book may be held accountable for its opinions and perhaps even for its publication. If this becomes the general view, we shall have a choice between only two options: either to refuse help or advice to anyone but graduate students preparing dissertations under our direction or, alternatively, to imitate civil service procedures and require all persons consulting us to submit a final text for approval before publication. This would be a sad end to the already endangered freedom of our republic of letters.

Tenure

The academic tenure system, in one form or another, exists in most if not all of the universities of the free world. Its purpose is to protect the freedom of university teachers. It is to enable them in their writings and more importantly in their teaching, to express their opinions freely, and more specifically, to protect them from pressure by academic, religious, political or other forces, notably—and in some places most dangerously—by donors. It is often used to ensure that university teachers enjoy a level of job security shared by no other profession except perhaps the civil service and the priesthood. This system has from time to time been questioned, notably by British Prime Minister Margaret Thatcher, who saw no reason why university faculty should enjoy such a unique privilege. She changed it.

In many respects the tenure system has worked very well and has enabled university faculty, in their teaching and in their publications, to express their opinions with a degree of freedom and immunity that is rare even in the modern democratic world. But it also has its drawbacks. A not uncommon figure is the university teacher who, having reached the level of publication required to achieve tenure, stops working once he has achieved it, and devotes the rest of his life to idleness or other activities, with only the normal minimum teaching requirement. Tenure can thus be used to protect laziness or incompetence. This is not common, but it happens from time to time and represents a real danger.

A truly disastrous innovation was the abolition of compulsory retirement at the age of seventy. There were of course good reasons for enabling professors still competent and in full possession of their faculties to continue their work beyond that age, but some better way could have been found of achieving this, based on individual achievement and assessment. The blanket abolition of mandatory retirement enabled professors to continue indefinitely, irrespective of their competence either in teaching or in research. This had two harmful consequences; one was that it could leave university departments burdened with professors who were at best useless and sometimes harmful; the second was that it blocked the path of advancement of rising talents in the next generation. A whole practice has developed of finding some way to bribe professors to retire by offering financial or other inducement. This has in many respects had a devastating effect. The desired result could have been achieved more easily by allowing an extension beyond the age of retirement in individual cases based on individual merit for a specified period of time. This would have enabled the universities to retain those worth retaining without obliging them to retain those who are not.

A still greater danger to academic freedom is the use of tenure to ensure conformity, the exact opposite of its original purpose. The damage is particularly great when university teachers are appointed for some reason other than competence in scholarship and/or teaching. This is not common, but again it is not unusual. With such appointees, incompetence is the least of the problems. In some areas, notably in Middle Eastern studies, it has become commonplace that certain lines of thought (if that is the right word) must be accepted and applied if one wishes to achieve appointment, promotion and tenure. This kind of enforced orthodoxy can extend even to learned journals and publishing houses and has been used to bring about a level of intellectual conformism unknown for centuries.

Fortunately, there are signs of change. To general astonishment, a group of scholars in the field established a new organization to counter the straitjackets of MESA, the Middle East Studies Association. ASMEA, the Association for the Study of the Middle East and Africa, was established in 2007 to provide a platform and a medium for ideas and opinions that deviate from currently enforced orthodoxy, and to do this—and this is profoundly important—without establishing a similarly repressive alternative. I was very happy to accept the chairmanship of this organization and took the opportunity to express my views on these matters at the inaugural meeting. The response has been gratifying, to say the least. But the danger remains. The battle is now engaged—not between rival ideologies, but between enforced ideology and freedom.

The Annenberg Center

In 1986, on reaching the then mandatory retirement age of seventy, I formally stepped down from my two positions—at Princeton University and at the Institute for Advanced Study. My esteemed colleague and friend Charles Issawi retired at the same time. His comment at our joint party was, "There are five ages of professors—tireless, tiring, tiresome, tired and retired; but for people like Bernard and me, retirement means a new set of tires and full speed ahead." (At the retirement party for Carl Brown and John Marks, Issawi's memorable quip was, "How much more dramatic it would have been if they had been Karl Marx and John Brown.")

Since then, the rules have changed, and professors can stay on for as long as they wish and are deemed to be reasonably competent. This has sometimes created problems, and ways have been found to offer inducements to retire, in order to make room for the rising next generation. But this is a more recent development, and when I reached the age of seventy, more than twenty-five years ago, retirement was obligatory and final. As I approached that point I began to wonder what I was going to do after retirement. Since I was still quite active and healthy I felt that I should go on and do something else. A number of invitations and offers came in, including one from the University of Paris, one from the University of California and others. The two which I found most attractive and which I had in principle decided to accept, were from the Hoover Institution in California, to spend part of the year with them on research projects of my choice, and from Brandeis University, to spend part of the year there as a visiting professor. Both made it clear that it would be possible for me to combine the two if that was what I wished to do. This was more or less settled, and then came a different invitation from the Annenberg Research Institute for Judaic and Near Eastern Studies in Philadelphia, which I was invited to head.

This was a new institution and, as director, I could play a leading role in its creation and development. I had no experience in administration and no great desire for it, but this was irresistible—the opportunity to craft a totally new institute from scratch and develop it in accordance with my ideas. The Institute also had another advantage; it was inheriting the assets of Dropsie College, a well-known center for Hebrew and Judaic studies with a very rich library including many rare manuscripts. I accepted the invitation and met with Walter Annenberg on several occasions and with the board of governors that he had appointed.

It was a fascinating project and I was very excited. We were starting something completely new, with a superb library, supplemented by the fact that it could be augmented in almost any direction we wanted by CD-ROMs, which had just been introduced. That meant, for example, that one could have the whole of ancient Greek literature on one small disk. There was also a remarkable computer program which was able, on the insertion of a single phrase, to find allusions, references and variants of that phrase in a number of ancient and other languages. An extraordinary tool for the researcher.

The new Institute was to be devoted exclusively to research and publication. It would not have students in the normal sense of that word, nor would it grant degrees. It would have a small permanent faculty and a number of invited guest fellows every year who would be given the opportunity to do research on some approved project. The person most directly involved was David Goldenberg, the last director of Dropsie College, who now became my deputy director. I was apprehensive about my relationship with him since I was in effect replacing him as the head of this institution. But I needn't have worried. He was in every respect cooperative and I could not have hoped for a more competent and loyal colleague.

And now I had an entirely new experience—dealing with a board of directors. The chairman was Judge Arlen Adams, a respected member of the Philadelphia community; the other directors were businesspeople. Normally their principal function as directors of a nonprofit institution would have been to give or find funds, but as this was endowed by Annenberg, one of the wealthiest men in the United States, it was generally assumed that no fund-raising or fund-giving was necessary. Since the board was not fulfilling its normal function, it was not quite clear what their function was and how power and responsibility were to be allocated between the chief executive, me, on the one hand and the board of directors on the other.

This led to growing tension. It soon emerged that their perceptions and expectations were entirely different from mine and indeed from those of the academic world in general. As people with business experience they had what one might call quarterly expectations. Academic research and publication work on a different time scale, a very much longer one. I remember a conversation with Buntzie Ellis Churchill, president of the World Affairs Council of Philadelphia, then housed in a building around the corner from the Institute. She explained to me how boards of directors of nonprofit organizations work. The boards function on the principle that the directors will contribute one of the three "W's"—work, wealth or wisdom, or they can provide one of the three "G's"—give, get or get off. My immediate reaction was to comment that my board offered the three "I's"—ignorance, incompetence and interference.

One of the problems was Walter Annenberg himself. As he was providing all the funding he assumed that he would have the final say on all issues. Unfortunately he had no direct knowledge or experience of academic life but nevertheless expected to have the final say on all academic issues. I found him a difficult man with whom to work, and eventually, impossible.

A particular issue was the Jewish aspect. Dropsie College had been a center for Jewish studies. The Annenberg Institute had "Judaic and Near Eastern Studies" in its title. I didn't realize this at first but Walter was very anxious to de-emphasize the Judaic aspect and in general to reduce greatly the Jewish connections.

Let me give some examples. Visiting fellows would need a kitchen to provide a place for them to have lunch or refreshments. I assumed that this would be kosher since a proportion of the visiting fellows would probably be observant Jews. Annenberg vetoed this emphatically. I then suggested that a corner might be made available where kosher food could be brought in from outside. He vetoed that too. And in one way after another he was adamant that the Institute de-emphasize, if not conceal, any Judaic connection.

I found this a depressing experience. Annenberg was arrogant and peremptory and took it for granted that his wishes on all issues, even including those on which he was ignorant, would be immediately accepted and enforced. The directors, with few and rare exceptions, were deferential and submissive and just assumed that whatever he said or did was right and must be obeyed.

In the world of business in which he moved Mr. Annenberg was accustomed to immediate and total assent and obedience. This was his expectation in other matters too and any sort of question, even a request for further information, came as a surprise, evoking first shock and then, if pursued, anger. In the academic world we are accustomed to a different approach. The question first arose with a quotation which he found somewhere and liked; he gave orders that it be inscribed in the entrance hall. I recognized the quotation and had two problems with it: the text was inaccurate and the attribution was incorrect. I don't know where he found the quotation but it was obviously not a reliable source. I suggested we correct it and that evoked a curious mixture of bewilderment and fury. I was being "insubordinate and ill-mannered."

During my time at the Annenberg Center Pope John Paul II came on a visit to the United States. Annenberg decided that he, Al Wood, then chairman of the board, and I, as director of the Institute, should go to Miami to welcome the Pope. There was a gathering of about fifty people from various organizations standing in a semicircle and the Pope made the usual round, exchanging politenesses, receiving the appropriate deference from Catholics and courtesy from others. When he came to me it was different. As I have explained elsewhere, I was on friendly, personal terms with this Pope and when he saw me, he smiled, greeted me by name, said how much he had enjoyed my last visit to Castel Gandolfo and was looking forward to my next.

Al Wood, standing next to me, was beside himself. He repeated several times: "If I had not seen this with my own eyes I would never have believed it." Annenberg saw the exchange from a distance but could not hear the conversation; he came over and demanded to know what had happened. I explained to him and his reaction was mixed. Clearly he would have preferred the Pope's friendly gesture to be made to himself rather than to one of his employees.

In 1990 I decided to leave. Academic progress at the Institute was virtually nil. My resignation was accepted with alacrity and eventually the Institute was taken over by the University of Pennsylvania. My connection had lasted four years.

I returned to Princeton and decided this time not to take up any other academic appointments but instead to devote myself to my own work, research and writing. Paradoxically, the period of my life which began at the age of seventy-four has been the most productive of all. I produced more books and articles in the fifteen years that followed than in all my previous life. I would regard the four years I spent at the Annenberg Institute as a total failure and a personal tragedy except for one thing. I became friends with Buntzie Churchill and later that friendship developed in new and undreamt-of ways. Who would expect, at the age of eighty, to fall in love?

Buntzie and I met in 1989 at the reception before a meeting of the Philadelphia Committee on Foreign Relations. We talked and laughed and discovered that my office was around the corner from hers. We had lunch every couple of months and became friends. Many of our interests coincide. She enjoys playing with languages, uses English masterfully and loves puns. She had an early interest in the Middle East, having done undergraduate and graduate papers on Nasser and Egypt. During the period when she was studying at the University of Pennsylvania my available work was on Turkey and the medieval Islamic period—not her interests. She didn't know who I was.

I waited a year and a half after her husband died of a heart attack in 1994 before "making my move." It's been a wonderful relationship. The only thing that I felt was lacking was a shared, private language. With my ex-wife I had Danish and with my subsequent companion, Turkish. Both languages were little known in the Western world and assured us a convenient privacy. For a while, until I got used to it, I felt the lack of this. In compensation we shared the richness and depth of the English language and in particular enjoyed discovering and sharing our regional deviations. Buntzie gave me a better and deeper understanding of American culture, both popular and historic, in a way that I would probably otherwise never have achieved.

For example, I didn't know what "the yellow brick road" was. At my first Halloween instead of offering candy to the children who came to the door I offered a plate of apricot rugelach which someone had given to me. Not what they were expecting! There are, however, some things I just can't fathom—what is the appeal of computer games?—although that's probably a function of age rather than culture.

Buntzie, by the way, has provided an interesting tabulation of what she considers the three main sources of my professional success: a long attention span, a good memory and an ability to produce convincing imitations of unfamiliar noises—all useful for learning and retaining languages and remembering history.

Periodically we have discussed getting married but she has her life in Philadelphia and I have mine in Princeton, and we always have the weekends and trips to which to look forward. We used to go back and forth on the marriage issue regularly, with one of us tilting one way and in the next discussion tilting the other way. At one point Buntzie said the only reason to get married was that that way, after I died, she'd have societal support for six months, whereas as my "girlfriend" she'd have societal support for six days. I mused, "Does that mean you don't want to be my wife but you do want to be my widow?"

The status quo works for us.

11.

Judgment in Paris

In my book *The Emergence of Modern Turkey,* first published in 1961, I referred to the massacres of Armenians by the Turks in 1915 using the word "holocaust" to describe them. This did not prevent the book from being acclaimed in Turkey and translated into Turkish. In the third edition, published in 1962, I replaced the word "holocaust" with "slaughter"—not to question or minimize what happened, but to avoid a comparison with the destruction of six million Jews in Nazi-ruled Europe, for which "holocaust" had by then become almost a technical term. I gave the number as "a million and a half," the commonly accepted estimate.

When Turkey became a member of NATO in 1952, the Russians, not surprisingly, saw this as a major strategic threat to the Soviet Union. Indeed, the presence of a Turkish Muslim republic as a NATO member in the region of the Black Sea and the Caucasus could raise problems for them both at home and abroad. The Soviets therefore responded in their usual way by making trouble for the Turks. They did this in two ways, first domestically and then internationally. They resorted to the familiar method of mobilizing and encouraging internal opposition. In Turkey, this meant the left-wing elements among the Turks and the Kurdish ethnic minority. The Soviets also tried to make problems for the Turks abroad and more particularly in the United States. There too they sought to mobilize anti-Turkish forces and turned in the first instance to the significant Armenian community in the United States.

The Armenian massacres of 1915 left very bitter memories in that community. In the post–World War I period friendly relations developed between some Turks and some Armenians in the United States as elsewhere. The revival of the Armenian issue proved a powerful and effective weapon, mobilizing not only Armenians, a significant community in many American states, but also other groups who sympathized with them.

In 1985, a campaign began to persuade the United States Congress to recognize the Armenian massacres as a genocide. There were a number of different groups who objected to this—first of course, the Turks, but then others who felt that it was not the business of the U.S. Congress or indeed of any legislative body to write or rewrite history and that such a resolution could do no good and might do considerable harm. At the time I was asked to sign a letter of protest against this bill and agreed, as did many others in the academic profession.

In November 1993, I spent a few days in Paris where, coincidentally, two of my books were being published in French translation by two different publishing houses. At their request I gave a number of interviews to the media including one in *Le Monde.* One of the questions put to me concerned the proposed resolution before Congress and more generally the nature of the Armenian massacres. My answers gave rise to further discussion in the paper in which I participated.

My point was that while the Armenians suffered appalling losses, the comparison with the Holocaust was misleading. The one arose from an armed rebellion, from what we would nowadays call a national liberation struggle. The Armenians, seizing the opportunity presented by World War I, rose in rebellion against their Turkish overlords in alliance with Britain and Russia, the two powers with which Turkey was at war. The rebellions of the Armenians in the east and in Cilicia achieved some initial successes but were eventually suppressed, and the surviving Armenians from Cilicia were ordered to be exiled. During the struggle and the subsequent deportation, great numbers of Armenians were killed.

The slaughter of the Jews, first in Germany and then in German-occupied Europe, was a different matter. There was no rebellion, armed or otherwise. On the contrary, the German Jews were intensely loyal to their country. The attack on them was defined wholly and solely by their alleged racial identity and included converted Jews and people of partly Jewish descent. It was not local or regional, but was extended to all the Jews under German rule or occupation, and its purpose was to achieve their total annihilation.

When the survivors of the Armenian deportation arrived at their destinations in Ottoman-ruled Iraq and Palestine they were welcomed and helped by the local Armenian communities. The German Jews deported to Poland by the Nazis received no such help, but joined their Polish coreligionists in a common fate.

The first difference was thus that some of the Armenians were involved in an armed rebellion; the Jews were not, but were attacked solely because of their identity. A second difference was that the persecution of Armenians was mostly confined to endangered areas, while the Armenian populations in other parts of the Ottoman Empire, notably in big cities, were left more or less unharmed. I say "more or less" because there were some attacks on individual Armenians accused of anti-Ottoman acts, but the Armenian populations in general were not persecuted.

It was these statements and explanations that led to four lawsuits, two criminal and two civil, arising from my interview and the subsequent discussion. Three actions were against *Le Monde* and me; the remaining civil action was against me alone. The common theme of all of them was an accusation of an offense tantamount to "Holocaust denial," a crime in French law. Judgment was pronounced on November 18, 1994. *The Armenian Report International* of October 20 noted,

"It is unlikely that punishment will be meted out to *Le Monde* and/
or Professor Lewis, even if the court upholds that the Armenian genocide is fact; the reason is that the French law adopted in 1990 called
Gaysod [sic] prohibiting the publication of any literature that questions the veracity of genocide pertains only to the Jewish holocaust of
World War II. The pursuance of this case by the Armenian National
Committee of France was ultimately aimed at having a similar law
adopted in France which would apply to the Armenian genocide." My
interview, and I, were used to serve this purpose.

The courts dismissed the three actions against both *Le Monde*
and me and gave partial acceptance only to the civil action directed
against me alone. My French friends were for the most part of the
opinion that the whole interview and its subsequent development
were a deliberate entrapment. The ensuing course of events lends considerable plausibility to this explanation. The court explicitly dis-
claimed any intention to "arbitrate and decide" historical polemics
and controversies and ruled that "it is not for the court to evaluate
and say whether the massacres committed from 1915 to 1917 against
the Armenians do or do not constitute the crime of genocide as defined by law." According to the judges I was required to do so even in
the narrow compass of a newspaper interview. My opponents, on the
other hand, even in books and articles, with ample space at their
disposal, were free to ignore such argument or evidence and even to
demand its suppression and the punishment of those who adduced it.
Specifically they remain free to maintain their total disregard of the
mass of published documents, as well as the many studies and monographs published by scholars of many nationalities and of different
allegiances or none, unless they totally accept and reaffirm the view
which the genocide proponents have maintained, unchanged for
three-quarters of a century. Even to name this "the Armenian version," as I did, and thus injure the feelings of those who uphold it is,
in French law, a tort, the commission of which can give rise to an

order for damages. There is no limitation on hurting Turkish feelings, whether by naming and condemning the "Turkish version," by accusations of genocide directed not only against the alleged perpetrators but against the whole nation, past and present, or by either denying or approving the massacres of Turkish, Kurdish and other Muslim villagers by Armenian guerrillas. Some of the arguments and imputations of the prosecution—on the one hand alleging a continuity of Turkish genocide from the Armenians in 1915 to the Kurds at the present day, and on the other concerning the inadmissibility of Turkish scholars and of evidence adduced by them—suggest the kind of prejudice that the Forum of Armenian Associations' junior partner, the Ligue Internationale Contre le Racisme et l'Antisémitisme (LICRA), is pledged to oppose.

The court held that "while it was in no way established that I had pursued any purpose foreign to my mission as a historian" I was at fault in "hiding (*occultant*) elements contrary to [my] thesis . . . and had thus been lacking in [my] duty of objectivity and prudence, in expressing [myself] without nuance on so delicate a subject; that [my] remarks, likely to revive unjustly the pain of the Armenian community, are at fault and justify indemnity." My "failure" in my *"devoir d'objectivité et de prudence"* provoked some reflection, notably that those who were of a different view were under no such obligation to refrain from "hiding" elements contrary to their thesis, nor to maintain even a pretense of "objectivity and prudence."

I was ordered to pay 1 franc each in damages to the Forum of Armenian Associations and to LICRA, and to pay for excerpts from this judgment to be published in *Le Monde,* to the amount of 20,000 francs, and to pay costs in the amount of 10,000 francs for the Armenian Forum and 4,000 francs for LICRA. In the unsuccessful cases brought by the Armenian Medical Association and AGRIF each was ordered to pay me 8,000 francs, leaving me slightly ahead in the absurd arithmetic of these proceedings.

In all these lawsuits, the plaintiffs proceeded on certain assumptions:

1. In history, as in mathematics, there is one right answer to a problem, all others being wrong.

2. This answer is fixed and unchanging and cannot be in any way affected by such ephemeral phenomena as the discovery of new evidence, the questioning of old evidence or the development of new lines and methods of inquiry.

3. The proper place to determine which is the right answer is a court of law.

4. The right answer having been determined, all other answers must be suppressed and those who advance them punished.

To these assumptions the lawyers conducting the case for the plaintiffs added a fifth, that the proper way to disprove a historical view is to launch an all-out attack, unconstrained by any concern for truth, not to speak of decency, on the professional, personal and financial integrity of the historian who advances that view.

One example, among many, of the dangers of press falsification is an article in *L'Express* which stated that I "benefited from three scholarships accorded by Turkey." This is totally false. In fact, I have never accepted any grant or subvention from the Turkish nor for that matter from any other foreign government. Although in the vast majority of cases such grants and subventions are without political strings, I have preferred, because of the sensitivities of the field in which I work, to avoid such complications. During the lawsuit in Paris the Turkish Embassy in France offered to pay all my legal bills. I refused that offer and thus incurred a considerable expenditure. When I refused the offer of the Turkish Embassy my French lawyer expressed his relief and gratification. The court only awarded the plaintiffs 1 franc in damages, but there was still the matter of the lawyers' bills and other costs.

The ethical question arose again some years later when I was awarded the Atatürk Prize by the Turkish Academy of Sciences. The prize was $50,000. I accepted the honor but not the monetary portion which I asked be given to three Turkish nonprofit organizations. My hosts insisted on giving me two gold coins as a personal souvenir of the event. These I gave to Buntzie, who had them made into earrings.

There remains the plaintiffs' general implication that by receiving a "bourse" a scholar becomes at least suspect of being a servant of a foreign state. Great numbers of scholars young and old in France and elsewhere benefit every year from scholarships and fellowships sponsored directly or indirectly by foreign governments. Do they thereby all lay themselves open to the suspicion of becoming agents of those governments? The attack on me personally misfires, since it is based on a lie. The imputation against the academic profession remains.

The Armenians appealed, both against the unfavorable verdicts and the payments to Le Monde and myself. The appeals from both parties were rejected, with costs. After the verdict against me the question arose whether I should appeal. I had ample grounds. I refrained for a very simple and cogent reason: a lack of faith in a judicial system that could perpetrate, and might therefore uphold, such absurdities.

Throughout this case I refused requests for press interviews. My reason for refusing French requests is obvious. It would be foolhardy, even foolish, to accord an interview in a country where a historian who is bold enough to answer questions put by an interviewer about history may thereby make himself liable to extensive and expensive litigation, possibly leading to criminal penalties and/or civil damages. My reasons for refusing interviews in the English language press in Britain and in the United States were different. Those who asked for interviews were clearly more sympathetic to my cause than to that of the prosecution which some of them regarded with disapproval or even derision. But I had no wish to participate in deriding French freedom and French justice.

I had one other reason for refusing interviews all around. I was born and brought up in a country where there is a rule of law, strictly enforced, against the public discussion of matters that are still sub judice. There is no such rule in either France or the United States, but my experience in the one and my observations in the other have convinced me of the wisdom and value of such a rule.

The press coverage was, in fact, minimal—for which I suppose I should be grateful, given the quality and accuracy of that coverage.

The plaintiffs showed great skill in their handling of the press. Their Paris press conference, of which I received a detailed report from a friend, was efficiently conducted. The folders of press cuttings, documents and other material which they distributed on that and subsequent occasions were misleading but plausible, and indeed, persuasive. The results can be seen in the reporting of the four lawsuits that were brought against me. The hearings and judgments in the three cases where the court found in my favor were not reported at all, nor were they mentioned in the handouts that I saw, as far as I am aware. They might have caused embarrassment to the plaintiffs, and were therefore passed over in silence.

The fourth, and in many ways the most important, case provides perhaps the best illustration of their skilled press management. On the main accusation, that of "negationism," the court refused to pronounce and instead found for the plaintiffs on a relatively minor issue. For those who had transformed the cautiously noncommittal "take note" of a subcommission into a ringing endorsement of their point of view by the United Nations, it was child's play to magnify this verdict into a "condemnation of negationism," and to manipulate the press accordingly.

This transformation was effected overnight and appeared in the reports of the judgment in the three main Paris papers, all of which, it would seem, took their versions of the judgment not from the judges but from the plaintiffs. The three newspapers, *Le Monde, Liberation* and *Figaro,* with striking unanimity, reported inaccurately that the court had "condemned" me for "negationism," which the judges had made great efforts not to do. *Liberation* and *Figaro* followed their inaccurate reports with interviews with the two principal propagandists for the Forum of Armenian Associations. *Le Monde* needed no such adventitious aid and managed to cap a fairly accurate account of the judgment with a highly inaccurate headline.

On the advice of my lawyer, I sent a letter drafted by him to all three papers in which I protested, not of course the judgment, but their misreporting of the judgment. They refused to print my letter until obliged to do so by a court order. *Le Monde'* s unwillingness to print my letter concerning their misreporting of the judgment until compelled to do so by court order might be ascribed to discourtesy rather than disloyalty, and perhaps to prudence more than discourtesy. Their refusal to print a letter signed by a number of distinguished French Turcologists rebutting the slurs leveled by the plaintiffs against their entire profession may be similarly explained. It is reasonable to assume that this refusal was motivated by fear of further costly and troublesome legal proceedings. In the circumstances, one must recognize that this was a wise precaution.

Some inaccuracies live forever. A good example of the misreporting of the trial is provided by Norman G. Finkelstein in his 2008 book *Beyond Chutzpah* (University of California Press) where he says that I was "indicted and convicted by a French court for denying the Armenian holocaust." It would appear the author lives up to the title of his book.

The coverage in the foreign press was limited and dealt predominantly with the issue of freedom of speech. The London *Eve-*

ning Standard of May 23, 1995, under the headline "Sued over a History Lesson," speaks of "one of the strangest trials to take place for some years" and concludes that "the professor's real mistake was to suppose that he was addressing the descendants of Voltaire." Christopher Hitchens, writing in *The Nation,* made it clear that he had no sympathy whatever either with Turkey or with me, but did not miss the opportunity for a sneer at what he called "the magnificent hypocrisy of French law and the French intellectual climate." The London *Jewish Chronicle* concluded, "Lewis was right, but even if he had been wrong he should still have been at liberty to utter his views. Being manifestly in error is, for a historian, a serious reflection on his professional competence but not an act of wanton criminality.

"The Gayssot law is a serious impediment to free speech but it was passed because the French, with good cause, have a conscience about the events of the war years, and there is, for obvious reasons, a similar law in Germany. There is none in America because it would be contrary to the American constitution and happily, there is none in Britain because it would be contrary to common sense."

An article in the *Frankfurter Allgemeine Zeitung* of June 26, 1995, examined the entire proceedings and condemned it as an offense at once against academic independence, freedom of expression and civilized discourse.

Perhaps the Armenians' most remarkable success in media management was in what did not appear. References to the lawsuits in British, American and German and perhaps other newspapers drew attention to the basic issue of freedom of expression that, one way or another, was involved. I saw only one reference to this issue in the French press coverage and it was clearly a minority view. I still find it strange that the main point that was of relevance to Frenchmen at the time, not the events of 1915 but the lawsuit of 1995, should have evoked so little concern among French journalists and intellectuals.

With astonishingly few exceptions the attitude of the French academic and literary communities to these proceedings ranged from approval through acquiescence to indifference. Of those whom I regarded as friends and colleagues in France, some were silent even when invited to speak. This saddened me. Others sent letters of sympathy and volunteered public support. I shall not endanger them by naming them, but they will recognize themselves if ever these words are published in France.

The same disparity of resources and effort displayed in public relations can also be seen in the pleadings where five plaintiffs in four lawsuits had a battery of lawyers against my single, valiant defender. Against such odds, I had about as much chance as the Polish cavalry confronting the German tanks in 1939.

A dramatic response came from the Institut de France, the most distinguished academic body in the country, which elected me a Corresponding Fellow of the Académie des Inscriptions et Belles-Lettres, one of its major branches. This would have been an honor at any time but it was particularly dramatic that they chose that moment. What was at issue was not the correctness of my opinion but my right to express it, or, more specifically, to express it in France. And since I am neither a citizen nor a resident of France, nor, since this incident, a visitor, that is not, in the last analysis, my problem.

I abstained from any discussion of the main issue at the time for practical and personal reasons. I prefer not to discuss history in a place where historical opinion is subject to judicial review, where judicial verdicts can be rewritten, revised and even reversed by journalists and their mentors and, most important of all, where the rules of debate are not the same for all participants.

In sum, as far as I was concerned, two lessons emerged clearly from these proceedings: first, a court of law is not the best place to debate, still less to resolve, a historical problem, and second, that the press is not the best platform to discuss or contest a lawsuit.

I understand the anguish of the survivors and descendants of the Armenian deportees and their insistence that the term "genocide," first commonly used to designate the destruction of the Jews in Nazi-ruled Europe, should also be applied in their case, and their anger when it is refused—the more so in our day when this same word "genocide" is used widely and loosely for all kinds of situations in various parts of the world, where the destruction and the loss of life are no greater than that suffered by the Armenians and sometimes significantly less. If the term denotes large-scale suffering and death, much though not all of it deliberate, then it can hardly be withheld. But if, as the plaintiffs clearly intend, the word "genocide" is to be used in its original and legal meaning—the deliberate, planned extermination or attempted extermination of a people, such as was conducted and in large measure completed in Nazi Europe, then the appropriateness of this term to the Armenian massacres of 1915 remains unproven. However, language changes, and looking at this again twenty years later it is clear that the word "genocide" has developed a broader and less precise meaning today.

For the victims, their families, their compatriots and their descendants who are still seared by the memory of these terrible events, this lexical distinction makes little difference. But for the historian, these things matter; and not only for the historian, but also for those who look to the future and who cherish a hope for better relations and better understanding between two peoples who can only be still further divided by the reiteration of old grievances and the rekindling of old hatreds.

12.

Writing and Rewriting History

Style merits a very high place in the writing of history. I don't mean a sort of makeup which is added afterward. It's not something which is applied. I've heard people suggest that one man writes and then another applies the style, and some see this as the function of the editor appointed by a publisher. I don't accept that at all. I think that style is part of the actual thought and writing process—thought especially. Clarity of thought will normally produce clarity of style; obscurity of thought will produce obscurity of style. Writing history is not the same as writing a novel or a poem, but one should have some thought for elegance. Historical writing should have certain essential qualities—clarity, precision and elegance.

Clarity means that you say what you mean to say and your meaning is unambiguous. Precision is saying just what you mean to say and not something else. Time and time again things are so clumsily and carelessly written that what the person intends to say and what he actually says are significantly different. If a book is poorly presented and poorly written it's not good history. It may be good scholarship but it is not good history. Elegance speaks for itself.

The study and the writing of history are constantly being enriched by new insights and new experience. Every generation brings something fresh to the study of the same topics and periods. Two things are always added. One is new methods, new documents, and new sources. The other is that every generation brings some fresh experience and the experience of one's own time can be useful, if only by suggesting new lines of inquiry, new questions which can be put to the evidence of the past.

History at one time was military and political and nothing else. It was the story of kings and wars, sometimes described as drums and trumpets. Kings and wars are important, and at times we have tended to go overboard in rejecting them, but a history which is purely political and military is no longer acceptable. Over the last fifty years we have added a psychological dimension and an economic dimension; we now have cultural history, social history, intellectual history, economic history and so on. The addition of the psychological method may prove as fruitful as the addition of the sociological method to the study of history. However much one may believe in impersonal, historical forces which determine the course of events, people are important, and individual decisions and actions are in part at least psychologically determined. Psychology is of value to the biographer, and what is of value to the biographer is ipso facto valuable to the historian.

But one needs to be careful because there are certain questions which one can never ask, or rather, to which one cannot hope to find answers. The psychologist, like the social scientist, asks questions and pursues his questions because he has living subjects to whom he talks. A historian can't do that. If we want to write a social history of the past, we have to make do with the evidence available. This is the great difference between the historical method and the social science method. In the historical method you have evidence left behind from an era which is gone; the activities of people who are no longer around. This limits the use of the sociological method, and to an even greater extent it limits the use of the psychological method. It is no use building theories based on evidence which we don't possess and can never hope to acquire. The psychological method should be used with caution, bearing in mind that you can't put Julius Caesar or Martin Luther or Kemal Atatürk on the psychoanalyst's couch.

Since most modern psychology is the work of Westerners working on Western patients, asking Western questions and getting Western answers, it is extremely dangerous to assume that one can simply take the whole caboodle and apply it to another society without making the necessary adjustments. That way you get the same sort of nonsense as if you try to explain the Ottoman Empire in terms of medieval Europe or of industrial Germany, which is what some people have done.

Take, for example, the Oedipus complex. This is something which relates to the European family, the theoretically monogamous nuclear family in Christian Europe and other Christian countries. How does this work in an Islamic royal family of the past where the mother is a nameless bought concubine and the father an absentee polygamist? One can't just take one set of psychological determinants and apply it to another time or place.

The psycho-biographer has one advantage that the psychoanalyst does not have, in that he confronts a total career. A psychoanalyst who might have met Abraham Lincoln would have met him at a certain point in his career, whereas the psycho-biographer sees the entire life and times. He has a further advantage in that he doesn't have to cure him.

Sensitive Subjects

A few years ago, one of the questions I was asked in the course of an interview was, "Why do you always deal with sensitive subjects?" I responded by explaining that the answer to his question was contained in the metaphor he used. The sensitive place in the body, physical or social, is where something is wrong. Sensitivity is a signal the body sends that something needs attention, which is what I try to give. I don't agree with the implicit meaning of the question that there should be taboo subjects. In any society there are, in fact, taboo subjects. In ours, it usually takes the form of political correctness maintained by social, cultural and professional pressure, but it is not completely enforced.

I have in particular given some attention to two major points of sensitivity—the treatment of non-Muslims in general and Jews in particular in Muslim countries, and the related questions of race and slavery. My first essay on Islam and the non-Muslims was published in the French review *Annales* in the summer of 1980. This formed the introductory chapter of a book, *The Jews of Islam* (1984), dealing with the classical, Ottoman and, more briefly, the modern periods. I dealt with this last at greater length in a succeeding volume, *Semites and Anti-Semites* (1986). Both of these books were translated into a number of European languages. Unlike most of my other books, with one exception they were not translated into Arabic. Nor was my book on race and slavery. The exception, *Semites and Anti-Semites,* is available in Arabic thanks to the effort of an Egyptian lawyer, the late Muhammad Mahmud 'Umar, who felt that this book should be accessible to the Arab reader. After trying in vain to find a publisher he finally decided to do it himself. He translated it into Arabic and had it printed and distributed at his own expense. I greatly appreciate his effort and feel free to draw attention to it as he is safely dead.

My interest in race and slavery began with an invitation I received in the late 1960s from a political scientist in England who was running a project on tolerance. He formed a group of scholars to examine the problems of tolerance and intolerance, and asked me whether I would contribute a paper to a conference on tolerance and intolerance in Islam. At first, I took these words in the conventional sense, meaning willingness or unwillingness to coexist with people of another religion. As I was preparing the paper it suddenly struck me that the true test of tolerance is willingness to accept diversity in matters that really concern us. The fact that we are nowadays tolerant in religion doesn't indicate much since for many people religion has become unimportant. To test tolerance one must look at how people react in matters about which they are passionately concerned, and in much of the modern world that often means race and color. This led me to look at racial attitudes in Middle Eastern history and literature, to consider how far they indicate tolerance or intolerance, and to ask how much truth there was in the commonly accepted stereotypes, both positive and negative.

I presented my paper at the conference and thought that would be the end of the matter. It was not. One of those attending the conference came from the Institute of Race Relations in London. He expressed interest in what I had to say and asked whether I would be willing to give a paper on the same subject at his Institute. I agreed and we set a date for December 2, 1969. When he wrote to confirm the date he informed me that in view of the importance of the subject he had arranged for it to be a joint meeting of the Institute of Race Relations, the Royal Institute of International Affairs, and the Royal Anthropological Institute.

This, to be frank, caused me some anxiety. It is one thing to do a paper and present it to a colloquium or a small group of colleagues. It is quite another to make a formal presentation at a meeting of three august learned societies. I therefore felt obliged to drop everything else and set to work to produce a paper which would be adequate for the occasion.

In due course the paper was completed and delivered, and once again I thought this was the end of the matter. Again it was not. The editor of *Encounter,* a London monthly, was present, and said that he wanted to publish my paper. I agreed, on condition that he include all my footnotes, which he accepted. Monthly literary and political magazines do not normally publish heavily footnoted articles, but with a subject as sensitive as this I did not wish to make statements without providing the documentation.

The article appeared in *Encounter,* with all its footnotes, in August 1970. It brought me a letter from a publishing firm in New York, saying that they had read the article, and would like to have a longer version for book publication, as one of a series of short paperbacks that they had in hand. This was not difficult, since the *Encounter* article had been abridged from a much longer draft. The resulting booklet, *Race and Color in Islam,* was published in 1971.

The publication of a French translation in 1982, more than ten years later, gave me the opportunity to make a number of substantial changes. In addition to correcting some errors I added new documentation and discussed some topics not touched upon in the earlier versions. I also appended a selection of relevant original sources, most of them translated from Arabic.

The study of race led inevitably, in the Islamic world as in other societies, to the problem of slavery, by which both race relations and racial attitudes were profoundly affected. This raised serious difficulties. One of them is the remarkable dearth of scholarly work on the subject. The bibliography of studies on slavery in the Greek and Roman worlds, or in the Americas, runs to thousands of items. Even for medieval Western Europe, where slavery was of relatively minor importance, European scholars have produced a significant literature of research and exposition. For the central Islamic lands, despite the subject's importance in virtually every area and period, a list of serious scholarly monographs on slavery—in law, in doctrine, or in practice—could be printed on a page or two. The documentation for a study of Islamic slavery is almost endless; its exploration has barely begun.

Perhaps the main reason for the lack of scholarly research on Islamic slavery is the extreme sensitivity of the subject. This makes it difficult, and sometimes professionally hazardous, for a young scholar to turn his attention in this direction. In time, we may hope, it will be possible for Muslim scholars to examine and discuss Islamic slavery as freely and as openly as European and American scholars have been willing to discuss this unhappy chapter in their own past.

But that time is not yet. Meanwhile, Islamic slavery remains both an obscure and a highly sensitive topic, the mere mention of which is often seen as a sign of hostile intentions. Sometimes indeed it is, but it need not and should not be so. The imposition of taboos on topics of historical research can only impede and delay a better and more accurate understanding.

My book on the subject was published by the Oxford University Press under the title *Race and Slavery in the Middle East* in 1990. As with *The Muslim Discovery of Europe,* I was able to draw on extensive pictorial evidence of how slaves and people of other races were perceived in the Middle East. This time I was very happy to have twenty-four illustrations in full color. In this book, I tried to deal fairly and objectively with a subject of great historical and comparative importance and to do so without recourse to either polemics or apologetics.

It is an interesting reflection on the subject that *Race and Slavery,* of all my books, is the poorest seller and the least translated.

Once when I was attending a conference in Spain I was sitting and chatting with Patrick Harvey, the distinguished historian of Spanish Islam, when an African American acquaintance joined us. At some point in the conversation I asked him a question that had been puzzling me. "Why is it that so many African Americans who are not converts to Islam are giving their children Muslim names like Ahmad and Ali and Fatima? I can understand that converts to Islam would do that. That would be very natural, but why do people who are not converted to Islam give their children Muslim names?" He replied with some passion, "We don't want to go on carrying the names of the people who bought us." To which Patrick Harvey responded, "But what do you gain by adopting the names of the people who sold you?" It was an interesting point. The European and later American slave dealers who went to West Africa to get slaves did not go and capture them themselves. They bought them from local slave merchants. The identity of those slave merchants is well known but rarely mentioned.

The Middle East and the West

I have always been interested in the relations between the Middle East and what we now call the West, the impact of both Western action and Western civilization on the Islamic peoples and societies of the Middle East and the successive phases of Middle Eastern response. My book *The Middle East and the West* consisted originally of a series of six public lectures delivered at Indiana University in Bloomington in March and April 1963, and published in the following year. I attempted to look at the Middle East as a historical, geographical, and cultural entity; to show what the West has meant and means to Middle Easterners; to trace the processes of Western intrusion, influence, domination, and partial withdrawal; and to deal with political and intellectual movements in the Middle East in recent and modern times in three main groups—liberal and socialist, patriotic and nationalist, and Islamic. Finally, I felt it was important to examine the place and role of the countries of the Middle East in international affairs and so consider some of the factors affecting Western policy toward them.

This book, published in 1964, was reprinted a number of times in both Britain and the United States and was translated into several languages, including Norwegian, Greek, Arabic and Hebrew. It was translated into Hebrew by the publishing house of the Israel Defense Ministry, and was translated into Arabic by the Muslim Brothers. I felt that a book which could appeal to such diverse clients must have some merit, at least from the point of view of objectivity. I particularly liked the preface to the Arabic translation in which the translator says, "I don't know who this person is but one thing is clear. He is, from our point of view, either a candid friend or an honest enemy and in any case one who disdains to distort the truth."

In 1993, thirty years after the delivery of the original lectures, I prepared a revised edition which appeared in 1994 with a new title,

The Shaping of the Modern Middle East. It was promptly translated into German and French. During those intervening years, vast changes had taken place in both the world and the region. The Arab states and Israel fought several more wars and Palestinians formed their own organization. Egyptian and Israeli statesmen negotiated and accomplished the first peace treaty between Israel and an Arab state. A revolution in Iran evoked responses all over the Middle East and indeed all over the Islamic world and transformed the region through the emergence of a new regional power and a new Islamic ideology, radical in both its objectives and its methods. Saddam Hussein in Iraq invaded and annexed Kuwait, thus flouting the rules of both inter-Arab and international coexistence, and provoking a massive intervention and involvement of the United States.

A second and more sizable work, *The Muslim Discovery of Europe,* was first published in 1982. It had however a long prehistory. I had for many years been preoccupied with the idea of looking at relations between Europe and the Middle East from the other side—the same curiosity that brought me to the Middle East in the first place. I set to work to explore what Muslims in the Middle East knew about Europe, where they got their information, how good that information was, and what they thought about Europe—if indeed they thought about Europe at all. I presented my first statement on this topic to the International Congress of Historians in Rome in 1955 and discussed it at greater length in some broadcasts on the BBC, and in a series of public lectures at the Collège de France in 1980. In the book I tried to draw these different threads together and, using Arabic, Persian and Turkish materials, to look at ourselves and at our culture from the outside.

In many of my books I use illustrations to make the subject matter more accessible and more intelligible to the general reader. In two cases, the illustrations were an essential part of my narrative, in *Race and Slavery* and, still more so, in *The Muslim Discovery of Europe.* For these, the way in which slaves in the one case and Europeans in the other were portrayed by Muslim artists was of central and obvious importance.

For *The Muslim Discovery of Europe* I collected thirty pictures, most of them from the seventeenth and eighteenth centuries, portrayals of European men and women as seen by Middle Eastern, mostly Turkish and Persian, artists. I was eager to have them in color but my American publisher told me that this was quite impossible as it would drive the price per copy to an unacceptable height. He agreed reluctantly to let me have my thirty illustrations, but only in black and white. As the usual sequence of translations began, the situation got worse. The German publisher accepted only eight illustrations, the French publisher none. Then came a moment of utter delight. I received a letter from the Italian publisher saying that he would prefer to have the illustrations in color, did I have prints available? I had some, but not all, and the Italian translation of *The Muslim Discovery of Europe* had sixteen pictures in color and twelve in black and white. Among other translations, the Persian included twenty-eight pictures in black and white, the Japanese and Indonesian translations included none.

The question arose again with my book *Race and Slavery,* where I thought it would be interesting and relevant to show how Muslim artists perceived and portrayed their slaves. Here the response filled me with delight. The original English edition, published by the Oxford University Press, contained twenty-four pictures, all in color. All twenty-four reappeared, again in color, in the French translation.

One interesting and perhaps significant detail is that in the paperback edition of *Race and Slavery in the Middle East,* one of the pictures, a portrayal of a slave market from a thirteenth-century manuscript, was also used by the publishers on the cover. The upper part of the picture shows the merchants, with scales and money. The lower half of the picture shows the merchandise, black slaves and their custodians. Interestingly, this picture was used in a television program about Islam to illustrate the vigor of medieval Islamic trade. But they used only the upper half, showing the merchants. The lower half, showing the merchandise, was omitted.

Poems in Translation

No publisher ever asked me for translations of poetry, and it was not always easy to get them into print. Mostly this happened by some fortunate chance. A few were contributed to literary journals, a few more to anthologies of one sort or another. The only translation that actually came out at book length was the *Keter Malchut* (*The Kingly Crown*) by the medieval Spanish Jewish poet Solomon Ibn Gabirol. It was a poem which impressed me enormously as a religious statement in itself and as an expression of a whole worldview of a medieval man. There was already a complete English translation by Israel Zangwill. I suppose I was being overly ambitious in trying to compete with a writer of the distinction of Zangwill but I wasn't happy with his translation. He was a fine novelist but I don't think he was a poet, and his translation at times seemed to me rather awkward and not true to the original. So I tried my hand at it. My version of *The Kingly Crown* was published in London in 1961.

During my first visit to Tel Aviv in 1938 I had a very brief meeting with the Hebrew poet Shaul Tchernikhovsky. I had neither a book for him to inscribe nor did he give me one, and unfortunately I have no recollection of our conversation. I was particularly intrigued by one of his works, a cycle of sonnets, *On the Blood*. Each one is in the correct European sonnet form, and the fifteenth and last sonnet consists of the first lines of the previous fourteen. This was a challenge I could not resist, and I set to work to do the same in English. I can't claim it was a great success, but I don't think it was too bad.

I should perhaps mention one other not very large group of poetic translations: those included in my various books on history. A poem is also a historical document, a record of a culture, a mood, even an event; no less important, in its way, than the narratives of chroniclers or the files in the archives. In recent years I have been publishing my translations in small batches, as contributions to this or that Festschrift or, latterly, in a memorial volume in honor of one of my colleagues. I still have quite a number in reserve. Many of these translations of poetry were made during the war, that is, more than sixty years ago.

Translating Turkish poems was almost a vocation and I was pleased that my translations appeared in two anthologies, *The Penguin Book of Turkish Verse* and *An Anthology of Turkish Literature*, edited by Kemal Silay. Finally, in 2001, Princeton University Press gave me the opportunity to publish some of my translations in book form. *Music of a Distant Drum* contains translations from Arabic, Persian, Turkish and Hebrew. With the exception of the Turkish section, which continues to the eighteenth century, all the poems are from the medieval period. The Hebrew poems are limited to those of poets who lived in Islamic lands, and thus formed part of the Judeo-Islamic tradition.

While most of my books have been translated into other languages I did not, for obvious reasons, expect this one to be translated. A translation of a translation, especially of verse, does not normally make good sense. To my astonishment, and I must add, delight, the Italian publishing house of Donzelli produced an Italian version, with a different title, *Ti Amo di due Amori* (*I Love You with Two Loves*). A few of the texts were translated from the English, but most of them were directly translated from the originals by Italian experts in those languages. The book is illustrated with no fewer than thirty-eight full-page color prints from originals in Turkish, Persian, Arabic and Hebrew manuscripts. On the title page I am credited with having "chosen and introduced" the poems, but not translated them. This was of course correct for the Italian volume.

One of my favorite comments about translations is the Italian phrase with two words that sound almost the same, "*Traduttore, traditore*" ("Translator, traitor").

The *Encyclopedia of Islam*

One of the major works of reference in the field of Islamic studies is the *Encyclopedia of Islam*. Edited and published in the Netherlands, under the auspices of the Royal Netherlands Academy and the house of Brill, it had the cooperation of British, French and German institutions and individuals and was published simultaneously in three languages. Sometime after the war it was decided that the time was ripe for a new edition, but with some changes. For obvious reasons, German was omitted, and the new edition was to be published only in English and French. There were three editors—one in England, Sir Hamilton Gibb, one in France and a general editor in the Netherlands. When Gibb accepted an appointment at Harvard and left England for the United States, he and his colleagues felt he could no longer adequately discharge his editorial duties from so far away, and they decided to put a substitute in his place. The choice fell on me and I gladly accepted. I served for a number of years on the editorial board, attending meetings by rotation in London, Leiden and Paris, and participating in various ways in the complex, ongoing editorial process. My own migration to the United States created a similar problem, but this time they decided to keep me on the board and appoint an additional English editor, in England. This second edition of the *Encyclopedia of Islam* was published in fascicles from 1954 to 2005 with some supplementary materials up to 2007.

Rewriting One's Own Words

During the last few weeks of 1992, at age seventy-six, I spent most of my time reading and rereading three of my earlier works, which were all sent to me at about the same time and for the same purpose—the preparation of new and revised editions. No doubt the publishers who sent them had been aiming at the Christmas vacation, when I was deemed to be free and available. The result of this was that for a period of something like six weeks, I had an almost unrelieved diet of eating my own words, a diet which I found neither tasty nor nourishing. I had, after all, read it all before. This provoked a number of reflections, some of which I incorporated and published in a new preface; others I will share with my readers now.

The most important, which I shall discuss here, was the oldest of the three books, *The Arabs in History,* first published in 1950, whose genesis I have already described. As time passed, I became less and less satisfied with what I had written in the last months of 1946 and the early months of 1947. The publisher, Hutchinson, brought it out again and again, and for each reprint invited me to make some changes. The changes that I could make were very limited. They insisted on maintaining the type, so that any omission had to be compensated by an addition, and vice versa, and any change affecting the length of a line had to be compensated before the end of the paragraph. One line more or less would have been a disaster, I was told, reverberating to the end of the chapter. Obviously there are limits to what one can do while maintaining the existing type. It gave me the opportunity to correct a few statements which, for one reason or another, were no longer true. I could for example switch from one Yemen to two Yemens and then back to one Yemen, and adjust the number of member states of the Arab League as required—such changes were fairly easy. I was even able to make a few more substantial changes by careful juggling with the number of words in a line and to do some scholarly updating; but all that was very limited. I could cope with simple updates—for example to record, in successive editions, the 1958 creation and 1961 dissolution of the United Arab Republic, but no more.

After the sixth edition, in the early 1990s, the original publisher, Hutchinson of London, decided that they had had enough; and as part of a general restructuring of their activities, in which the whole series to which my book belonged was abandoned, they said that they would let it go out of print. Oxford University Press became interested; they said they would like to take my book over, but they wanted me to do a thorough revision. They were prepared to reset the whole thing from scratch, so I was no longer bound in the chains of type, and had a chance to reexamine the book more thoroughly and undertake a more comprehensive overhaul.

Their intention, and initially mine too, was to revise principally the last part. After all, we agreed, the earlier history hadn't changed very much. It was the most recent part which would be most in need of revision, as quite a lot had happened in the Middle East since the early months of 1947. At first, I shared this view. But the idea that the earlier history hadn't changed was deeply flawed, as I should have seen from the start. Rereading the text that I wrote almost forty-five years earlier, I soon realized that many more changes would be needed before I could in honesty present it as a "revised and updated" edition. The publishers would not be satisfied with anything less. Understandably, they wanted to market this by now old book as a revised and updated edition, and I would have to honor those words. The result was a whole series of changes, on virtually every page of the book—an interesting indication of the scholarly, intellectual and even verbal changes that take place over almost half a century.

Many of the changes were purely verbal. There were even a number of places in the book where I had to change the text in order to retain the original sense, because the English language had developed in the meantime, and many words had changed their connotation or even their meaning. One example is the use of the words "race" and "racial." In England in 1946 and 1947, these words were almost invariably used where nowadays one would use such words as "ethnicity" or "ethnic." When I joined the British Army in 1940, I was given a form to fill in and one line said "Race." This was the first time I had ever encountered the word "race" in an official document, and I didn't know what they wanted. If I had been joining the German Army, I would have known what they meant, but I was joining the British, not the German, Army. I went to the sergeant in charge and asked him if he could explain to me what "race" meant, and he gave me the sort of pitying look that sergeants had for the raw recruits with whom they had to cope. He tried to explain, but I didn't really get much from his explanation. So I asked, "Well, am I supposed to put 'Jewish' here?" "No," he said, "that's your religion. They don't ask you two different questions with the same answer. We've already got a line for that. This is your race." So I said, "Well, what?" Nowadays I suppose I would say "white" or "Caucasian," but that wouldn't have entered my mind at that time. White was a color—or the lack of one; Caucasian meant people from the Caucasus with names like Djugashvili. So he explained to me, slowly and carefully, that as far as the British Army was concerned, there were four races, and I had a free choice among the four: English, Scottish, Welsh and Irish.

To use the word "race" in a book published in 1993 in this sense would be offensive and, what is more important, misleading. In most places where I had used the words "race" or "racial" in the original edition, I substituted "ethnic." The word "race" has virtually disappeared from the book since I was not talking about differences of race in the modern Americanized sense of the word, actually the old anthropological meaning which has now become general.

Another word, "class," has also changed in content and significance, both in the common usage of our time and in my own perception of it. In the first edition, I frequently used "class" in ways that now seem to be loose and inaccurate, and at times even tendentious. I retained it where it seemed appropriate but in most places where I had used the word "class" I replaced it with other terms, more precise where the evidence permitted, less specific where the evidence did not permit.

There are other words that have changed or lost their meaning, and words that have simply become unacceptable. Sometimes, as I said, even where I had no desire to change the meaning of words that I used in 1948, I found it necessary to change the words themselves in order to convey the same meaning more accurately to the present-day reader.

Rereading the old text, I was also jarred in a number of places by the use of what now struck me (though obviously it didn't then) as ideologically slanted language; terms, forms of words which were fashionable and acceptable at that time but are no longer in accord with contemporary opinion, including, more especially, my own.

All these were verbal changes. Of far greater importance were those that affected the substance. These were of several kinds. One kind might reasonably be described as corrections, that is, changes, the purpose of which is to bring the text into line with the current state of knowledge and climate of opinion among scholars. Since the book was originally published in 1950 many scholars in many countries had worked on most of the subjects and periods discussed in it and, to quote the University of London requirements for a Ph.D., they had contributed to knowledge "through the discovery of new evidence and the achievement of new insights," and thus in significant respects transformed our perception of the Arab past. Obviously I had to take account of this in a book marketed as "revised and updated."

The progress of research in history, as in other fields, has as at least part of its general purpose to make clear what was obscure. But students of medieval Islamic history will recognize what I mean when I say that very often its result is to make obscure what was once clear. In certain subjects our knowledge diminishes from year to year with the progress of scholarship and research, as one generally accepted view after another is attacked, leaving a terrain strewn with demolished or endangered hypotheses and assumptions.

When I wrote my chapter on the Prophet in 1947 (a book on Arab history obviously has to have a chapter on the Prophet), there were many disagreements among scholars as to the authenticity of this or that tradition, of this or that narrative, but the broad outline of the Prophet's career, as also the actions and achievements of his companions and successors, was generally accepted. Writing at the time, I was able to present the advent of Islam in the form of a narrative of events and then try to interpret its significance in the framework of Arab, Muslim and general history. I was at that time blissfully unaware of a group of iconoclast scholars in the Soviet Union (Klimovitch, Belayev, Tolstov and others) who already, before the outbreak of World War II, had begun to question the historical authenticity of the Koran and the historicity of the prophetic biography, some of them even the historicity of the Prophet himself. Later, of course, similar and even more radical criticism developed in the Western world, and while one need not go all the way with the more radical critics, obviously one can no longer proceed blithely with the kind of narrative which was normal until that time.

Radical, critical scholarship has called one source after another, one narrative after another, into question. In a brief but broad-ranging historical essay of this type, it would not be possible, nor indeed would it be appropriate, to examine the arguments of the radical critics of early Islamic history, but neither is it possible to disregard them. Matters previously presented as simple statements of fact must now be presented in a more tentative, a more hypothetical, form. Nor can they simply be omitted, which would be the easy way of handling it, because their importance, their influence, still remains. The past as remembered, the past as perceived, the past as narrated, is still a powerful, at times a determining, force in the self-image of a society and in the shaping of its institutions and laws, even if the factual base on which this image rests is shown by historians, centuries later in distant countries, to contain more fantasy than fact.

This is probably the most important of the major changes due to historical scholarship of which I had to take account, and probably the most difficult—to preserve a chapter on the Prophet, retaining as much of the traditional narrative as was necessary in order to make the Muslims' own perception of their past intelligible, without committing myself as narrator to too many simple declaratory statements.

Another view that needed modification was of the role of the half-Arabs in the early Islamic empire. The tendency at one time was to divide the Muslim population of the early empire into the Arabs and the non-Arab converts to Islam, known as the Mawali. In 1947 I, like others at the time, gave far too little importance to another group—the half-Arabs, that initially small but rapidly growing population who were the children of an Arab father and a non-Arab mother. The exercise by the conquerors of the rights of conquest had rapidly created a considerable number of such people. These, belonging on their father's side to the ruling conquistador aristocracy, and on their mother's side to a conquered and subjugated population, formed an extremely important intermediate social group. By the mid-eighth century the distinction between these and the "pure" Arabs was ceasing to matter, and even the Caliphs were now the sons, not of free Arab ladies, but of foreign slave concubines. In the period of the Conquests, the half-Arabs played a role of some significance, which was underestimated by earlier historians, including myself.

It is hardly necessary for me to add to this list of subsequent research and revision the extensive work that has been done on the Arab world in the Ottoman period—a subject which had been barely touched upon at the time when I was writing, before the opening of the Ottoman archives.

A second category of changes derived not so much from the advancement of scholarship as from something of a more personal character—the evolution of my own views, my own interests, my own concerns. This was, after all, my book—I wrote it, it had my name on the title page and it was shaped inevitably by my own preoccupations then and my different preoccupations now.

Looking back, I felt that the amount of space I allocated to the Isma'ili movement was disproportionate. I was, shall we say, somewhat obsessed with the Isma'ilis; I had done my doctoral dissertation on the Isma'ilis; my earliest attempt at fieldwork had been in the Isma'ili villages in Syria; most of my other early work had been in connection with the Isma'ilis and for me at that time they were the most important thing in Arab history. So I gave them a whole chapter and they tended to infiltrate from that chapter even into other places. It was too late to do anything much about that. Restructuring to the point of omitting a chapter would have been much too difficult, but I did try to restore some better proportion between the Isma'ilis and other elements in the history of the time.

If I paid too much importance to the Isma'ilis, there were other subjects to which, looking back, I felt I gave too little importance, and I tried to remedy that in the new edition. One might argue (and I think I would have to concede some truth in this) that I was merely replacing my old obsessions by my current obsessions. Slavery, for example, hardly occurred in the old edition, whereas it figured quite prominently in the new one. But that again, I think, is not only inevitable but quite reasonable.

There are many other things in Arab history, as in other topics in general, which I no longer saw, or for that matter see now, as I did in 1947. It would have been self-defeating and utterly pointless to try to rewrite the book as I would have written it forty-five years later. I was indeed inspired, a few years later, to attempt a longer view of a broader topic, in my book *The Middle East: A Brief History of the Last Two Thousand Years,* first published in 1995. The aim of the revisions of the earlier book was more modest: to remove statements which I now found unacceptable, to use cautious language where I was no longer as sure as I was half a century ago (and that applies to practically everything in this world and the next), to add new material where this seemed necessary in order to present a balanced picture. In both respects I proceeded by addition, by omission, by emendation while still preserving the original structure of exposition and analysis.

I began by saying that the original idea of the publishers and of myself was to update the book by rewriting the sections dealing with more recent history and current events, and obviously there were major changes in the Arab world and beyond during the years that had passed since this book was written and first published. These events are important in themselves and some of them at least had to be discussed. They are important in another respect, and that is in the way in which they affect the perception and presentation of the past. It is commonplace that we use the past to illuminate the present and perhaps the future; it is also true though less realized that we sometimes use the present to illuminate our understanding of the past.

Let me illustrate this with some examples. In 1947, when I first wrote this book, the Cold War had not yet begun; in 1992, when I prepared the new edition, it was over. Looking back at my chapter on pre-Islamic Arabia, I could not but be struck by the parallels between the situation of the modern Middle East between the two rival superpowers and the position of the Arabian peninsula between Byzantium and Persia, for the most part beyond the direct rule of either but affected in many ways by the competing strategic, commercial and diplomatic efforts of both superpowers of the time, in war, in peace, then in war again. The impact of their rivalry on Arabia provoked new reflections on the ending of the Cold War and its probable consequences for the Middle East.

Another topic where recent and current events could help achieve a better understanding of the past is the relative importance of socio-economic and ethnic-national factors. In the nineteenth century, in the age of liberalism and nationalism, it was assumed generally by scholars that the great struggles of the early caliphate were basically national: especially Persian nationalism in revolt against Arab domination. By the time that I was writing this book, these ideas had been generally abandoned and we were all quite sure that nationality did not matter very much, that ethnicity was of secondary importance, that what really mattered were the economic and social factors. So, along with most others at the time, I presented these early struggles in primarily socioeconomic terms. Looking at the world in 1992, who would say that ethnicity doesn't matter? Who could say with certainty that socioeconomic factors are more important and more decisive than ethnic, and one might add religious, loyalties and allegiances? There again, I felt that some revision was required.

Arab history offers a wide range of experiences where one may engage in the usual exercise of looking into the past to help understand the present and even prepare for the future. We have a wonderful selection of seemingly relevant events in the Arab past: invasions from the north, south, east and west; triumphs and defeats; the waxing and waning of imperial power, their own and that of others; the blooming and withering of cultures; tensions and releases in economic and social change. Not least important of the lessons of the past are the things that didn't happen—the changes resisted or attempted without success, the revolutions that failed or, to borrow a phrase, the roads not taken.

The events of the last few decades have demonstrated with blinding clarity the impact of technological change, both in peace and in war; and the penalties paid by those who fail to keep pace. This may help us now to achieve a better understanding than before of the impact of firearms in late medieval and early modern times in the Middle Eastern Islamic world and the cultural causes and political consequences of the late and reluctant adoption of modern weaponry. The communications revolution of our time and its consequences have illuminated another contrast in the Arab and Islamic past: the swift and early acceptance of paper—an import from China which made possible the rapid and relatively inexpensive production of more durable books and affected not only literature and science but also government and commerce; and after paper, the long-delayed and reluctant acceptance of printing. Social choices of this type are no less important, and at the present time a good deal more relevant, than cataclysmic events like the Crusades and the Mongol conquests.

Of all the pages in the original edition, the ones that had become most badly out-of-date were of course the ones that at the time of writing were the most up-to-date—the final pages dealing with recent and current affairs. These date very rapidly, even in the brief interval between proofreading and publication. I was more careful this time. I did, of course, rewrite these final pages to take some account of the massive changes that had taken place in the Arab world since the first edition appeared, but after some reflection I decided not to include even the barest outline of recent and current history. In a region and in a period of rapid and often violent change, some distance is needed for serious evaluation and any attempt to keep pace with new developments is swiftly outdated. The past is more stable.

Iceland

Sometime in the early fifties, when I was spending the summer months in Denmark as I usually did at that time, I received a request to contribute to a Festschrift, to be published in Turkish, in honor of a distinguished Turkish colleague. The deadline was dangerously near.

For social, personal and professional reasons I could not refuse but the question was how on earth was I to write anything being so far away from all my books and notes and files? In desperation, I went to the Royal Danish Library to see if I could find anything there and looked up the terms "Turks" and "Turkey" in the various subject catalogs. To my surprise and delight I found several items relating to a raid by Barbary Corsairs on Iceland in the year 1627. The raid seems to have received very little attention from historians (except of course in Iceland). The published material was very limited and almost all of it was in either Danish or Icelandic. I eagerly accessed the available publications and decided that this would provide me with the basis for an article suitable for the Festschrift in honor of my colleague. The Turks were of course not Turks in the sense in which that term is used today—that is, people from Turkey. At that time the term "Turk," like "Moor" and "Saracen" in earlier times, was used simply to designate Muslims. The raiders in question came from North Africa; many of them came originally from Christian Europe. In the Christian perspective they were renegades, in the Muslim perspective, converts to the true faith.

I was able to read the Danish material without much difficulty. The Icelandic stuff was more of a problem but I managed to get the general sense. With this material I was able to write a short article, "Corsairs in Iceland," and sent it to Ankara for publication. It was duly included, in Turkish translation, in a special Festschrift issue of a Turkish journal in 1953. Unsurprisingly, it received very little attention in Turkey and none at all anywhere else. Some twenty years later I was asked to contribute to a French journal devoted to the "Muslim Occident" for a special issue in honor of the birthday of a distinguished French historian, an expert on the Islamic Far West. It occurred to me that the unpublished English original of my "Corsairs in Iceland" piece might be suitable. The original Turkish publishers had no objection to my reusing it; the French publishers had no ob-

jection to my using a piece previously published in Turkish and therefore unknown in the Western world. The article was duly published
in the English language, in a French journal, on an Icelandic subject.
Unsurprisingly, it remained obscure and unknown and I assumed
that it would remain so.

I was mistaken. In 2000 Buntzie and I went on a ten-day holiday
in Iceland. It is a relatively short journey with very little jet lag. Iceland is a beautiful country with excellent food, especially fish, and
neither of us had been there before. It seemed a good idea for an interesting, relaxing and not too expensive holiday. We booked a four-
day tour to see waterfalls and glaciers and found ourselves part of a
group of about a dozen tourists. On the first day we were sitting and
having coffee with a guide, who suddenly asked me if I was the Bernard Lewis who had written about the Turkish raid on Iceland. I was
astonished at this reference to an obscure piece, written on an obscure
subject and published in an obscure place more than a quarter of a
century earlier. I admitted that I was indeed the author of that piece
and the guide became very excited. He explained that he was a historian by profession and was doing tours as a sideline to make a little
extra money. He had just finished reviewing for accuracy the script
for a program about the raid that was being produced for an Icelandic
TV station. Would I agree, he asked, to be interviewed by the director of the program, and for the interview to be included in the broadcast? I did and I was, and the incident certainly lent a distinctive
flavor to the rest of the trip.

Another incident during that trip is one which I remember only
because Buntzie won't let me forget it. When traveling abroad I usually go into bookstores and look particularly at the history sections,
to see what historians are writing and people are reading. In a bookshop in Reykjavik I found something I had never seen before—an
Icelandic grammar in English. Icelandic, originally a dialect of Old
Norse, is what one might call the classical Scandinavian language and

since I had a fairly good knowledge of Danish, I found that the "buy one, get one free" principle applied here. If one knows Danish, Norwegian is easy and Swedish accessible. Icelandic is somewhat more difficult, but not excessively so. After spending about ten minutes leafing through the Icelandic grammar in the bookshop, I remarked: "I think I could learn to read Icelandic in about a week." Buntzie found this startling and amusing and teases me about it.

13.

Politics and the Iraq War

When Saddam Hussein invaded and occupied Kuwait in 1990, the United States, with the support of the international community, decided that something had to be done. Almost every Middle East expert in the country was invited to Washington and was asked for his comments on the situation. That was my first meeting with high-level official Washington, and more important, my first meeting with Dick Cheney, at that time Secretary of Defense. We met on subsequent occasions over the years.

I gather that my assessment and recommendations were radically different from those of almost all the other "experts" they had consulted. The general feeling was that this was going to be a major and difficult struggle. It could be "another Vietnam," a phrase that came up frequently during the discussions. In general, preparations were being made as if the United States were about to confront the Third Reich in its prime. One senior officer even said, in terms of great alarm, that he feared that this might be a repetition of the Russo-Japanese War when a major European power was defeated by an upstart Asian power, and the beginning of a new era in East-West relations.

I took a different view, reinforced by a recent conversation with the Turkish President Turgut Özal. I told them that I thought that the war, when it came, would be "quick, cheap and easy." In this I was echoing what President Özal had told me shortly before when I was in Turkey on university business. Özal and I spent an evening together.

I knew him well, long before he rose to high office and our conversation was more relaxed than would be normal between a head of state and a visiting foreigner. We talked of many things and then inevitably we talked about the crisis in Iraq. Saddam Hussein had invaded and occupied Kuwait and President Bush was still wondering what to do. Turgut Özal said, "You remember when I visited Washington a few months ago?" I remembered because we had had lunch together. He said, "I spoke with your President. He is an indecisive sort of character, but I think he has made up his mind this time. There will be war, and," Özal added, "when it comes, it will be quick, cheap and easy." This was startling. I said, "What makes you think that?" and so he gave me an enigmatic Turkish smile, and said, "We like to know what is happening among our neighbors." In other words, they had good intelligence. "Let me give you an example," he continued. "Not a week passes without many Iraqi soldiers, including officers, deserting from the Iraqi Army, crossing our frontier and asking for sanctuary. An army from which officers are deserting before the battle begins is not in good shape." I had to agree. Then I said, "If it comes to war, will you be with us?" "Of course," he said. I asked, "May I ask why?" Again he gave me his enigmatic Turkish smile and said, "For the same reason we declared war on the Axis in February 1945. When the fighting stops and the talking starts, we want to be at the victors' table, and we want to be there on the guest list, not on the menu."

The really tough problem was political, how to deal with the country after military victory was achieved. The results of the invasion amply confirmed President Özal's judgment and therefore my reputation with Cheney. Incidentally we were not entirely alone in our view. An Israeli general who happened to be passing through Washington at the time was asked if he thought the preparations were adequate and he replied that they were adequate in all respects but one. "You haven't made enough arrangements to accommodate prisoners of war and deserters."

The prompt and effective American response not only saved Kuwait but also Saudi Arabia, which was threatened and whose rulers relied entirely on American action to save them. Indeed, a quip at the time was that the marching song of the Saudi Arabian armed forces was "Onward Christian Soldiers."

During the Eight-Year War (1980–88) between Iraq and revolutionary Iran, Saddam Hussein was able to count on a considerable measure of American tolerance and even, on occasion, help. One of the factors that helped end the war was that U.S. forces shot down and destroyed an Iranian passenger aircraft. The American statement, and I have no doubt that it was the truth, was that it was an accident. But neither the Iranians nor the Iraqis believed it. The Iranians, whose army had weakened considerably, decided that the Americans were becoming serious, and that they had better make peace on the best terms that they could get. Although the UN brokered a cease-fire (Security Council Resolution 598) Saddam Hussein felt that he could count on American support, or at least acquiescence, in whatever he decided to do next.

His next step was to invade and annex Kuwait—an independent state since the eighteenth century, long before the creation of modern Iraq in the twentieth. According to Saddam Hussein, it was an integral part of Iraq and should be returned to its motherland. The Arab world in general was outraged at this annexation which was rightly seen as an immediate threat to the Gulf states and Saudi Arabia and a more general threat to the rest of the Middle East. Action was demanded and the U.S. administration of Bush Sr. first gave a deadline for withdrawal from Kuwait and then sent forces into Iraq to compel Saddam Hussein to withdraw. But having accomplished this immediate and limited purpose, the U.S. government, to everyone's astonishment, promptly made peace. Saddam Hussein was left in control of the state, his army and most particularly of his revolutionary guards, and he was free to use them as he chose, except in two separate no-fly zones set up to protect the Kurds in the north and the Shi'a in the south. These zones were enforced by the United States, the United Kingdom and France, which sent out aircraft patrols.

I was not consulted on what followed in Iraq and do not feel it was handled wisely. Saddam Hussein was soundly defeated but the victorious Americans treated him with extraordinary gentleness. Instead of a picture of defeat and surrender, the reality of the situation, he was allowed, even encouraged, to cherish and spread the illusion of a compromise truce. Worse was to follow. The United States had called upon the oppressed people of Iraq to rise against the tyrant, and some of them, notably the Kurds and the Shi'a, had done so. The victorious Americans now sat back and watched while Saddam, using the Republican Guard which he had been allowed to retain, proceeded to wreak ferocious vengeance on both groups. Not surprisingly, this had a discouraging effect the next time around.

An argument was put forward at that time that it was on Saudi advice, indeed insistence, that the Americans had stopped their advance and left Saddam Hussein in power. I had an opportunity to discuss this with the Saudi ambassador in Washington at that time, Prince Bandar, and asked him if this were true. He replied with considerable emphasis that it was totally untrue. "On the contrary," he said, "we urged them to go ahead and finish the job."

The general impact all over the Middle East of the tolerance and acceptance of Saddam Hussein's tyranny was catastrophic. I remember suggesting at the time that instead of the code name "Desert Storm," the operation should have been named "Kuwaitus Interruptus."

But the first Iraq war was by no means entirely a failure. Kuwait recovered its independence and the neighboring Gulf states were no longer under immediate threat. More important, a significant part of Iraq, about a fifth of the country in the north, was no longer ruled by Saddam Hussein but by an autonomous regime, an alliance of Kurds and mostly Shi'ite Arabs.

The running of the northern zone was a remarkable success story. With astonishing speed life returned to normal—the economy, education, both at the school and university level, and civil life in general. The groups who were running the north did an excellent job in creating an effective, smoothly functioning independent society. I was in touch with some of the leaders of the north and was told that they also had a substantial following in the remainder of Iraq, including many senior army officers, and that when the time was ripe they would be able to take over.

The method they proposed was that they would establish and proclaim a "provisional government of free Iraq." A government of free Iraq proclaimed in New York or Washington or Europe would be meaningless, but such a government proclaimed on the soil of Iraq, with a base in that country, was another matter. The rulers of the north were quite convinced that they could do this and that they would immediately get powerful support in the rest of the country. They proposed this on at least two occasions to the U.S. government, once during the first Bush administration, the second time during the Clinton administration. On both occasions their proposal was the same. They did not ask for any military help as they felt confident that they could handle the military side themselves. All they asked for was political support and a clear statement of recognition.

They were not able to get either. I and others pleaded for action along these lines, but there were always reasons to postpone and delay. I still feel that the liberation of Iraq could have been achieved far more peacefully and more effectively by collaborating with the rulers of the free zone in the north rather than by a second war against Saddam Hussein.

I have sometimes been blamed by the media for the second invasion of Iraq. This is the opposite of the truth. What I actually proposed, the recognition of a "Free Government of Iraq," would have given international legitimacy to a homegrown, independent movement and thus would have accelerated the overthrow, from within, of the already crumbling tyranny of Saddam Hussein.

But it was not to be.

"The Lewis Doctrine"

A changing and multifaceted aspect of my life has been the so-called "Bernard Lewis Doctrine," which has appeared in a variety of different and sometimes contradictory forms. It was invented by Lyndon LaRouche, a well-known political eccentric, in the late 1970s. According to LaRouche and his publications, I had not, as was the general view, discerned the development of Muslim radicalism. I had caused it. I had deliberately fomented this in order to serve my ulterior purposes. It was in this capacity that, among other things, I organized and conducted the Iranian Revolution and other later examples of Muslim extremism.

As absurd as this may appear, his explanation is even more so. In doing all this I was acting as a secret agent of British intelligence; the purpose of all my nefarious activities was to restore British imperial power and extend it in new directions.

For a while I was subjected to a treatment which might not unfairly be described as harassment by Lyndon LaRouche agents. Some of them attended my lectures, interrogated my audiences and more generally my students, and tried in various ways to prove my guilt. The reason why Islamic radicalism served British imperial purposes was never made clear, but neither reason nor clarity ever ranked high among the LaRouche objectives.

The LaRouche connection gradually faded but the "Lewis Doctrine" survived, and metamorphosed into often mutually exclusive forms. The most remarkable was a front-page article in *The Wall Street Journal* in 2004 by Peter Waldman, a journalist. This was published with no interview or inquiry to me directly. The article was an interesting selection of nonsense. The most recent and the most persistent form of the "Lewis Doctrine" makes me responsible for the policies of the Bush administration, and more particularly for the invasion of Iraq.

The story of my connection with the Bush presidency did have some slender basis in fact, but was wildly exaggerated, distorted and misrepresented. It began with my acquaintance with Dick Cheney, and it was chiefly with the Vice President's office that I maintained contact.

I was invited to Cheney's home twice after 9/11 to dine with him and a small group of staff. My task was to talk about the Middle East and Islam and I found them a receptive audience asking excellent questions. I also met with this group in Cheney's office several times. My job was not to offer policy suggestions but to provide background—some of the detail and information which is taken into consideration when policy decisions are made.

My role in policy making was, at most, minimal. The exaggeration of this in some of the media was absurd. This experience deepened my mistrust of what I read and heard about goings-on in the administration.

I was sadly reminded of the old British principle that intelligence and policy must be totally separate. Intelligence people provide information but make *no* recommendations so that policy people get just the facts and make decisions with unvarnished information. The danger to be avoided is that intel should be selected and presented to promote a policy line or a course of action. This "separation of powers" is an important part of effective democracy and its erosion can be dangerous.

I found Cheney to be thoughtful and unusual among politicians in that he wanted to hear what I had to say. We discussed the challenge posed by specific countries as well as issues facing the region. He asked excellent questions, listened intently to my answers and asked probing follow-ups.

During the last two years of the Bush administration the Vice President's office was virtually sidelined, to the detriment of U.S. policy and interests. I was saddened by the willful vilification of Cheney by the liberal media. The Cheney that they described was not the Cheney I knew and respected.

On one occasion I was invited to give an off-the-record talk to the White House staff. It was a pleasant occasion, socially interesting and intellectually stimulating. My most vivid recollection is of a wide-ranging conversation with Condoleezza Rice, the National Security Advisor, who asked me to come to her office for a private discussion. I hope I was helpful.

I was invited to meet President George W. Bush on three occasions—a small group discussion after 9/11, a large black-tie dinner at the White House in 2005 and at an awards presentation in 2006. I was told that if I wished to make any suggestions I should e-mail them to Stephen Hadley, who was by then the National Security Advisor. I did send a few e-mails to him, but they were about Iran and not Iraq and were sent long after the Iraq War. In the interest of dispelling conspiracy theorists, or perhaps offering them more grist for their feverish speculation, allow me to offer up some excerpts from those 2006 e-mails:

> We must be conscious of what we say as much as what we do. Sir Harold Nicolson once said that one can never be certain what is in the mind of the oriental but we must leave the oriental no doubt what is in our mind. . . .
>
> Let us not forget that we have tried a number of times since the Iranian revolution to negotiate with the [Iranian] regime, starting when President Carter addressed Khomeini during the hostage crisis "as a believer to a man of God" and continuing through various phases of apology and other expressions of good will and even praise. The result was always the same—a refusal and a snub. To seek to negotiate now—from a position

of weakness in Iraq, uncertainty at home and insult from Iran can only be seen as an expression of weakness and fear on our part. When defeated in battle, it makes good sense to try and get the best possible terms of surrender. We are not yet at that stage.

Over the years, a pattern has evolved in the Middle East whereby the people of "friendly" countries hate us because they see us, often correctly, as supporting the tyrants that misrule them, while the people of "hostile" countries, i.e., those ruled by hostile rulers, turn to us as their best hope of liberation from those rulers. I remember being told by a highly placed Iranian that, "There is no country in the world where pro-American feeling is stronger, deeper and more widespread than Iran." I have ample independent confirmation of this, for example, in the often repeated remark from Iranians that, "You should have tackled your problems in this region in alphabetical order," i.e., first Iran, then Iraq. . . .

What we need to do is encourage the people and scare the leadership. To negotiate in present circumstances would do exactly the reverse. A better line would be to show some encouragement and even support for opposition movements and sympathy for the sufferings of the Iranian people under their corrupt and tyrannical masters.

We might say things like, "We have the greatest respect for their culture. . . . We share their hatred of their tyrannical and predatory rulers who are dishonoring their country, their people and their faith, which their rulers pretend to represent." The regime has only two policies—tyranny at home and terror abroad, both serving the same purposes. . . .

Particular importance should be attached to the policies, and perhaps still more the attitudes, of the present rulers of Iran, who seem to be preparing for a final apocalyptic battle between the forces of God [themselves] and of the Devil [the Great Satan—the United States]. They see this as the final struggle of the End of Time and are therefore undeterred by any level of slaughter and destruction even among their own people. "Allah will know his own" is the phrase commonly used, meaning that among the multiple victims God will recognize the Muslims and give them a quick pass to heaven.

In this context, the deterrent that worked so well during the Cold War, namely M.A.D. (Mutual Assured Destruction), would have no meaning. At the End of Time, there will be general destruction anyway. What will matter is the final destination of the dead—hell for the infidels, and the delights of heaven for the believers. For people with this mindset, M.A.D. is not a constraint; it is an inducement. . . .

I have been reading with increasing alarm stories in the press about how we are making diplomatic approaches to Iran to help us extricate ourselves from the "mess" in Iraq. What matters most is the immediate message this will convey to both our enemies and our friends in the Middle East—an encouragement to the first, a sign of desperation, even of abandonment and betrayal, to the second.

In considering any step, there are two questions which we must ask. Will it work? What will be its immediate impact?

It will obviously take time to formulate an answer to the first question. My conviction is that it will fail but I can see that others think differently. We can agree to disagree. But the answer to the second question is immediate, clear and devastating. It will be seen as a sign of American fear and weakness, as seeking the help of an enemy to betray a friend. Ahmadinejad has made no secret of his attitudes, and the attempt by diplomacy to ingratiate ourselves with him and his faction will be seen as a frantic attempt by us, in retreat and defeat, to solicit Iranian help in withdrawing from Iraq. This will be seen as confirming

Ahmadinejad's boast when he assumed office, "I know how to deal with the Americans."

This e-mail correspondence makes it quite clear that my primary concern was Iran's nuclear program, and not toppling Saddam Hussein.

The first invasion of Iraq, after its conquest of Kuwait, was unquestionably legitimate and necessary. Iraq had committed a blatant act of military aggression which could not be tolerated. I, along with most, thought that corrective action was necessary. The second invasion of Iraq in 2003 was another matter. This is sometimes ascribed to my influence with Vice President Cheney. But the reverse is true. I did not recommend it. On the contrary, I opposed it. It is, to say the least, annoying to be blamed for something I did not do. Advice, whether given or not, is impossible to prove. The best I can do to prove my point is to note that I am nowhere mentioned in the 530 pages of Cheney's memoir, *In My Time*.

It is often said that an American connection or American support is the kiss of death for a Middle Eastern politician. This may be true if the support is fluctuating, uncertain and applied in accordance with what often seems to be the guiding principle of American foreign policy—we must not get too close to our friends for fear of antagonizing our enemies. But even now, despite the damage caused by the second Iraq war, there are still reserves of goodwill toward the United States. American support could even again become an asset in a domestic political struggle provided that the support is clear and effective—that there are rewards for friendship and penalties for hostility to the United States and not, as often appears to be the case, the other way round.

To achieve these results it is necessary to project an image of firmness and reliability. Experts in public relations would no doubt be able to devise many ways of doing this. But to project an image of firmness and reliability, there is one essential prerequisite—to be firm and reliable.

The OIC and EU Foreign Ministers Conference

In February 2002, at the invitation of the Turkish government, a joint meeting was held in Istanbul of two organizations, the OIC (Organization of the Islamic Conference) and the European Union. Each member nation of the two organizations was invited and was asked to be represented by its minister of foreign affairs. In addition, the Turkish government invited a small number of individuals to come as guests. They invited two from the United States, Edward Said and myself; a curious combination, to say the least. Professor Said pleaded a previous engagement and sent his regrets. I accepted with alacrity, the more so since my invitation included Buntzie Churchill. We were treated royally. In this, as in so many other matters, the Turks were well informed. We were given two rooms in one of the most luxurious hotels in Istanbul, a car and driver, and driving to and from the meetings we were preceded by a police motorcycle escort.

I was astounded that in order to move us quickly from the hotel to the meeting and to avoid traffic, our car and the escorts raced down the fenced-in trolley corridor. What would have happened if a trolley had come along is a mystery.

The opening reception was very much Western-style. Turkey at that time was still rigorously secular. Press photographers were darting around trying to take pictures of us and I saw that the Iranian representatives were visibly anxious that they not be photographed with miniskirted waitresses carrying trays of alcoholic drinks.

They also had some other concerns. To my surprise, the Iranian minister of foreign affairs came up to me and introduced himself. This was very shortly after President Bush had delivered his "Axis of

Evil" speech and the Iranians were visibly worried about what he was going to do next. This emerged still more clearly when, to my astonishment, I found myself scheduled to participate in one of the major debates. The stage was occupied by a panel of four speakers—the ministers of foreign affairs of Iran and Egypt, and two professors, an Egyptian and myself. We were each asked to make a brief statement, and then to answer questions from the floor.

The speeches from the two ministers of foreign affairs were precisely the opposite of what one would expect. The Iranian foreign minister, still under the impact of the "Axis of Evil" speech, was very cautious. He had some criticism of American policy but the strongest word he used was "misguided." The Egyptian foreign minister, followed by the Egyptian professor, felt free to denounce America in the strongest terms. They started with the atrocities of the first European colonists who landed on the shores of the New World and dispossessed, evicted, and in various ways persecuted the original inhabitants. Later Americans enslaved and ill-treated millions of black Africans. When it was my turn to speak, I took the opportunity to make a response. I pointed out that the enslavement of black Africans had begun centuries before Columbus discovered America and continued for a long time after slavery was abolished in America. And most of these slaves went east, not west. This brought some smiles of approval and even a timid round of applause from some of the darker-skinned members of the conference. It is worth noting that slavery was not abolished in Saudi Arabia until 1962, and continues in all but name in some countries in the Middle East to this day.

In response to a question the Egyptian professor stated that while slavery in America was vicious, slavery in the Arab world was "benign."

One amusing interaction occurred when Buntzie went to buy a knockoff Hermès purse in a Grand Bazaar shop recommended by the wife of the Turkish ambassador to one of the EU countries. As a very determined Buntzie had only approximate directions and had to ask for help en route, the two motorcycle policemen and I tagged along to assist—me to translate and the policemen to ensure we didn't get lost as I have an abominable sense of direction. She found the tiny shop, went in, and told the proprietor what she wanted. He was delighted to help her until the two large, very intimidating motorcycle policemen clothed in black leather and I came in. Our presence filled the shop. The owner paled and signaled to Buntzie that she go up the narrow, rickety stairs at the rear. He stayed downstairs with us while his assistant helped her on the tiny second floor. There was no doubt that he was most eager to have us leave as soon as possible. The mission was accomplished in record time and the purse was, and still is, proudly worn.

In Oman

The following year, I was invited to the Emirate of Oman. I went there as a guest of the Ministry of Religious Affairs to give a couple of lectures, one in the Grand Mosque of Muscat and one in the Ministry of Foreign Affairs. The first was for a public audience; the second was private, at the ministry. The second of these lectures, but not the first, was followed by a lively question and answer session.

I also had some private conversations with my host, the minister of religious affairs. At one point he startled me by remarking, "I understand that you visit Israel every year." I agreed that this was so. "Why not come here every year too?" he said. To this I gave a diplomatic answer.

After I had completed my assignment I was invited to go on a tour of the country, and provided with a car, driver and guide to do the honors. It was an interesting trip and I enjoyed it. In the course of the trip we came to a small town called 'Ibri. That is the Arabic word for Hebrew and this struck me as a rather odd name for a town in southern Arabia. I asked how it came to have this name. My guide responded, "We believe that this was originally a Jewish settlement, but there are no Jews here now; it's entirely Arab Muslim." Then I asked the usual historian's question, "Apart from the name, is there any sort of evidence of a Jewish connection in this place?" The answer surprised me. "Well, two things. One, the people here tend to be lighter in color than others in the neighborhood. And two, they tend to be more intelligent."

A Guest of Gaddafi

In the fall of 2006 I was more than astonished to receive an invitation from Colonel Muammar Gaddafi to visit Libya as his guest, for some private conversations. The invitation came through Monitor, a London public relations firm, which was to make all the arrangements. I was somewhat suspicious at this invitation, wondering what on earth he could be wanting from me. After inquiries with the London firm revealed nothing that caused alarm, I agreed to go, accompanied by Buntzie. They offered an honorarium of $15,000, which I refused as I did not want to be in the pay of a Middle Eastern government. We flew to London for a day of briefings and then on to Tripoli, where we were met and escorted to the largest, highest, most luxurious hotel in the city and to our rooms on the top floor. The next day we were to meet the head of state. The journey to the meeting took place in several stages: first, a thirty-minute drive to a small airport; then a flight into the desert followed by a drive to a camp where The Leader was awaiting us in his tent.

The tent was very large and could have held a banquet for hundreds of people. Its walls were swaths of cloth with geometric patterns in white, green and gold. In the far side of the tent I could see Oriental carpets but where the meeting was held, at the front of the tent, the floor coverings were plastic rugs that could be rolled up. The lighting was bare bulbs hanging at infrequent intervals. It was spare, functional and certainly not elegant. At the opening of the tent, where there was daylight, Gaddafi was seated behind a table and at right angles were chairs in front of a low table for Buntzie and me. We were served coffee. On each table was a two-foot-long switch of thin branches gathered and wrapped tightly with tinfoil around the bottom six inches. They were to swish over one shoulder and then the other in order to brush away the flies.

Gaddafi was wearing a black, long-sleeved T-shirt and what appeared to be a brown blanket wrapped around his body and over one shoulder like a toga.

In the actual discussion there were three people: Gaddafi, the interpreter and me. Gaddafi spoke Arabic, I spoke English and the interpreter, a Libyan professor from Purdue University, translated. In the course of the discussion I could not resist my professional teacher's impulse to correct Gaddafi on a point of medieval Islamic history and the interpreter on a nuance of Arabic. They did not seem to mind and these minor interruptions led to interesting digressions in the conversation.

Gaddafi's main message, that for which he had brought me to hear and pass on to Washington, was something of a surprise. You are all worried about Iran, he said, as if that were the principal threat to the world. You are quite wrong. Iran is not important and is not a real danger. The real danger, the source of all your troubles, of all the terrorism, of all the radical violence, is Saudi Arabia. He went on to express his deep concern at what he called "the cozy relationship" between the house of Bush and the house of Saud. "It is the Saudis who fund and train Al-Qaida and all the other terrorist movements," he said. "It is they who are trying to stir up the whole Muslim world against you." A valid complaint against the Saudis is that they sponsor and export Wahhabism, a particularly extreme and militant version of Islam.

In the course of our two-hour meeting Gaddafi also mentioned that the United States must develop alternative sources of energy. This was a rather odd comment coming from the head of an oil-producing country. It took several moments but finally I realized that by "alternative source of energy" he meant that the United States should buy its oil from Libya, and not Saudi Arabia.

Gaddafi was enthusiastic about a one-state solution to the Palestinian problem. I hear, he said, that a million or more Arabs live peacefully in Israel, alongside their Jewish neighbors. I agreed and pointed out that this was due to the nature of the Israeli state and society. This he brushed aside. This proves, he said, that Jews and Arabs can live peacefully side by side in the same state. In that case, why should there not be a single state of the whole area, comprising both the Jewish and the Arab regions? He thought the state should be called Isratine. With such a solution Israel wouldn't have to give back the settlements, and Palestinians and Israelis could cohabit in the same state. I understand that he promoted the same solution on other occasions.

Later in the day we were hosted at a dinner in our honor at the sumptuous home of Abdullah Senussi, Gaddafi's chief of military intelligence and one of his brothers-in-laws. This was a party of fifteen people and, surprisingly for an Arab Muslim party, it included a number of women, two of whom were Senussi's daughters. I was seated next to our host.

Senussi, unsurprisingly, was preaching the same doctrine as his master: the Saudi menace and the unimportance of Iran. We had a long and interesting conversation which, over the course of the evening, degenerated from high politics at the table to low humor in a corner of the hall as we were preparing to leave. Our host bestowed upon us a number of gifts, a watch for me and a small rug for Buntzie. His sotto voce parting suggestion was, "I hope you'll come again, but next time come alone. We'll find you a younger woman."

My hosts had asked me where we were planning to go after leaving Libya. I replied that our next stop would be Israel. There is, of course, no direct communication between Libya and Israel, but I thought it might be possible to cross into Egypt and get a plane from there. The Libyans did not like this idea as their relations with Egypt at that time were far from cordial. Instead, they chartered a small Maltese plane for us which stopped in Cyprus for a brief twenty minutes to change the documentation, and then flew on to Ben Gurion Airport.

It was a fascinating forty-eight hours.

The Arab Spring, or the Winter of Their Discontent

In January 2011, a young vendor in Tunisia immolated himself and sparked a mass expression of the Arab peoples' outrage against injustice. From there protests spread to Egypt, Yemen, Oman, Bahrain, Jordan, Syria and occurred sporadically in other Middle Eastern states. It was no coincidence that the unrest erupted first in Tunisia, the one Arab country where women play a significant part in public life. The role of women in determining the future of the Arab world will be crucial.

Developing a democracy is a slow and difficult business. We must be patient and give emerging democracies a chance to develop. Look around the world today and make a list of secure and successful democracies, those countries in which democracy has existed for a long time and where you could reasonably predict that democracy will still be functioning years from now. You will find that almost all of them are monarchies, mostly Protestant—Norway, Sweden, Denmark, Holland, Belgium, the United Kingdom and the British Dominions. The only non-monarchical countries which have a long, uninterrupted record of democracy are Switzerland and the United States. Even the United States had a bumpy road in developing its democracy—notably coping with such problems as slavery and the total disenfranchisement of women. However, problems can be overcome.

In the West, we tend to get excessively concerned with elections, regarding the holding of elections as the purest expression of democracy, as the climax of the process of democratization. Well, the second may be true—the climax of the process. But the process can be a long and difficult one. Consider, for example, that democracy was fairly new in Germany in the interwar period and in 1933 Hitler came to power in a free and fair election.

The Arab masses certainly want change. And they want improvement. But what does "democracy" mean in a Middle Eastern context? It's a word that is used with very different meanings, even in different parts of the Western world. And it's a political concept that has no history, no record whatever in the Arab, Islamic world.

Many believe the Arabs want freedom and democracy. Westerners tend to think of democracy in our own terms—that's natural and normal—to mean periodic elections in our style. But it's a mistake to try to think of the Middle East in those terms and that can only lead to disastrous results, as we've already seen in various places. Hamas did not establish a democratic regime when it came to power through a free and fair election.

I am mistrustful and view with apprehension a genuinely free election—assuming that such a thing could happen—because the religious parties have an immediate advantage. First, they have a network of communication through the preacher and the mosque which no other political group can hope to equal. Second, they use familiar, indigenous, language. The language of Western democracy is for the most part newly translated and the concepts are not readily intelligible to the general population. A dash toward Western-style elections, far from representing a solution to the region's difficulties, constitutes a dangerous aggravation of the problem and I fear that radical Islamic movements are ready to exploit so misguided a move.

In genuinely fair and free elections, the Muslim parties are very likely to win. A much better course would be a gradual development of democracy, not through general elections, but rather through civil society and the strengthening of local institutions. For that, there is a real tradition in the region.

An anxious West tries to work out what signals it should be sending and what processes it should be encouraging. What opportunity do America and the free world have to influence this process? I'd rather take it from the other side and say what signals the West should not be sending. And that is not pressing for elections. This idea that a general election, Western-style, is a solution to problems is a dangerous fallacy which can lead to disaster. We should let them do it their way by consulting with groups of various kinds. There are all sorts of possibilities.

The anger and resentment in the Middle East are universal and well grounded. They come from a number of elements. First, there's the obvious one—the greater awareness that they have, thanks to modern communications, of the difference between their situation and the situation in other parts of the world. I mean, being abjectly poor is bad enough. But when everyone around you is not abjectly poor, it becomes intolerable.

Another thing is the sexual aspect of it. Remember that in the Muslim world, casual sex, Western-style, doesn't exist. If a young man wants sex, there are only two possibilities—marriage or prostitution. There are vast numbers of young men with normal testosterone levels growing up without the money either for the brothel or the bride price. It can lead to the suicide bomber who is attracted by the virgins of paradise—the only ones available to him—or to unquenchable frustration.

The protesters who rose up in the Arab Spring are all agreed that they want to get rid of the present leadership, but they are not agreed on what they want in its place. For example, we get different figures from polls as to the probable support for the Muslim Brothers. The Muslim Brotherhood is a very dangerous, radical Islamic movement. If it obtains power, the consequences could be disastrous for Egypt. I can imagine a situation in which the Muslim Brotherhood and other organizations of the same kind obtain control of much of the Arab world. I would not say it's likely, but it is not unlikely. If that happens, they would gradually sink back into medieval squalor. According to their own statistics, the total exports of the entire Arab world, other than fossil fuels, amount to less than those of Finland, one small European country. Sooner or later the oil age will come to an end. Oil will be either exhausted or superseded as a source of energy and then they will have virtually nothing. In that case it's easy to imagine a situation in which Africa north of the Sahara becomes not unlike Africa south of the Sahara, with growing emigration.

It's not easy to define what they are for. It's much easier to define what they are against. They are against the tyrannies which, as they see it, not only oppress them but dishonor their name, their religion, their nationhood. They want to see something better. What that something better would be is differently defined. They are not usually talking in terms of parliamentary democracy and free elections and so on. That's not part of the common discourse. For different groups it means different things. But usually, it's religiously defined. That doesn't necessarily mean the Muslim Brothers' type of religion. There is also an Islamic tradition which is not like that—the tradition of consultation. It is a form of government.

If you look at the history of the Middle East and its own political literature, it is totally against arbitrary and tyrannical rule. Islamic tradition always insisted on consultation. This is not just a matter of theory. There's a remarkable passage, for example, in the report of a French ambassador to the sultan of Turkey a few years before the French Revolution. The French ambassador was instructed by his government to press the Turkish government in certain negotiations and was making very slow progress. Paris said angrily, "Why don't you do something?" The ambassador replied that one must understand that here things are not as they are in France, where the King is sole master and does as he pleases. Here, the sultan has to consult with the holders of high office. He has to consult with the retired former holders of high office. He has to consult with the merchants, the craft guilds and all sorts of other groups.

This is absolutely true. It's an extraordinarily revealing and informative passage and the point comes up again and again through the nineteenth and twentieth centuries.

There was a traditional system of consultation with groups which were not democratic as we use that word in the Western world, but which had a source of authority other than the state—authority which derived from within the group, whether it be the landed gentry, the civil service, the scribes or whatever. That could be a better basis for the development of free and civilized government.

The authoritarian, even dictatorial regimes that rule most of the countries in the modern Islamic Middle East are a modern creation—the result of modernization. The premodern regimes were much more open, much more tolerant. You can see this from a number of contemporary descriptions. A nineteenth-century British naval officer named Slade put it very well. Comparing the old order with the new order, created by modernization, he said, "In the old order, the nobility lived on their estates. In the new order, the state is the estate of the new nobility."

The value systems of the West and the Middle East are different. Opinion surveys show overwhelming proportions of Middle Easterners taking very bleak views on some aspects of human rights, supporting terrible punishments for adultery, benighted attitudes to homosexuality and so on.

Yet, one has to understand not so much the differences between the West and the Arab world as the differences in the political discourse. In the Western world, we talk all the time about freedom. In the Islamic world, freedom is not a political term. It's a legal term: Freedom as opposed to slavery. In the past this was a society in which slavery was an accepted institution existing all over the Muslim world. You were free if you were not a slave. It was entirely a legal and social term, with no political connotation whatsoever. You can see in the debate in Arabic and other languages the puzzlement with which the use of the term "freedom" was first perceived. They just didn't understand it. They wondered what this had to do with politics or government. Eventually, they got the message. But it's still alien to many. In Muslim terms, the measure of good government is justice.

The major contrast is not between freedom and tyranny, between freedom and servitude, but between justice and oppression, or, between justice and injustice. Looking at it this way makes it much easier to understand the mental and therefore the political processes in the Islamic world. Corruption and oppression are corruption and oppression by whichever system you define them. There's not much difference between their definition of corruption and our definition of corruption. In the Western world one makes money in the marketplace and then uses it to acquire political influence or access. In the Middle East the traditional practice is to seize power and use that power to get money. Morally I see no difference between them; economically, the Middle Eastern method does greater damage.

What bothers me about the Middle East at the present day is not so much what they are doing but what we are saying. We are transmitting the wrong signals. We must be more clear and more definite on the need for freedom in the Middle East and our desire to help those who work for freedom.

There is a question of whether democracy can work in the Arab world. There are different views on this. One of them says that these people are not like us; they have different ways, different traditions. We should admit that they are incapable of setting up anything like the kind of democracy we have. Whatever we do, they will be governed by tyrants. The aim of our policies should therefore be to maintain stability and ensure that they are ruled by friendly rather than hostile tyrants. This is known as the pro-Arab point of view. In fact, of course, it is in no way pro-Arab. It shows ignorance of the Arab past, little concern for the Arab present, and even less for the Arab future.

The other point of view says that these are the heirs of an old and great civilization. They have gone through some bad times but there are elements in their society which will help, which can be nurtured to develop into some form of limited consensual government in their own cultural tradition. Oddly enough, this is sometimes denounced as the imperialist strategy. But I think it shows far greater respect for the ambitions and aspirations of the people of the region. Western ideas may have helped precipitate such Middle Eastern crises of transition as the Suez War of 1956, and more recently the Arab Spring of 2011, but only the people themselves can resolve these crises. We must beware of proposing solutions which, however good, are discredited by the very fact of our having proposed them. Our politics and diplomacy are not welcome, though our weaponry and our money are.

In Sum

For my ninetieth birthday the World Affairs Council of Philadelphia sponsored a daylong conference attended by over six hundred people on "Islam and the West." It featured an encomium by Vice President Dick Cheney and presentations by Henry Kissinger, Fouad Ajami, Ayaan Hirsi Ali, and others.

Buntzie says that when she called Fouad to tell him about my forthcoming milestone he exclaimed, "Ninety! Oh, don't tell him."

During my ninetieth year, I had the usual messages of congratulations and goodwill, including one from an Israeli friend using a common Israeli formula but with an interesting difference. The common Israeli phrase when offering birthday greetings to the elderly is to say, *Ad me'a ve-esrim*—"Till a hundred and twenty." The change of one Hebrew consonant made this *Ad me'a ke-esrim*—"Till a hundred, like twenty." Much preferable.

I am ninety-five years old now. When I was young at eighty I didn't know how true it would be when I murmured to Buntzie Robert Browning's lines "Grow old along with me!/The best is yet to be,/The last of life, for which the first was made . . ." She has improved and lengthened my life.

On walks now I must use a cane or a walker. I need hearing aids. I take naps. My short-term memory is not what it used to be. (Buntzie says that soon I will be normal!) I have deteriorated physically and mentally, but not emotionally.

I have loved my life. I have had a rewarding career. Thirty-two books translated into twenty-nine languages isn't bad. I have explored places and cultures and been able to play with fifteen languages. Even those who dislike me or with whom I have heartily disagreed are usually interesting and sometimes even stimulating. I have a family and devoted friends whom I cherish.

I have been, and am, very fortunate.

Appendix I

The Dirge
(September 29, 1945)

In the bleakness of German plains,
In the stillness of English woods,
In the squalor of Polish towns,
In the clamour of London streets,
      I see them die.

In the eyes of indifferent friends,
In the sullen spite of slaves,
In the haughtiness of lords,
In their brothers that forget,
      I see them die.

In the agony of thought,
In the grey relief of toil,
In the fret of idleness,
In the black-ribbed page of print,
      I see them die.

In the feckless, flirting pairs,
In the dishes full of food,
In the wineglass, in the wine,
In the sleek, contented smile,
      I see them die.

In the soft webs of sleep,
In the pallor of awakening,

In the light, in the shadows,
In the passion, in the regret,
    I see them die.

In the pain of remembered joy,
In the sear of remembered pain,
In the hope, in the forgetting,
In the anguish of self,
    I see them die.

They the lost, the forgotten,
They the unnumbered, the despairing,
In the camps of reluctant death,
By the barred gates of hope,
    I see them die.

In the softness of the strings,
In the discords of the city,
In the golden wildness of autumn,
In the green brilliance of summer,
    I see them die.

In the furnaces of hate,
In the pigeon-holes of neglect,
In the prejudice of fools,
In the wisdom of the warped,
    I see them die.

In the ecstasy of liberation,
In the sadness of liberty,
In the captivity of distant friends,
In the remoteness of conquerors,
    I see them die.

In bondage in the wilderness,
In the dream of a Promised Land,
In the tents of Japhet,
By the tent-ropes of Israel,
    I see them die.

They the lost, the forgotten,
They the unnumbered, the despairing,
In the camps of reluctant death,
By the barred gates of hope,
    I see them die.

Appendix II
Honors and Publications

Born
London, England, May 31, 1916

Education
B.A. (First Class Honours in History), University of London, 1936
Diplôme des Études Sémitiques, University of Paris, 1937
Ph.D., University of London, 1939

Present
Cleveland E. Dodge Professor of Near Eastern Studies Emeritus, Princeton
  University, 1986–

Previous Positions
Assistant Lecturer in Islamic History, School of Oriental and African Studies,
  University of London, 1938
Lecturer, School of Oriental and African Studies, University of London, 1940
Senior Lecturer, School of Oriental and African Studies, University of London, 1946
Reader, School of Oriental and African Studies, University of London, 1947
Professor of the History of the Near and Middle East, School of Oriental and
  African Studies, University of London, 1949–74
The Encyclopedia of Islam, member, Editorial Committee, 1960–91
Cleveland E. Dodge Professor of Near Eastern Studies, Princeton University,
  1974–86
Long-term Member of the Institute for Advanced Study, Princeton, New Jersey, 1974–86

Visitor, Institute for Advanced Study, Princeton, New Jersey, 1986–87
Director, Annenberg Research Institute, Philadelphia, Pennsylvania, 1986–90
Honorary Incumbent, Kemal Atatürk Professorship in Ottoman and Turkish
   Studies, Princeton University, 1992–93

Visiting Appointments

University of California at Los Angeles, 1955–56
Columbia University, 1960
Indiana University, 1963
Princeton University, 1964 (to deliver the class of 1932 lectures)
Institute for Advanced Study, 1969
Collège de France, Paris, 1980
The Sackler Institute of Advanced Studies, Tel Aviv, 1980–
École des Hautes Études en Sciences Sociales, Paris, 1983
Committee on Social Thought, University of Chicago, 1985
Andrew D. White Professor-at-Large, Cornell University, 1984–90
Scholar in Residence, University of Wisconsin, Milwaukee, 1988
École des Hautes Études en Sciences Sociales, Paris, 1988
Dayan Center, Tel Aviv University, 1990–

War Service

British Army, 1940–41
British Intelligence, 1941–45

Honors

Citation of Honor, Turkish Ministry of Culture, 1973
Honorary Doctorate, Hebrew University of Jerusalem, 1974
Fellow, University College, London, 1976
The Harvey Prize, The Technion, Haifa, 1978
Honorary Doctorate, Tel Aviv University, 1979
Annual Education Award for Outstanding Achievement in the Promotion of
   American-Turkish Studies, 1985
Honorary Doctorate, State University of New York, Binghamton, 1987
Honorary Doctorate, University of Pennsylvania, 1987
Honorary Doctorate, Hebrew Union College, Cincinnati, 1987
Tanner Lecturer, Oxford University, 1990

Jefferson Lecturer in the Humanities, National Endowment for the Humanities, 1990

Honorary Doctorate, Haifa University, 1991

Honorary Doctorate, Yeshiva University, New York, 1991

Honorary Doctorate, Bar-Ilan University, 1992

Henry M. Jackson Memorial Lecture, Seattle, 1992

Honorary Doctorate, Brandeis University, Waltham, 1993

Honorary Doctorate, Ben-Gurion University, Beersheba, 1996

Honorary Doctorate, Ankara University, Ankara, 1996

Honorary Member, Turkish Academy of Sciences, 1997

Atatürk Peace Prize, 1998

George Polk Award, Long Island University, New York, 2001

Honorary Doctorate, New School University, New York, 2002

Atatürk Society of America Award for Peace and Democracy, 2002

Honorary Doctorate, Princeton University, Princeton, 2002

Honorary Doctorate, Northwestern University, Evanston, 2003

Honorary Doctorate, University of Judaism, Los Angeles, 2004

Golden Plate Award, Academy of Achievement, Washington, D.C., 2004

National Humanities Medal, National Endowment for the Humanities, 2006

Irving Kristol Award, American Enterprise Institute, 2007

Academies

Fellow of the British Academy, 1963

Corresponding Member of Institut d'Égypte, Cairo, 1969

Honorary Member, Turkish Historical Society, Ankara, 1972

Member, American Philosophical Society, 1973

Member, American Academy of Arts and Sciences, 1983

Honorary Member, Société Asiatique, Paris, 1984

Honorary Member, Atatürk Academy of History, Language, and Culture, 1984

Honorary Fellow, School of Oriental and African Studies, 1986

Board of Directors, Institut für die Wissenschaften vom Menschen, Vienna, 1988

Corresponding Member, Institut de France, Académie des Inscriptions et des Belles-Lettres, 1994

Societies

Royal Asiatic Society
Royal Historical Society
Royal Institute of International Affairs
American Oriental Society
American Historical Association
Council on Foreign Relations
Association for the Study of the Middle East and Africa

Books

The Origins of Ismailism. Cambridge: W. Heffer & Sons, Ltd., 1940; reprinted AMS, New York, 1975.

Handbook of Diplomatic and Political Arabic. London: Luzac & Co., Ltd., 1947; reprinted London, 1956.

The Arabs in History. London: Hutchinson & Co., Ltd., 1950, reprinted 1954, 1956; 2nd ed. 1958; reprinted 1960, 1962; 3rd ed. 1964; 4th ed. 1966; reprinted 1968; 5th ed. 1970; reprinted 1975; New York: Oxford University Press, 6th ed., 1993.

Notes and Documents from the Turkish Archives. Jerusalem: Israel Oriental Society, 1952.

The Emergence of Modern Turkey. London and New York: Oxford University Press, 1961; rev. ed. 1968; new ed. 2001.

The Kingly Crown (trans. from Ibn Gabirol). London: Vallentine Mitchell, 1961.

Istanbul and the Civilization of the Ottoman Empire. Norman, OK: University of Oklahoma Press, 1963; reprinted 1968, 1972.

The Middle East and the West. Bloomington: Indiana University Press, and London: Weidenfeld & Nicholson, 1964; reprinted (paperback) New York: Harper & Row, and Weidenfeld & Nicholson, 1964; reprinted (paperback) Harper & Row, 1966, 1968.

The Assassins. London: Weidenfeld & Nicolson, 1967; New York: Basic Books, 1968, 1970; reprinted 1972, 1980; New York: Oxford University Press, 1987.

Race and Color in Islam. New York: Harper & Row, 1971; reprinted New York: Octagon Books, 1979.

Islam from the Prophet Muhammad to the Capture of Constantinople. 2 vols.

New York: Walker, 1974; (paperback) New York: Harper & Row, 1974; New York: Oxford University Press, 1987.

History—Remembered, Recovered, Invented. Princeton: Princeton University Press, 1975; reprinted 1976; (paperback) New York: Simon & Schuster, 1987.

Population and Revenue in the Towns of Palestine in the Sixteenth Century. Co-author with Amnon Cohen. Princeton: Princeton University Press, 1978.

The Muslim Discovery of Europe. New York: W. W. Norton, 1982, paperback ed. 1985; rev. ed. 2001.

The Jews of Islam. Princeton: Princeton University Press, 1984, reprinted 1986; paperback ed. 1987.

Semites and Anti-Semites. New York: W. W. Norton, 1986; London: Orion Publishing, 1997; rev. ed. 1999.

The Political Language of Islam. Chicago: University of Chicago Press, 1988.

Race and Slavery in the Middle East: An Historical Enquiry. New York: Oxford University Press, 1990. A revised and expanded edition of *Race and Color in Islam,* 1979.

Islam and the West. New York: Oxford University Press, 1993.

Shaping of the Modern Middle East. New York: Oxford University Press, 1993. A revised and recast edition of *The Middle East and the West,* 1964.

Cultures in Conflict: Christians, Muslims and Jews in the Age of Discovery. New York: Oxford University Press, 1995.

The Middle East: Two Thousand Years of History from the Rise of Christianity to the Present Day. London: Weidenfeld & Nicolson, 1995. National Book Critics Award Finalist.

The Multiple Identities of the Middle East. London: Weidenfeld & Nicolson, 1998.

A Middle East Mosaic: Fragments of Life, Letters and History. New York: Random House, 2000.

Music of a Distant Drum. Princeton: Princeton University Press, 2001.

What Went Wrong? Western Impact and Middle Eastern Response. New York: Oxford University Press, 2002.

The Crisis of Islam: Holy War and Unholy Terror. New York: Random House, 2003.

From Babel to Dragomans: Interpreting the Middle East. New York: Oxford University Press, 2004.

Islam: The Religion and the People. Coauthored with Buntzie Ellis Churchill. Upper Saddle River, NJ: Wharton School Publishing, 2008.

Faith and Power: Religion and Politics in the Middle East. New York: Oxford University Press, 2010.

The End of Modern History in the Middle East. Stanford, CA: Hoover Institution Press, 2011.

Books (edited or coedited)

Land of Enchanters. Editor, London: The Harvill Press Ltd., 1948; reprinted Princeton: Wiener Publishers, 2001.

Historians of the Middle East. Coeditor with P. M. Holt. London: Oxford University Press, 1962; reprinted 1972.

Encyclopedia of Islam. 2nd ed. Coeditor and author of numerous articles. Leiden: Brill, 1970–80.

The World of Islam. Editor. London: Thames & Hudson. *Islam and the Arab World.* New York: Knopf, 1976. (Editions of the same book.)

Christians and Jews in the Ottoman Empire. Coeditor with Benjamin Braude. 2 vols. New York: Holmes & Meier Publications, Inc., 1982.

Religionsgespräche im Mittelalter. Coeditor with Friedrich Niewöhner. Wiesbaden: Herzog August Bibliothek, Wolfenbüttel, 1992.

Collections

Islam in History. London: Alcove Press Ltd., 1973; Chicago: Open Court, 1993; new ed. 2001.

Studies in Classical and Ottoman Islam, 7th–16th Centuries. London: Variorum reprints, 1976.

Le Retour de l'Islam (translations from my works). Paris: Gallimard, 1985.

Islam (translations from my works). Paris: Quatro Gallimard, 2005.

Political Words and Ideas in Islam. Princeton: Markus Wiener Publisher, 2008.

Booklets

British Contributions to Arabic Studies. London: Longmans, Green & Co., Ltd., 1941.

The Future of the Middle East. London: Phoenix/Orion Publishing Group, 1997.

Europe and Islam. American Enterprise Institute for Public Policy Research, Irving Kristol Lecture, March 7, 2007.

Contributions

Constantine Porphyrogenitus: De Administrando Imperio. Coeditor with others. Vol. II, commentary, London: Athlone Press, 1962.

The Cambridge History of Islam. Coeditor with others. Cambridge: Cambridge University Press, 1970.

Introduction to Islamic Theology and Law. (Introduction and additional notes.) Ignaz Goldziher, trans. by Andras and Ruth Hamori. Princeton: Princeton University Press, 1981.

As Others See Us: Mutual Perceptions East and West. Coeditor with Edmund Leites and Margaret Case. New York: International Society for the Comparative Study of Civilizations, 1985.

Muslims in Europe. Coeditor with Dominique Schnapper. London: Pinter Publishers, 1994.

Other

Uno sguardo dal Medio Oriente. (A long interview with me.) Rome: Di Renzo Editore, 1999, 2002.

Articles

"The Islamic Guilds," *Economic History Review* viii (1937): 20–37.

"An Isma'ili Interpretation of the Fall of Adam," *BSOAS* iv (1938): 179–84.

"A Jewish Source on Damascus just after the Ottoman Conquest," *BSOAS* x (1939):179–84.

"An Arabic Account of a Byzantine Palace Revolution," *Byzantion* xiv (1939): 383-86.

"Jewish Science according to an Arabic Author of the 11th Century," *Sinai* iv (1940): 25–29.

"An Epistle on Manual Crafts," *Islamic Culture* xvii (1943): 142–51.

"Arabic Sources on Maimonides," in S. Rawidowicz (ed.), *Metsuda*, London, 1945, 171–80.

"An Apocalyptic Vision of Islamic History," *BSOAS* xiii (1950): 308–38.

"The Legend of the Jewish Origin of the Fatimid Caliphs," *Melilah* iii–iv (1950): 185–87. (In Hebrew.)

"The Near and Middle East," in C. H. Philips (ed.), *Handbook of Oriental History*, London, 1951.

"Recent Developments in Turkey," *International Affairs* xxvii (1951): 320–31.

"The Danish East India and Asiatic Company Records in the State Archives

(Rigsarkiv) in Copenhagen," *The Indian Archives* (New Delhi) v (1951): 138–40.

"The Ottoman Archives as a Source for the History of the Arab Lands," *JRAS* (1951): 139–55.

"Population and Revenue in Palestine in the 16th Century, according to Turkish Documents," *Jerusalem* iv (1952): 133–37.

"Islamic Revival in Turkey," *International Affairs* xviii (1952): 38–48.

"The Privilege Granted by Mehmed II to His Physician," *BSOAS* xiv (1952): 550–63.

"The Sources for the History of the Syrian Assassins," *Speculum* xvii (1952): 475–89.

"Saladin and the Assassins," *BSOAS* xv (1952): 239–45.

"Some Observations on the Significance of Heresy in the History of Islam," *Studia Islamica* i (1952): 43–63.

"The Impact of the French Revolution on Turkey," *Journal of World History* i (1952): 105–25. Revised version in G. S. Metraux and F. Crouzet (eds.), *The New Asia: Readings in the History of Mankind*, New York, 1965, 31–59.

"Three Biographies from Kamal ad-Din," in *Melanges Fuad Köprülü*, Istanbul, 1953, 325–44.

"Izlanda'da Türkler," *Türkiyat Mecmuası* x (1953): 277–84.

"Europe and the Turks," *History To-Day*, October 1953, 673–80.

"An Arabic Account of the Province of Safed," *BSOAS* xi (1953): 477–88.

"The Fatimids and the Route to India," *Review of the Faculty of Economics* (Istanbul) xi (1950–53): 1–5.

"History Writing and National Revival in Turkey," *Middle Eastern Affairs* iv (1953): 218–27.

"Communism and Islam," *International Affairs* xxx (1954): 1–12.

"Nationalism and Patriotism in the Middle East," *World Affairs Interpreter*, 1954, 208–12.

"Ägypten von der Eroberung durch die Araber bis zur Besetzung durch die Osmanen," in A. Randa (ed.), *Handbuch der Weltgeschichte*, I. Olten, 1954, 1001–16.

"Studies in the Ottoman Archives I," *BSOAS* xvi (1954): 469–501.

"Islam," D. Sinor (ed.), *Orientalism and History*, Cambridge, 1954; reprinted Bloomington, 1970, 16–33.

"Early Educational Reforms by Middle Eastern Government," *Yearbook of Education* (1954): 446–51.

"A Note on Some Danish Material in the Turkish Archives in Istanbul," *Acta Orientalia* xxii (1955): 75–76.

"An Historical Document in the Responsa of R. Samuel de Medina," *Melilah* v (1955): 169–76. (In Hebrew.)

"Constantinople and the Arabs," in *The Fall of Constantinople*, London, SOAS, 1955, 12–17.

"The Concept of an Islamic Republic," *Die Welt des Islams*, n.s., iv (1955): 1–9.

"Democracy in the Middle East," *Middle Eastern Affairs* vi (1955): 101–8.

"Jerusalem in the XVIth Century," *Jerusalem* v (1955): 117–27.

"The Isma'ilites and the Assassins," in K. M. Setton (editor-in-chief), *A History of the Crusades*, i, M. W. Baldwin (ed.), *The First Hundred Years*, Philadelphia, 1955; 2nd ed. Madison, 1969, 98–132.

"Some Danish-Tatar Exchanges in the 17th Century," in *Symbolae in Honorem Z. V. Togan*, Istanbul, 1955, 137–46.

"Turkey: Westernization," in G. E. von Grunebaum (ed.), *Unity and Variety in Muslim Civilization*, Chicago, 1956, 311–31.

"The Middle Eastern Reaction to Soviet Pressures," *Middle East Journal* x (1956): 125–37.

"The Ottoman Archives, a Source for European History," *Supplement to Research Bibliography*, Middle East Institute, Washington, D.C.

"The Muslim Discovery of Europe," *BSOAS* xx (1957): 409–16.

"A Karaite Itinerary through Turkey in 1641–42," *Vakıflar Dergisi* (Ankara), iii (1957): 97–106 and 315–25.

"The Islamic Middle East," in W. Burmeister (ed.), *Democratic Institutions in the World Today*, London, 1958, 45–61.

"The Middle East in World Affairs," in P. W. Thayer (ed.), *Tensions in the Middle East*, Baltimore, 1958, 50–60.

"On Writing the Modern History of the Middle East," *Middle East Forum* (Beirut), June 1958, 15–17.

"An Islamic Mosque," in Walter James (ed.), *Temples and Faiths*, London, 1958, 47–50.

"Some Reflections on the Decline of the Ottoman Empire," *Studia Islamica* ix (1958): 111–27.

"The Mughals and the Ottomans," *Pakistan Quarterly*, Summer 1958, 4–9.

"Der Islam im Osten: Vorderasien, Agypten, Balkan," *Historia Mundi*, vi, Berne, 1958, 474–510.

"Men, Women and Traditions in Turkey," *The Geographical Magazine*, December 1959, 346–54.

"The Near and Middle East and North Africa," *The New Cambridge Modern History* xii (1960): 207–12.

"The Ottoman Archives, a source for European History," *Archives* iv (1960): 226–30.

"The Political Ideas of the Young Ottomans," *International Islamic Colloquium Papers,* December 29, 1957–January 8, 1958, Lahore, 1960, 97–99.

"Ibn Dihya's Account of the Embassy of Al-Ghazal," In W. E. D. Allen, *The Poet and the Spae-Wife*, Dublin, 1960, 19–25.

"Mas'udi on the Kings of the Franks," *Al-Mas'udi Millenary Commemoration Volume*, Aligarh, 1960, 7–10.

"The Invading Crescent," in *The Dawn of African History,* Oxford, 1961, 30–36.

"The Use by Muslim Historians of Non-Muslim Sources," B. Lewis and P. M. Holt (eds.), *Historians of the Middle East,* London, 1962, 180–91.

"Contribution to Constantine Porphyrogenitus," *De administrando imperio*, ii, *Commentary* (ed. R. J. H. Jenkins), London, 1962.

"Islam Devlet Müessese ve telakkileri üzerinde bozkir ahalisinin tesiri," *Review of the Institute of Islamic Studies* (Istanbul) ii (1962): 209–30.

"Approaches to Islamic History in Europe and America," *Colloque sur la Sociologie musulmane 11–14 September 1961, Correspondance d'Orient*, no. 5, Brussels, 1962, 103–17.

"Quelques themes andalous de la litterature turque au xixe siecle," in *Études d'Orientalisme dédiées a la memoire de Levi-Provençal*, Paris, 1962, 185–90.

"Ottoman Observers of Ottoman Decline," *Islamic Studies* (Karachi), i (1962): 71–87.

"Maimonides, Lionheart, and Saladin," *Eretz-Israel*, vii (L. A. Mayer Memorial Volume), Jerusalem, 1963, 70–75.

"Registers on Iran and Adharbayjan in the Ottoman Defter-i Khaqani," *Melanges Massé*, Tehran, 1963, 259–63.

"Problems as the Outcome of Changing Social Values in Developing Countries," *Social Aspects of Economic Development*, Istanbul, 1964, 109–24.

"Orta Şarkın Tarihi Hüviyeti," *Ankara Universitesi Ilahiyat Fakültesi Dergisi* vii (1964): 75–81.

"Islah al-anzima al-baladiyya fi 'ahd al-imbaraturiyya al-'uthmaniyya," *Takhtit al-mudun fi'l-'alam al-'arabi,* Cairo, 1964, 99–108.

"The Ottoman Empire in the mid-nineteenth Century: a Review," *Middle Eastern Studies* i (1965): 283–95.

"Arabic Dawn Poetry" (with S. M. Stern), in A. T. Hatto (ed.), *Eos*, The Hague (1965): 215–43.

"Nazareth in the Sixteenth Century According to the Ottoman Tapu Registers," *Arabic and Islamic Studies in Honor of Hamilton A. R. Gibb*, Leiden (1965): 416–23.

"Government, Society and Economic Life under the Abbasids and Fatimids," *Cambridge Mediaeval History* (new ed.), iv (1966): 638–61.

"Kamal al-Din's Biography of Rašid al-Din Sinan," *Arabica* xiii (1966): 225–67.

"Turkey," in *Dustur: A Survey of the Constitutions of the Arab and Muslim States*, Leiden (1966): 6–24.

"The Sources for the History of Iran," *Rahnema-ye Ketab* (1967): 228–32.

"Paltiel: a note," *BSOAS* xxx (1967): 177–81.

"The Consequences of Defeat," *Foreign Affairs* (1968): 321–35.

"Friends and Enemies—Reflections after a War," *Encounter* (February 1968): 3–7.

"Some English Travellers in the East," *Middle Eastern Studies* iv (1968): 296–315.

"The Pro-Islamic Jews," *Judaism* (New York), xvii (1968): 391–404.

"Jaffa in the Sixteenth Century, According to the Ottoman Tahrir Registers," *Necati Lugal Armaganı*, Ankara, 1968, 435–45.

"The Mongols, the Turks and the Muslim Polity," *Transactions of the Royal Historical Society*, 5th series, vol. 18, 1968, 49–68.

"The Regnal Titles of the First Abbasid Caliphs," *Dr. Zakir Husain Presentation Volume*, New Delhi, 1968, 13–22.

"The Great Powers, the Arabs and the Israelis," *Foreign Affairs* (1969): 642–52.

"Sources for the Economic History of the Middle East," M. S. Cook (ed.), *Studies in the Economic History of the Middle East from the Rise of Islam to the Present Day*, London (1970): 78–92.

"Race and Colour in Islam," *Encounter* xxxv (1970): 18–36.

"Russia in the Middle East," *The Round Table* (1970): 257–63.

Joseph Schacht (obituary), *BSOAS*, xxxiii (1970): 378–81.

"On the Revolutions in Early Islam," *Studia Islamica* xxxii (1970): 215–31.

"Semites and Anti-Semites," *Survey* 2, no. 79 (1971): 169–84.

"Small Print of the Soviet-Egyptian Treaty," *The Times*, October 8, 1971, 16.

"The Contribution to Islam," *The Legacy of Egypt*, Oxford (1971): 456–77.

"Assassins of Syria and Isma'ilis of Persia," *La Persia nel Medioevo*, Rome (Accademia Nazionale dei Lincei) (1971): 573–80.

"The Study of Islam," *Encounter* (1972): 31–41.

"An Interpretation of Fatimid History," *Colloque international sur l'histoire du Caire*, Cairo (1972): 287–97.

"Islamic Concepts of Revolution," P. J. Vatikiotis (ed.), *Revolution in the Middle East* (1972): 30–40.

"Corsairs in Iceland," *Revue de l'Occident Musulman et de la Méditerranée* (1973): 139–44.

"Fatimids," *Encyclopaedia Britannica* (1974): 193–94.

"On That Day, a Jewish Apocalyptic Poem on the Arab Conquests," *Mélanges d'Islamologie, volume dedié à la memoire de Armand Abel*, Leiden (1974): 197–200.

"Politics and War (in Islam)," in J. Schacht and C. E. Bosworth, *The Legacy of Islam*, 2nd ed., New York, Oxford University Press, 1974, 156–208.

"On Some Modern Arabic Political Terms," *Orientalia Hispanica*, ed. J. M. Barral, vol. 1, *Arabica-Islamica*, E. J. Brill (1974): 465–71.

"Ali Pasha on Nationalism," *Middle Eastern Studies* 10, no.1 (January 1974): 77–79.

"An Anti-Jewish Ode: The Qasida of Abu Ishaq Against Joseph Ibn Nagrella," *Salo Wittmayer Baron Jubilee Volume*, American Academy for Jewish Research, Jerusalem (1975): 657–68.

"Gibbon on Muhammad," *Daedalus, Journal of the American Academy of Arts and Sciences* 105, no. 3 (Summer 1976): 89–101.

"The Anti-Zionist Resolution," *Foreign Affairs* 55, no. 1 (October 1976): 54–64.

"The African Diaspora and the Civilization of Islam," *The African Diaspora: Interpretive Essays*, edited by M. L. Kilson and Robert A. Rotberg. Cambridge, MA: Harvard University Press, 1976.

"The Palestinians and the PLO," *Commentary* (January 1975): 32–48.

"Return of Islam," *Commentary* (January 1976): 39–49.

"Cold War and Detente in the 16th Century," *Survey*, nos. 3/4 (100/101) (Summer/Autumn 1976): 95–96.

"Settling the Arab-Israeli Conflict," *Commentary* 63, no. 6 (June 1977): 50–56.

"Right and Left in Lebanon," *The New Republic* 177, no. 11 (September 1977): 20–23.

"Turkey," *The Washington Review* 1, no. 1 (January 1978): 103–6.

"Turkey Turns Away," *The New Republic* (February 18, 1978): 18–21.

"Turkey—A Loyal United States and NATO Ally," *NATO, Turkey and United States Interests,* American Foreign Policy Institute (1978): 22–27.

"The Egyptian Perspective," *Commentary* 66, no. 1 (July 1978).

"The State of Middle Eastern Studies," *The American Scholar* 48, no. 3 (Summer 1979): 365–81.

"Ottoman Land Tenure and Taxation in Syria," *Studia Islamica*, Fasc. 50 (1979):109–24.

"Palestine: On the history and Geography of a Name," *The International History Review* 11, no. 1 (January 1980): 1–12.

"Translation from Arabic," *Proceedings of the American Philosophical Society* 124, no. 1 (February 1980): 41–47.

"The Ottoman Empire and its Aftermath," *Journal of Contemporary History* 15 (1980): 27–36.

Türkiye'nin Sosyal Ve Ekonomik Tarihi (1071–1920), Ankara (1980): 215–26.

"Some Statistical Surveys of 16th Century Palestine," *Middle East Studies and Libraries, A Felicitation Volume for Professor J. D. Pearson*, edited by B. C. Bloomfield, London (1980): 115–22.

"The Bases of Political Power and Perceptions in the Middle East," *The Political Economy of the Middle East: 1973–78, A Compendium of Papers Submitted to the Joint Economic Committee Congress of the United States,* Washington, D.C. (April 21, 1980): 503–20.

"L'Islam et les non-musulmans," *Annales,* nos. 3–4 (May–August 1980): 784–800.

"The United States, Turkey and Iran," Haim Shaked and Itamar Rabinovitch, eds., *The Middle East and the United States: Perceptions and Policies*. New Brunswick, NJ: Transaction Books, 1980, 165–80.

"Acre in the Sixteenth Century According to the Ottoman Tapu Registers," *Bibliothèque de l'Institut français d'études anatoliennes d'Istanbul, Memorial Ömer Lutfi Barkan*, Paris (1980), xxviii, 135–39.

"A Letter from Little Menahem," *Studies in Judaism and Islam*, in honor of Professor S. D. Goitein's eightieth birthday, Jerusalem (1981): 181–84.

"Panarabismo," *Enciclopedia del Novecento*, Rome (1981): 67–78.

Loyalties to Community, Nation and State," George S. Wise and Charles Issawi (eds.), *Middle East Perspectives: The Next Twenty Years*, Princeton (1981): 13–33.

"Assassins," *Dictionary of the Middle Ages.* New York: Charles Scribner's Sons, 1981, 2–5.

"Kimlik ve Politika," *Türkiye ve Müttefiklerinin Güvenliği*, Ankara, 1982, 19–33.

"The Question of Orientalism," *New York Review of Books*, New York, 1982, 44–48.

"Meşveret," *Tarih Enstitüsü Dergisi* xii, Istanbul (1981–82): 775–782.

"The Tanzimat and Social Equality," *Economie et Sociétés dans l'Empire Ottoman*, Jean-Louis Bacque-Grammont and Paul Dumont (eds.), Paris (1982): 47–54.

"Hûkumet and Devlet," *Belleten* xlvi, Ankara (1982).

"Judaeo-Osmanica," *Thought and Action, Essays in Memory of Simon Rawidowicz*, Haifa (1983): i–viii.

"The Revolt of Islam," *New York Review of Books,* New York, 1983, 35–38.

"Comment l'Islam regardait l'Occident," *L'Histoire,* no. 56 (May 1983): 44–55.

"The Judaeo-Islamic Tradition," *Pe'amim* (1984): 3–13.

"The Ottoman Obsession," *FMR* (1984): 89–99.

"Islamic Political Movements," *Middle East Insight* (1984): 12–17.

"Usurpers and Tyrants: Notes on Some Islamic Political Terms," *Logos Islamikos, Studia Islamica in honorem Georgii Michaelis Wickens,* Roger M. Savory and Dionisius A. Agius (eds.), Papers in Mediaeval Studies 6 (Toronto, Pontifical Institute of Mediaeval Studies) (1984): 259–67.

"The Impact of the Exotic," *New York Times Book Review,* December 1984, 15–16. (Review of *The Oriental Renaissance* by Raymond Schwab.)

"The Egyptian Murder Case," *New York Review of Books,* May 1984, 21-25. (Review of *Autumn of Fury: The Assassination of Sadat* by Mohamed Heikal.)

"How Khomeini Made It," *New York Review of Books,* January 1985, 10–13. (Review of *The Reign of the Ayatollahs: Iran and the Islamic Revolution* by Shaul Bakhash.)

"The Search for Symmetry," *New York Times Book Review,* April 1985, 10. (Review of *The Blood of Abraham* by Jimmy Carter.)

"Serbestiyet," *Ömer Lûtfi Barkan Memorial Volume, Journal of the Faculty of Economics of the University of Istanbul* 41, 47–52.

"The Crows of the Arabs," *Critical Inquiry* xii (Autumn 1985): 88–97.

"The Shiites," *New York Review of Books,* 32, no. 13, August 15, 1985.

"Siyasa," *In Quest of an Islamiç Humanism, Arabic and Islamic Studies in Memory of Mohamed al-Nowaihi,* A. H. Green (ed.), The American University in Cairo Press, 1986.

"On the Quietist and Activist Traditions in Islamic Political Writing," *Bulletin of the School of Oriental and African Studies* xlix (1986): 141–47.

"The Ras Burqa Affair," *The New Republic,* March 1986, 18.

"The New Anti-Semitism," *New York Review of Books,* March 1986, 28.

"Ibn Khaldun in Turkey," *Studies in Islamic History and Civilization in Honour of Professor David Ayalon,* edited by M. Sharon. Jerusalem: Cana and Leiden: E. J. Brill, 1986, 527–30.

"State, Nation & Religion in Islam," *Nationalism and Modernity: a Mediterranean Perspective,* edited by Joseph Alpher. New York, Westport, CT, and London: Praeger, 1986, 30–46.

"Islam and the West," in *National and International Politics in the Middle East, Essays in Honour of Elie Kedourie,* edited by Edward Ingram. London: Frank Cass, 1986, 16–30.

"The Shi'a in Islamic History," in *Shi'ism, Resistance and Revolution,* edited by Martin Kramer. Boulder, CO: Westview Press, and London: Mansell Publishing Company, 1987, 21–30.

"Some Notes on Land, Money and Power in Medieval Islam," in *Varia Turcica IX: Türkische Miszellen, Robert Anhegger Festschrift,* edited by Jean-Louis Bacque-Grammont, Barbara Flemming, Macit Gokberk, and Ilber Ortayli. Istanbul: Editions Divit Press, 1987, 237–42.

"Slade on the Turkish Navy," *Raiyyet Rusumu, Essays Presented to Halil Inalcık . . . , Journal of Turkish Studies* 11 (Harvard University Press, 1987): 1–10.

"The Central Ottoman Archives as a Source for Arab History," *Revue d'Histoire Maghrebine,* nos. 45–46 (Tunis, June 1987): 77–90.

"Malik," *Cahiers de Tunisie,* University of Tunis, Tome XXXV, nos. 139–40 (Tunis, 1987): 101–9.

"Islamic Revolution," *New York Review of Books,* January 21, 1988, 46–50.

"Islamic Revolution: An Exchange," *New York Review of Books,* April 28, 1988, 58–60.

"The Secret Temple by Ömer Seyfettin," *Die Welt des Islams,* xxviii, 1988 (translation), 301–8.

"Europa und der Islam," *Europa und die Folgen, IWM Castelgandolfo-Gespräche,* Klett-Cotta, Stuttgart, 1988, 256–83.

"Western Culture Must Go," *Wall Street Journal,* May 2, 1988.

"Metaphor and Illusion: Words of Islam," *Encounter,* May 19, 1988, 34–45.

"The Law of Islam," *Washington Post,* Washington, D.C., February 24, 1989.

"The Map of the Middle East: A Guide for the Perplexed," *The American Scholar,* 58, no.1 (Winter 1988–89): 19–38.

"State and Society under Islam," *The Wilson Quarterly* xiii, no. 4, Washington, D.C. (Autumn 1989): 39–51.

"The Maghribis in Jerusalem," *Arab Historical Review* x, nos. 1 and 2 (Tunisia, 1990): 144–46.

"The Roots of Muslim Rage," *The Atlantic Monthly,* September 1990, 47–60.

"Legal and Historical Reflections on the Position of Muslim Populations under Non-Muslim Rule," *Journal of the Institute of Muslim Minority Affairs* 13, no. 1 (January 1992): 1–16.

"Rethinking the Middle East," *Foreign Affairs* 71, no. 4 (Fall 1992).

"The Middle East Crisis in Historical Perspective," *American Scholar* (Winter 1992): 33–46.

"Women and Children, Slaves and Unbelievers," *17th International Congress of Historical Sciences,* Madrid, 1992.

"The Enemies of God," *New York Review of Books,* March 25, 1993, 30–32.

"Islam and Liberal Democracy," *The Atlantic Monthly,* February 1993, 89–98.

"In Defense of History," *Brandeis Review* 13, no. 2 (Fall 1993).

"What Went Wrong? Some Reflections on Arab History," *American Scholar* (Fall 1993).

"Why Turkey?" *Middle East Quarterly,* no. 1 (1994).

"Secularism in the Middle East," *Revue de Métaphysique et de Morale,* no. 2 (1995).

"Islam Partially Perceived," *First Things,* no. 59 (January 1996).

"Islam and Liberal Democracy," *Journal of Democracy* 7, no. 2 (April 1996).

"Jihad," *The Reader's Companion to Military History,* Boston, New York, 1996.

"Reflections on Islamic Historiography," *Middle Eastern Lectures,* no. 2 (Tel Aviv, 1997): 69–80.

"The West and the Middle East," *Foreign Affairs* 76, no. 1 (January/February 1997).

"Hopes and Fears about Peace," *Wall Street Journal,* July 10, 1996.

"Revisiting the Paradox of Modern Turkey," *Wall Street Journal,* November 12, 1996.

"How to Destroy 'Peace in Our Time,'" *Wall Street Journal,* November 26, 1997.

"Demokratie und Religion im Nahen Osten," *Transit Europäische Revue,* Heft 14 (Winter 1997): 118–31.

"Muslim Anti-Semitism," *Middle East Quarterly,* June 1998, 43–49.

"Historical Roots of Racism," *The American Scholar* 67, no. 1 (Winter 1998).

"License to Kill," *Foreign Affairs* 77, no. 6 (November/December 1998): 14–19.

"Islam and Liberal Democracy," *Common Knowledge* 7, no. 3 (Winter 1998): 84–103.

"From Babel to Dragoman: The Tortuous History of the Interpreter in the Middle East," *The Times Literary Supplement* 23, April 1999, 12–14.

"Poems from the Turkish," *Studies in Honour of Clifford Edmund Bosworth, Volume II, The Sultan's Turret: Studies in Persian and Turkish Culture,* Leiden, 2000, 238–45.

"Who Is Syria's Rightful Ruler?" *Wall Street Journal,* June 16, 2000.

"We Must Be Clear," *Washington Post,* September 16, 2001.

"The Revolt of Islam," *The New Yorker,* November 19, 2001, 50–63.

"A War of Resolve," *Wall Street Journal,* April 26, 2002.

"Osama and His Evil Appeal," *Wall Street Journal,* August 23, 2002.

"Targeted by a History of Hatred," *Washington Post,* September 10, 2002, A15; reprinted in *International Herald Tribune,* September 12, 2002, as "Inheriting a History of Hatred."

"A Time for Toppling," *Wall Street Journal,* September 28, 2002.

"A Question, and Answers," *Wall Street Journal,* April 3, 2003.

"I'm Right, You're Wrong, Go to Hell," *The Atlantic Monthly,* 291, no. 4, May 2003, 36–42.

"Put the Iraqis in Charge," *Wall Street Journal,* August 29, 2003.

"To Be or Not to Be," *Wall Street Journal,* November 15, 2004.

"Iraq at the Forefront," *Wall Street Journal,* February 11, 2005.

"A Democratic Institution," *Wall Street Journal,* May 24, 2005.

"Freedom and Justice in the Modern Middle East," *Foreign Affairs* 84, no. 3 (May/June 2005): 36–51.

"Rewriting Oneself," *The American Interest* 1, no. 3 (Spring 2006): 123–31.

"August 22," *Wall Street Journal,* August 8, 2006.

"The New Anti-Semitism, First Religion, Then Race, Then What?," *The American Scholar* 75, no. 1 (Winter 2006): 25–36.

"Was Osama Right?" *Wall Street Journal,* May 16, 2007.

"On the Jewish Question," *Wall Street Journal,* November 26, 2007.

"Second Acts," *The Atlantic,* November 2007, 23, 25.

"The Arab Destruction of the Library of Alexandria: Anatomy of a Myth," *What Happened to the Ancient Library of Alexandria?* edited by Mostafa El-Abbadi and Omnia Mounir Fathallah, Leiden-Boston, 2008, 213–17.

"Free at Last? The Arab World in the Twenty-first Century," *Foreign Affairs* (March/April 2009): 77–88.

"Israel's Election System Is No Good," *Wall Street Journal,* April 1, 2009.

"Moderate Islam: A History of Tolerance," *Wall Street Journal,* September 1, 2010.

Index